Frommer's® 97

Acapulco, Ixtapa & Taxco

by Marita Adair

Macmillan • USA

MACMILLAN TRAVEL

A Simon & Schuster Macmillan Company
1633 Broadway
New York, NY 10019

Find us online at **http://www.mgr.com/travel** or
on America Online at **Keyword: Frommer's.**

ISBN 0-02-861244-2
ISSN 1066-4939

Editor: Ian Wilker
Design by Michele Laseau
Digital Cartography by Ortelius Design
All maps copyright © by Simon & Schuster, Inc.
Page creation by Sean Decker, Heather Pope, Bryan Towse, Linda Quigley,
Christine Tyner, Angel Perez, Jerry Cole, Michelle Croninger, Karen Teo,
Tammy Ahrens, Joy Dean Lee, Tom Missler, Janelle Herber, and Stephanie Mohler

SPECIAL SALES

Bulk purchases (10+ copies) of Frommer's and selected Macmillan travel guides are
available to corporations, organizations, mail-order catalogs, institutions, and charities at
special discounts, and can be customized to suit individual needs. For more information
write to: Special Sales, Macmillan General Reference, 1633 Broadway, New York, NY
10019.

Manufactured in the United States of America

Contents

List of Maps

An Invitation to the Reader

In researching this book, I discovered many wonderful places—resorts, inns, restaurants, shops, and more. I'm sure you'll find others. Please tell me about them, so I can share the information with your fellow travelers in upcoming editions. If you were disappointed with a recommendation, I'd love to know that, too. Please write to:

Acapulco, Ixtapa & Taxco '97, 3rd Edition
Macmillan Travel
1633 Broadway
New York, NY 10019

An Additional Note

Please be advised that travel information is subject to change at any time—and this is especially true of prices. We therefore suggest that you write or call ahead for confirmation when making your travel plans. The authors, editors, and publisher cannot be held responsible for the experiences of readers while traveling. Your safety is important to us, however, so we encourage you to stay alert and be aware of your surroundings. Keep a close eye on cameras, purses, and wallets, all favorite targets of thieves and pickpockets.

A Few Words About Prices

In December 1994, the Mexican government devalued its currency, the peso. Over the ensuing months, the peso's value against the dollar plummeted from 3.35 pesos against U.S. $1 to nearly 7 pesos against U.S. $1. The peso's value continues to fluctuate—at press time it was around 7.5 pesos to the dollar. Therefore, to allow for inflation, prices in this book (which are always given in U.S. dollars) have been converted to U.S. dollars at a rate of 7 pesos to the dollar, with 15% added for inflation. Inflation for 1996/1997 is forecast at around 36%. Many moderate-priced and expensive hotels, which often have U.S. toll-free reservation numbers and have many expenses in U.S. dollars, do not lower rates in keeping with the sinking peso.

Mexico has a value-added tax of 15% (Impuesto de Valor Agregado, or IVA, pronounced "ee-bah") on almost everything, including restaurant meals, bus tickets, and souvenirs. (Exceptions are Cancun, Cozumel, and Los Cabos, where the IVA is 10%.) Hotel taxes are 17% everywhere except Cancun, Cozumel, and Los Cabos where they are 12%. The IVA will not necessarily be included in the prices quoted by hotels and restaurants. In addition, prices charged by hotels and restaurants have been deregulated. Mexico's new pricing freedom may cause some price variations from those quoted in this book; always ask to see a printed price sheet and always ask if the tax is included.

What the Symbols Mean

✪ Frommer's Favorites

Hotels, restaurants, attractions, and entertainment you should not miss.

⑤ Super-Special Values

Hotels and restaurants that offer great value for your money.

The following abbreviations are used for credit cards:

AE	American Express	EU	Eurocard
CB	Carte Blanche	JCB	Japan Credit Bank
DC	Diners Club	MC	MasterCard
DISC	Discover	V	Visa
ER	enRoute		

Getting to Know Southern Pacific Mexico

Experienced travelers who have watched modernity eclipse the color and tradition of the old ways in other countries covet their forays into Mexico—because "old" Mexico still exists. Travelers through this land still receive daily doses of cacti and burros, oxen-pulled plows, peasant folk, peasant ways, pre-Hispanic customs, and ancient architecture.

But the trappings of the modern world—tractors, skyscrapers, freeways, cellular phones, multinational businesses, beach resorts—are creeping up on Mexico. It's a curious thing, this juxtaposition of old and new. Go to a sophisticated Pacific Coast resort village and you may see a rural boy balancing huge natural gourds hung from a pole on his shoulders, mingling with tourists from Iowa and New York—he's journeyed from his village to sell *tuba,* a cool, sweet homemade drink. Go to any number of Mexico's modern cities and you'll see Nahuatl-speaking Indians rendered nearly invisible beneath armloads of huge, colorful baskets, or laden with hand-painted plates, clay necklaces, and colorful paintings on handmade paper; they've traveled all the way from their rural villages in Guerrero State.

For now these contrasting faces of Mexico coexist, making it one of the world's most fascinating countries to visit. Some people come to absorb as much of Mexico's rich cultural legacy as they can before it too disappears. Other people are perfectly content not to travel beyond the country's well-known beach meccas. Both kinds of travelers can enjoy Mexico.

And many of you will, of course, go to Mexico expecting both kinds of experiences from your visit. This book exists to help you help yourself. You'll find all the information and advice you'll need to plan a memorable beach vacation in the resort that fits your style. And if you want to hit the road in search of a more down-to-earth Mexico, you can choose between trips to three grand old Mexican colonial towns: Taxco, Cuernavaca, and Oaxaca.

1 The Land & Its People

Few regions in Mexico vary in terrain as dramatically as this coast. At **Zihuatanejo/Ixtapa** you'll find deep-green forests around the town; to the south, fruit plantations stretch almost all the way to **Acapulco,** affording brief glimpses of the ocean. Tree-covered mountains still remain around Acapulco, though hillside development has

Mexico

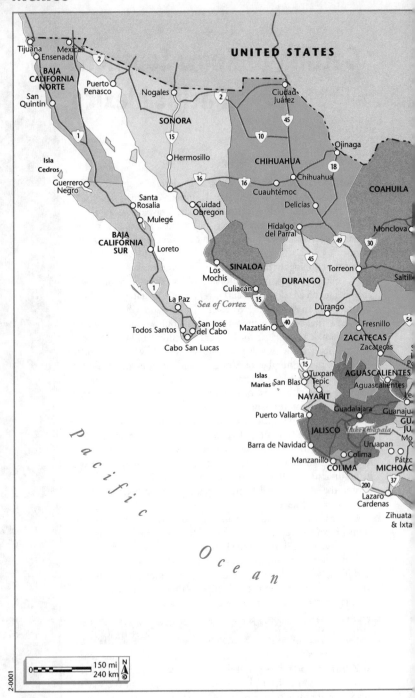

UNITED STATES

edras Negras

Nuevo Laredo

Matamoros

onterrey
EVO
ON   85

TAMAULIPAS

Ciudad Victoria

Ciudad Mante

AN LUIS
POTOSÍ

Miguel
llende

UERÉTARO

HIDALGO

eretaro

Pachuca

Mexico City

ca

rnavaca

MORELOS

xco   95

JERRERO

Chilpancingo

Acapulco

200

Gulf of Mexico

Tampico

Tuxpan

Poza Rica

180

Jalapa

Tlaxcala

TLAXCALA

Puebla

PUEBLA   Orizaba

Tehuacán

VERACRUZ

Coatzacoalcos

190D

175

186

Oaxaca

OAXACA

Salina
Cruz

Puerto Escondido

Huatulco

Puerto Angel

Bay of
Campeche

Veracruz

Catemaco

TABASCO

Villahermosa

Tuxtla
Gutierrez

CHIAPAS

Comitán

Gulf of
Tehuantepec

Tapachula

200

Progreso

Celestún

Campeche

CAMPECHE

261

Escarcega

Río Lagartos

Valladolid

Mérida

180

YUCATÁN   Playa del
Carmen

QUINTANA
ROO

Bacalar

Chetumal

186

San Cristóbal de las Casas

GUATEMALA

Isla
Mujeres

Cancún

Cozumel

Punta
Allen

Xcalak
Peninsula

Caribbean Sea

BELIZE

HONDURAS

EL
SALVADOR

3

marred them some, but in some places the natural vegetation has been replaced with tropical gardens around plush hillside villas. Farther south along the coast from Acapulco, the short, scrubby forests, interspersed with agricultural plots, give way to a boulder-laden scrub forest terrain around the nine gorgeous bays of **Huatulco.**

This book twice makes forays away from the beaches and up into the rugged Sierra Madre. Traveling inland from Acapulco to **Taxco,** the thinly covered mountainous landscape can be refreshing after the rainy season, but blisteringly hot and desertlike at other times. Taxco, a delightful hillside colonial-era city famed for its hundreds of silver shops, is surrounded by thinly forested mountains. And many people travel inland from the southernmost beach resorts—Puerto Escondido, Puerto Angel, and Huatulco—to experience the living color and texture of the Zapotec and Mixtec cultures around **Oaxaca.**

THE MEXICAN PEOPLE

The population of Mexico is 85 million; 15% are ethnically European (most are of Spanish descent, but a French presence lingers on from the time of Maximilian's abortive empire, and other Europeans are represented), 60% are *mestizo* (mixed Spanish and Indian), and 25% are pure Indian (descendants of the Maya, Aztecs, Huastecs, Otomies, Totonacs, and other peoples). Added to this ethnic mix are Africans brought as slaves (this group has been so thoroughly assimilated that it is barely discernible).

Although Spanish is the official language, about 50 Indian languages are still spoken, mostly in the Yucatán peninsula, Oaxaca, Chiapas, Chihuahua, Nayarit, Puebla, Sonora and Veracruz, Michoacán, and Guerrero.

Modern Mexico clings to its identity while embracing outside cultures—Mexicans enjoy the Bolshoi Ballet as easily as a family picnic or village festival. Mexicans have a knack for knowing how to enjoy life, and families, weekends, holidays, and festivities are given priority. They also enjoy stretching a weekend holiday into 4 days called a *puente* (bridge) and, with the whole family in tow, fleeing the cities en masse to visit relatives in the country, picnic, or relax at resorts.

The Mexican workday is a long one: Laborers begin around 7am and get off at dusk; office workers go in around 9am and, not counting the 2- to 3-hour lunch, get off at 7 or 8pm. Once a working career is started, there is little time for additional study. School is supposedly mandatory and free through the sixth grade, but many youngsters quit long before that or never go at all.

Sociologists and others have written volumes trying to explain the Mexican's special relationship with death. Death and the dead are at once mocked and mourned. The Days of the Dead, November 1 and 2, a cross between Halloween and All Saints' Day, is a good opportunity to observe Mexico's relationship with the concept of death.

Mexico's social complexity is such that it's difficult to characterize the Mexican people as a whole, but some broad generalizations can be drawn.

CLASS DIVISIONS IN MEXICO   There are vast differences in the culture and values of Mexico's various economic classes, and these gulfs have grown even wider over the last 10 years. On the one hand there are the fabulously rich; before the devaluation, according to *Forbes* magazine, Mexico had the fourth-most billionaires in the world, with at least 24. Upper-class Mexicans are extremely well educated and well mannered; they are very culturally sophisticated and often speak several languages. Many of Mexico's recent presidents have been educated in the United States.

The Mexican middle class—merchants, small restaurant and souvenir-shop owners, taxi drivers, and tour guides, etc.—swelled from the 1950s through the 1980s.

Impressions

Considering the variety of nations, tongues, cultures, and artistic styles, the unity of these peoples comes as a surprise. They all share certain ideas and beliefs. Thus it is not inaccurate to call this group of nations and cultures a Mexoamerican civilization. Unity in space and continuity in time; from the first millennium before Christ to the 16th century, these distinct Mexoamerican peoples evolve, re-elaborate, and re-create a nucleus of basic concepts as well as social and political techniques and institutions. There were changes and variation . . . but never was the continuity broken.

—Octavio Paz, 1990

Now, however, it's struggling to stay afloat after a decade of incredible inflation that was punctuated by the 1994 devaluation—the latter cut the value of an average Mexican's earnings in half. And yet these middle-class Mexicans are educating their children to higher standards—many young people now complete technical school or university. The middle-class standard of living includes trappings of life many take for granted in the States—maybe a phone in the home (a luxury that costs the equivalent of U.S. $600 to install), fancy tennis shoes for the children, occasional vacations, an economy car, and a tiny home or even smaller apartment in a modest neighborhood or high-rise.

Mexico's poorer classes have expanded. Their hopes for a decent future are dim and the daily goal for many is simple survival.

MACHISMO & MACHISMA Sorting through the world of machismo and machisma in Mexico is fraught with subtleties better suited to sociological studies. Suffice to say that in Mexico, and especially Mexico City, the roles of men and women are changing both slowly and rapidly. Both sexes cling to old sex roles—women in the home and men in the workplace—but they are relinquishing traditional ideas too. More women are being educated and working than ever before. And men are learning to work side by side with women of equal education and power.

Though women function in many professional positions, they encounter what they call the "adobe ceiling" (as opposed to the see-through "glass ceiling" in the United States): The male grip on upper-level positions in Mexico is so firm that women aren't able to even glimpse the top. Strong-willed women opt for setting up their own businesses as a result. Anyone used to a more liberated world may be frustrated by the extent to which Mexico is still a man's world—not uncommon are provocatively dressed women who pander to old-fashioned negative stereotypes, and flirtatious Mexican men who have difficulty sticking to business when dealing with a woman, even a serious businessperson who is dressed accordingly. Typically the Mexican man is charmingly polite, and affronted or embarrassed by the woman who won't permit him to open doors, seat her, and in every way put her on a respectful pedestal.

THE FAMILY As a rule, Mexicans are very family-oriented. Family takes priority over work. Whole extended families routinely spend weekends and holidays together, filling parks and recreational spots until the last minute of the holiday. During those times men are often seen playing with, tending to, and enjoying the children as readily as women. In the home, girls are supervised closely until they are married. But the untethering of boys begins around age 15, when they are given more freedoms than their sisters. It's customary, however, for all children to remain in the home until they marry, although there are more young people breaking the mold nowadays.

Family roles among indigenous people are clear-cut. Women tend the babies, the home, the hearth, and often the fields. Men do the heavy work, tilling the soil, but women often join them for planting and harvesting. Theirs is a joint life focused on survival. Though not so much an unbendable custom now among these cultures, it's common to see women walking behind her spouse, carrying a child on her back and heavy bundles on her shoulders. When these people reach Mexico City, these roles shift somewhat; for example, a husband and wife will take turns tending their street stall with a child sleeping in a box or playing nearby. But always she will prepare the food.

Generally speaking children are coddled and loved and are very obedient. Misbehaving children are seldom rebuked in public, since Mexican parenting style seems to favor gentle prodding, comforting, or nurturing instead.

THE MEXICAN CHARACTER   Describing the Mexican character is at least as complex as trying to describe the difference between New Englanders and Southerners in the United States. At the risk of offending some, I'll try and describe the values of the average Mexican. He or she is generous, honest, and loyal, and accepts acquaintances at face value. Visitors are far more likely to have something returned than to discover it stolen. But just as Mexicans are accepting, they can become unreasonably suspicious, and nothing will divert them from suspecting ill will.

The fierce Mexican dignity doesn't allow for insult. An insulting shopper, for example, may discover that suddenly nothing in the store is for sale, or that the prices have suddenly become ridiculously high for the duration of the shopper's visit.

Longtime friendships can fall apart instantly over a real or imagined wrong. Once wronged, Mexicans seldom forgive and never forget. The expression of indifference and distrust a Mexican wears when taking exception can appear to have been set in concrete. The more you try to right a wrong, or correct a wrong impression, the more entrenched it can become. This goes for personal friendships as well as dealings with the government.

Their long memories harbor the bad and the good. A Mexican will remember a kind deed or a fond, but brief, acquaintance until death. They will never forget the number of times the United States has invaded Mexico, or the government massacre of peaceful demonstrators at Tlaltelolco Square in the capital in 1968.

Mexicans seem to thrive on gossip. And it runs the gamut from what government is doing behind the public's back to neighborhood squabbles. It figures prominently in the breakdown of personal and business relationships as well as the lack of confidence that the public has in the government. During Mexico's recent investigation of the assassinations of two prominent government leaders, newspapers published the intrigue and conspiracy the public believed caused both events, alongside different official government reports. Mexicans often express the belief that their president takes his orders from the U.S. President.

No matter how poor or opulent their lives may be, all Mexicans love festivities, whether simple family affairs or the citywide parades on Revolution and Independence days. Often this celebratory spirit is just as evident at lunch in a festive place such as the Fonda del Recuerdo in the capital, known for its lively music and jovial atmosphere.

When it comes to foreigners, Mexicans want visitors to know, love, and enjoy their country and will extend many thoughtful courtesies just to see pleasure spread across the face of a visitor. They'll invite them to share a table in a crowded restaurant, go out of their way to give directions, help with luggage, and see stranded travelers safely on their way. An entire trip can be joyously colored by the many serendipitous encounters with the people of this nation, whose efficiency and concern will be as memorable as their warmth and good humor.

2   A Look at the Past

Mexico is undergoing fast-paced and far-reaching change, as are most countries touched by modern technology. Some changes are astounding in their rapidity—for example, the country's literally gone straight from manual typewriters to computers. Modern turnpikes are proliferating; though the tolls can be eye-popping, they've made getting from one place to another something of (dare I say it) a luxurious breeze. These new roads and the level of service provided by Mexico's luxury bus lines have made using public transportation worthy of anticipation.

On the other hand, many villages and most rural communities don't have electricity, running water, or a public sewer system; there's no natural gas pipeline servicing the country either.

And unreliable phone service is still one of the country's greatest obstacles to progress. But here as elsewhere forward progress is being made: The lofty aim of recent efforts to modernize the telephone system was to install at least one telephone in 70% of the villages without such service—and 1995 saw that goal achieved. Toll-free telephone numbers, and fax phones, almost unheard of as little 3 or 4 years ago, are common nowadays.

Despite Mexico's immense technological advances, some customs die hard: A handmade tortilla is still preferred over one made by machine; a housewife may have a tiny washing machine, but the maid is instructed to give the whole wash a thorough scrubbing *again* by hand on the cement washboard; clothes dryers are a rarity, never having won approval over line-drying in the open air—usually on the rooftop; orange juice—which most of us grew up drinking from the carton, heedless of the difference between pasteurized and fresh juice—is usually freshly squeezed while you watch; and prepackaged and frozen foods haven't yet overtaken dishes made from fresh ingredients bought at a colorful open-air market.

Whether small-scale traditions like these, or carefully observed manners and mores, or the ritualized pomp and circumstance of the country's many religious fiestas, Mexicans stubbornly cling to their traditional ways of doing things. And the country's traditions arise out of its long history—it's Mexican

Mexico Dateline

- **10,000–2300 B.C.** Prehistoric period.
- **1500** Preclassic period begins: Olmec culture develops and spreads.
- **1000–900** Olmec San Lorenzo center destroyed; Olmecs regroup at La Venta.
- **600** La Venta Olmec cultural zenith; Cholula begins 2,000-year history as ceremonial center.
- **500–100 B.C.** Zapotecs flourish; Olmec culture disintegrates.
- **A.D. 100** Building begins on Sun and Moon pyramids at Teotihuacán; Palenque dynasty emerges in Yucatán.
- **300** Classic period begins: Xochicalco established; Maya civilization develops in Yucatán and Chiapas.
- **650** Teotihuacán burns and by 700 is deserted. Cacaxtla begins to flourish.
- **750** Zapotecs conquer valley of Oaxaca; Casas Grandes culture begins on northern desert.
- **900** Postclassic period begins: Toltec culture emerges at Tula. Cacaxtla begins to decline.
- **978** Toltec culture spreads to Chichén-Itzá.
- **1156–1230** Tula and El Tajín are abandoned. Aztecs trickle into the Valley of Mexico.
- **1290** Zapotecs decline and Mixtecs emerge at Monte Albán; Mitla becomes refuge of Zapotecs.
- **1325–45** Aztec capital Tenochtitlán founded. Aztecs dominate Mexico until 1521,

continues

when they are defeated by Spaniards.

- **1519–21** Conquest of Mexico: Hernán Cortés and troops arrive near present-day Veracruz; Spanish gain final victory over Aztecs at Tlaltelolco near Tenochtitlán in 1521. Diseases brought by Spaniards begin to decimate native population.

- **1521–24** Cortés organizes Spanish empire in Mexico and begins building Mexico City atop ruins of Tenochtitlán; Spanish bring first cattle to Mexico.

- **1524** First Franciscan friars arrive from Spain.

- **1525–35** Cortés removed from leadership; Spanish king sends officials, judges, and finally an *audiencia* to govern.

- **1530** King Charles V of Spain declares Mexico City the capital of New Spain.

- **1535–1821** Viceregal period: Mexico governed by 61 viceroys appointed by King of Spain. Landed aristocracy, a small elite owning huge portions of land (haciendas) emerges.

- **1562** Friar Diego de Landa destroys 5,000 Mayan religious stone figures and burns 27 hieroglyphic painted manuscripts at Maní, Yucatán.

- **1571** The Inquisition is established in Mexico.

- **1767** Jesuits expelled from New Spain.

- **1810–21** Independence War: Miguel Hidalgo's *grito* starts independence movement; after a decade of war, Augustín Iturbide achieves compromise between monarchy and a republic. Mexico becomes independent nation.

- **1822–24** First Empire: Iturbide enjoys brief reign as emperor; is expelled; returns; and is executed by firing squad.

continues

history, in large part, that makes the country so rich for visitors.

PREHISPANIC CIVILIZATIONS The earliest "Mexicans" were Stone Age men and women, descendants of a people who had crossed the Bering Strait and reached North America before 10,000 B.C. These were *Homo sapiens* who hunted mastodons and bison and gathered other food as they could. Later, during the Archaic Period (5200–1500 B.C.), signs of agriculture and domestication appeared: baskets were woven; corn, beans, squash, and tomatoes were grown; turkeys and dogs were kept for food. By 2400 B.C., the art of making pottery had been discovered, a significant advance. Though life in these times was still very primitive, there were "artists" who made clay figurines for use as votive offerings or household deities. Many symbolized Mother Earth or Fertility. Use of these figurines predates any belief in well-defined gods.

It was in the **preclassic period** (1500 B.C.–A.D. 300) that the area known by archaeologists as Mesoamerica (running from the northern Mexico Valley to Costa Rica) began to show signs of a farming culture. The inhabitants farmed either by the "slash-and-burn" method of cutting grass and trees and then setting fire to the area to clear it for planting or by constructing terraces and irrigation ducts. The latter method was used principally in the highlands around Mexico City, where the first large towns developed. At some time during this period, religion became an institution as certain men took the role of shaman, or guardian of magical and religious secrets. These were the predecessors of the folk healers and nature priests still found in modern Mexico.

The most highly developed culture of this preclassic period was that of the Olmecs, which flourished from 1500 to 100 B.C. They lived in what are today the states of Veracruz and Tabasco, where they used river rafts to transport the colossal multiton blocks of basalt out of which they carved roundish heads that are the best-known legacy of their culture. These sculptures still present problems to archaeologists: What do they signify? The heads seem infantile in their roundness, but all have the peculiar "jaguar mouth" with a high-arched upper lip. Those with open eyes are slightly cross-eyed. The artists seemed obsessed with deformity, and many smaller carved or clay figures represent monstrosities or misshapen forms. Besides their achievements in sculpture, the Olmecs were the first in Mexico to use a calendar and to develop a written language, both of which were later perfected by the Maya.

The link between the Olmecs and the Maya has not been clearly established, but Izapa (400 B.C.– A.D. 400), a ceremonial site in the Chiapan cacao-growing region near the Pacific coast, appears to be one of several places where transition between the two cultures took place. When discovered, its monuments and stelae were intact, having escaped the destruction wrought on so many sites. El Pital, a large site being excavated in northern Veracruz state, may illuminate more links between the Olmec and other cultures.

Most of pre-Columbian Mexico's artistic and cultural achievement came during the **classic period** (A.D. 300–900), when life centered in cities. Class distinctions arose as a military and religious aristocracy took control; a class of merchants and artisans grew, with the independent farmer falling under a landlord's control. The cultural centers of the classic period were Yucatán and Guatemala (also home of the Maya), the Mexican Highlands at Teotihuacán, the Zapotec cities of Monte Albán and Mitla (near Oaxaca), and the cities of El Tajín and Zempoala on the Gulf Coast.

The Maya represented the apex of pre-Columbian cultures. Besides their superior artistic achievements, the Maya made significant discoveries in science, including the use of the zero in mathematics and a complex calendar with which priests were able to predict eclipses and the movements of the stars for centuries to come. The Maya were warlike, raiding their neighbors to gain land and subjects as well as to take captives for their many blood-centered rituals. Recent studies, notably *Blood of Kings* (Braziller, 1986) by Linda Schele and Mary Ellen Miller, debunked the long-held theory that the Maya were a peaceful people. Scholars continue to decipher the Maya hieroglyphs, murals, and relief carvings, revealing a world tied to the belief that blood sacrifice was necessary to communicate with celestial gods and ancestors and to revere the dynasties of earthly blood kin. Through bloodletting and sacrifice the Maya nourished their gods and ancestors and honored royal births, deaths, marriages, and accessions during a calendar full of special occasions. Numerous carvings and murals show that members of the ruling class, too, ritualistically mutilated themselves to draw sacrificial blood.

- **1824–55** Federal Republic period: In 1824, Guadalupe Victoria elected first president of Mexico; 26 presidents and interim presidents follow during next 3 decades, among them José Antonio Lopez de Santa Anna, who is president of Mexico off and on 11 times.
- **1835** Texas declares independence from Mexico.
- **1838** France invades Mexico at Veracruz.
- **1845** United States annexes Texas.
- **1846–48** War with United States concludes with United States paying Mexico $15 million for half of its national territory under terms of Treaty of Guadalupe Hidalgo.
- **1855–72** Era of Benito Juárez, literal or de facto president through Reform Wars and usurpation of Mexican leadership by foreign Emperor Maximilian. Juárez nationalizes church property and declares separation of church and state.
- **1864–67** Second Empire: Interim period; Maximilian of Hapsburg is Emperor of Mexico; Juárez orders execution of Maximilian and resumes presidency until his death in 1872.
- **1872–84** Post-reform period: Only four presidents hold office but country is nearly bankrupt.
- **1880** Electric lights go on in Mexico City for the first time.
- **1876–1911** Porfiriato: With one 4-year exception, Porfirio Díaz is president/dictator of Mexico for 35 years, leading country through rapid modernization.

continues

- **1911** Mexican Revolution begins; Díaz resigns; Francisco Madero becomes president.
- **1913** Madero assassinated.
- **1914, 1916** United States invades Mexico.
- **1917–40** Reconstruction: present constitution of Mexico signed in 1917. Land and education reforms are initiated and labor unions strengthened. Mexico expels U.S. oil companies and nationalizes all natural resources and railroads. Presidential term limited to one term of 6 years. Presidents Obregón and Carranza are assassinated as are Pancho Villa and Emiliano Zapata.
- **1940** President Lázaro Cárdenas leaves office; Mexico enters period of political stability, tremendous economic progress, and rising quality of life that continues to this day, though not without many continuing problems.
- **1942** Mexico enters World War II when Germans sink two Mexican oil tankers in the Caribbean.
- **1949** 10,000-year-old "Tepexpan Man" (really a woman) is unearthed near Mexico City.
- **1955** Women given full voting rights.
- **1957** Major earthquake rocks the capital.
- **1960** Mexico nationalizes electrical industry.
- **1968** President Díaz Ordaz orders army to fire on protesters at Tlaltelolco Plaza meeting, killing hundreds of spectators and participants. Olympic games are held in the capital.

continues

The identity of the people of Teotihuacán (100 B.C.–A.D. 700—near present-day Mexico City) isn't known, but it is thought to have been a city of 200,000 or more inhabitants covering 9 square miles. At its height, Teotihuacán was the greatest cultural center in Mexico; its influence extended as far southeast as Guatemala. Its layout has religious significance: High priests' rituals occurred on the tops of pyramids consecrated to the sun and moon, and these were attended, but not observed, by the masses of people at the foot of the pyramid. Some of the magnificent reliefs and frescoes that decorated the religious monuments can be seen in Mexico City's museums.

The Zapotecs, influenced by the Olmecs, raised an impressive culture in the region of Oaxaca. Their two principal cities were Monte Albán (500 B.C.– A.D. 800), inhabited by an elite of merchants and artisans, and Mitla, reserved for the high priests. Both cities exhibit the artistic and mathematical genius of the people; highlights include characteristic geometric designs, long-nosed gods with feathered masks, hieroglyph stelae, a bar-and-dot numerical system, and a 52-cycle calendar. Like the Olmecs, the Zapotecs favored grotesque art, of which the frieze of the "Danzantes" at Monte Albán—naked figures of distorted form and contorted position— is an outstanding example.

El Tajín (A.D. 300–1100), covering at least 2,600 acres on the upper Gulf coast of Veracruz, continues to stump scholars. The Pyramid of the Niches there is unique, and recent excavations have uncovered a total of 17 ball courts and Teotihuacán-influenced murals. Although Huastec Indians inhabited the region, the identity of those who built the site and occupied it remains a mystery. Death and sacrifice are recurring themes depicted in relief carvings. Pulque (pre-Hispanic fermented drink), cacao (chocolate) growing, and the ball game figured heavily into Tajín society.

In the **postclassic period** (A.D. 900–1500), warlike cultures developed impressive societies of their own, although they never surpassed the classic peoples. All paintings and hieroglyphs of this period show war, migration, and disruption. Somehow the glue of society became unstuck; people wandered from their homes, and the religious hierarchy lost influence. Finally, in the 1300s, the warlike Aztecs settled in the Mexico Valley on Lake Texcoco (site of Mexico City), with the island city of Tenochtitlán as their capital. Legend has it that as the wandering Aztecs were passing the lake, they saw a sign predicted by their prophets: an eagle perched on a cactus plant with a snake in its mouth. They built their city there, and it became a huge (pop. 300,000) and impressive capital. The Aztec empire was a more or less loosely united territory of great size. The high lords of the capital became fabulously rich in gold, stores of food, cotton, and perfumes; skilled artisans were prosperous; state events were elaborately ceremonial. Victorious Aztecs returning from battle sacrificed thousands of captives on the altars atop the pyramids, cutting their chests open with stone knives and ripping out their still-beating hearts to offer to the gods.

The legend of **Quetzalcoatl,** a holy man who appeared during the time of troubles at the end of the classic period, is one of the most important tales in Mexican history and folklore, and contributed to the overthrow of the Aztec empire by the Spaniards. Quetzalcoatl means "feathered serpent." Learned beyond his years, he became the high priest and leader of the Toltecs at Tula and put an end to human sacrifice. His influence completely changed the Toltecs from a group of warriors to peaceful and productive farmers, artisans, and craftsmen. But his successes upset the old priests, and they called on their ancient god of darkness, Texcatlipoca, to degrade Quetzalcoatl in the eyes of the people. One night the priests conspired to dress Quetzalcoatl in ridiculous garb, get him drunk, and tempt him to break his vow of chastity. The next morning the shame of this night of debauchery drove him out of his own land and into the wilderness, where he lived for 20 years. He emerged in Coatzacoalcos, in the Isthmus of Tehuantepec, bade his few followers farewell, and sailed away, having promised to return in a future age. Toltec artistic influences noted at Chichén-Itzá in the Yucatán seem to suggest that he in fact landed there and, among the Maya, began his "ministry" again, this time called Kukulkán. He supposedly died there, but the legend of his return in a future age remained.

THE CONQUEST OF MEXICO When Hernán Cortés and his fellow conquistadores landed in 1519 in what would become Veracruz, the enormous Aztec empire was ruled by Moctezuma (a name often misspelled Montezuma) in great splendor. It was thought that these strange visitors might be Quetzalcoatl and his followers, returning at last.

- **1982** President Echeverría nationalizes the country's banks.
- **1985** Deadly earthquake crumbles buildings in the capital and takes thousands of lives.
- **1988** Mexico enters the General Agreement on Tariffs and Trade (GATT).
- **1992** Sale of *ejido* land (peasant communal property) to private citizens is allowed. Mexico and the Vatican establish diplomatic relations after an interruption of 100 years.
- **1993** Mexico deregulates hotel and restaurant prices; New Peso currency begins circulation.
- **1994** Mexico, Canada, and the United States sign the North American Free Trade Agreement (NAFTA). An Indian uprising in Chiapas sparks protests countrywide over government policies concerning land distribution, bank loans, health, education, and voting and human rights. In an unrelated incident PRI candidate Luis Donaldo Colossio is assassinated 5 months before the election; replacement candidate Ernesto Zedillo Ponce de León is elected and inaugurated as president in December. Within weeks, the peso is devalued, throwing the nation into turmoil.
- **1995** The peso loses half its value within the first 3 months of the year. The government raises prices on oil and utilities. Interest on debt soars to 140%; businesses begin to fail; unemployment rises. The Chiapan rebels threaten another rebellion, which is quickly quashed by the

continues

government. Former President Carlos Salinas de Gortari, with the devaluation having left his reputation for economic leadership in a shambles, leaves Mexico for the United States. And Salinas's brother is accused of plotting the assassination of their brother-in-law, the head of the PRI. The United States extends Mexico $40 billion in loans to stabilize the economy following the peso crisis.

- **1996** Effects of the devaluation continue as in 1995, but many businesses without debt expand and prosper. Mexico begins repaying the loan extended by the United States in 1995; the wife of the president's brother is arrested attempting to remove millions of dollars from a Swiss bank, drug ties are alleged; former president Salinas's whereabouts unknown, though he speaks out on occasion; the Chiapan crisis remains unsettled.

Moctezuma was not certain what course to pursue; if this was in fact the god returning, no resistance must be offered; on the other hand, if the leader was not Quetzalcoatl, he and his men might be a threat to his empire. Moctezuma tried to bribe them with gold to go away, but this only whetted the Spaniards' appetites. Along the way from Veracruz to Tenochtitlán, Cortés made allies of Moctezuma's enemies, most notably the Tlaxcaltecans.

Though the Spaniards were outnumbered by the hundreds of thousands of Aztecs, they skillfully kept things under their control (with the help of their Tlaxcalan allies) until a revolt threatened Cortés's entire enterprise. He retreated to the countryside, made alliances with non-Aztec tribes, and finally marched on the empire when it was governed by the last Aztec emperor, Cuauhtémoc. Cuauhtémoc defended himself and his people valiantly for almost 3 months, but was finally captured, tortured, and ultimately executed.

What began as an adventure by Cortés and his men, unauthorized by the Spanish Crown or its governor in Cuba, turned out to be the undoing of a continent's worth of people and cultures. Soon Christianity was being spread through "New Spain." Guatemala and Honduras were explored and conquered, and by 1540 the territory of New Spain included Spanish possessions from Vancouver to Panama. In the 2 centuries that followed, Franciscan, Augustinian, and Dominican friars converted great numbers of Indians to Christianity, and the Spanish lords built up huge feudal estates on which the Indian farmers were little more than serfs. The silver and gold that Cortés had sought and found made Spain the richest country in Europe.

THE VICEREGAL ERA Hernán Cortés set about building a new city and the seat of government of New Spain upon the ruins of the old Aztec capital. Spain's influence was immediate. For indigenous peoples (besides the Tlaxcaltecans, Cortés's Indian allies), heavy tributes once paid to the Aztecs were now rendered in forced labor to the Spanish. In many cases they were made to provide the materials for the building of New Spain as well. Diseases carried by the Spaniards, against which the Indian populations had no natural immunity, killed millions.

Over the 3 centuries of the Viceregal period (1535–1821), Mexico was governed by 61 viceroys appointed by the King of Spain. From the beginning, more Spaniards arrived as overseers, merchants, craftsmen, architects, silversmiths, and others, and eventually African slaves were brought in as well. Spain became rich from New World gold and silver, chiseled out by backbreaking Indian labor. The colonial elite built lavish homes both in Mexico City and in the countryside. They filled their homes with ornate furniture, had many servants, and adorned themselves in velvets, satins, and jewels imported from abroad. A new class system developed: the *gauchupines* (Spaniards born in Spain), considered themselves superior to the *criollos* (Spaniards born in Mexico). Those of other races, the *castas* or castes, the pure Indians and

Impressions

When we [Cortés and Moctezuma] met, I dismounted and stepped forward to embrace him, but the two lords who were with him stopped me with their hands so that I should not touch him. . . . When at last I came to speak to Mutezuma himself I took off a necklace of pearls and cut glass that I was wearing and placed it around his neck; after we had walked a little way up the street a servant of his came with two necklaces, wrapped in a cloth, made from red snails' shells, which they hold in great esteem; and from each necklace hung eight shrimps of refined gold almost a span in length.

—Hernán Cortés, *Letters from Mexico* (1519)

When they arrived at the treasure house called Teucalco, the riches of gold and feathers were brought out to them: ornaments made of quetzal feathers, richly worked shields, disks of gold, the necklaces of the idols, gold nose plugs, gold greaves and bracelets and crowns. . . . The Spaniards . . . gathered all the gold into a great mound and set fire to everything else. . . . Then they melted down the gold into ingots.

—*The Broken Spears: The Aztec Account of the Conquest of Mexico* (1528)

Africans, and mixtures of Spanish and Indian, Spanish and African, Indian and African, all took the last place in society.

It took great cunning to stay a step ahead of the money-hungry Spanish crown, which demanded increasingly higher taxes and contributions from its well-endowed faraway colony. Still, the wealthy prospered grandly enough to develop an extravagant society.

However, discontent with the mother country simmered for years over issues such as the Spanish-born citizen's advantages over a Mexican-born subject, taxes, the Spanish bureaucracy, and restrictions on commerce with Spain and other countries. Dissatisfaction with Spain boiled to the surface in 1808 when, under the weak leadership of King Charles IV, Spain was invaded by Napoléon Bonaparte of France, who placed his brother Joseph in the Spanish throne. To many in Mexico, allegiance to France was out of the question—after nearly 300 years of restrictive Spanish rule, Mexico revolted.

INDEPENDENCE The independence movement began in 1810 when a priest, Father Miguel Hidalgo, gave the cry for independence from his pulpit in the town of Dolores, Guanajuato. The uprising soon became a revolution, and Hidalgo, Ignacio Allende, and another priest, José María Morelos, gathered an "army" of citizens and threatened Mexico City. Battle lines were drawn between those who sided with the Spanish crown and those who wanted Mexico to be a free and sovereign nation. Ultimately Hidalgo was executed, but he is honored as "the Father of Mexican Independence." Morelos kept the revolt alive until 1815, when he too was executed.

The nation endured a decade of upheaval (1810 until 1821), and then the warring factions finally agreed on a compromise, Augustín Iturbide's *Plan de Iguala*. It made three guarantees: Mexico would be a constitutional monarchy headed by a European prince; the Catholic church would have a monopoly on religion; and Mexican-born citizens would have the same rights as those born in Spain. He thoughtfully tagged on another proviso allowing for a Mexican emperor, should no European prince step forward to take the role of king. When the agreement was signed, Iturbide was positioned to take over. No suitable European monarch was located and the new Mexican congress named him emperor. His empire proved short-lived: The very next year his administration fell. The new nation became a republic, but endured a succession of presidents and military dictators, as well as invasions, a war, and devastating losses of territory to its neighbor to the north, the United States.

Characteristic of the Republic's turbulent history during the half-century following independence was the French Intervention, in which three old colonial powers—England, France, and Spain—and the United States demonstrated continued interest in meddling with Mexico's internal affairs. Together they sent troops and warships to Veracruz to pressure the Mexican Government for payment of debts. The English and Spanish withdrew before long, but the French remained and declared war on Mexico.

The Mexicans enjoyed a glorious victory over the French at Puebla (the event that birthed the nation's Cinco de Mayo celebrations), yet the victory proved hollow. The French marched on Mexico City, and the Mexican president, Benito Juárez, was forced to retreat to the countryside to bide his time. With the help of anti-Juárez factions, a naive young Austrian, Archduke Maximilian of Hapsburg, was installed by the French as king of Mexico. For 3 years Maximilian tried to "rule" a country effectively in the midst of civil war, only to be left in the lurch when the French troops that supported him withdrew at the behest of the United States. Upon his triumphant return, Juárez summarily executed the Austrian interloper. Juárez, who would be remembered as one of the nation's great heroes, did his best to strengthen and unify the country before dying of a heart attack in 1872.

THE PORFIRIATO & THE REVOLUTION   From 1877 to 1911, a period now called the "Porfiriato," center stage in Mexico was occupied by Porfirio Díaz, a Juárez general who was president for 30 years and lived in the Castillo de (Castle of) Chapultepec in Mexico City. He was a terror to his enemies—that is, anyone who dared challenge his absolute power. Nevertheless, he is credited with bringing Mexico into the industrial age and for his patronage of architecture and the arts, the fruits of which are still enjoyed today. Public opinion forced him from office in 1911; he was succeeded by Francisco Madero.

After the fall of the Porfirist dictatorship, several factions split the country, including those led by "Pancho Villa" (whose real name was Doroteo Arango), Alvaro Obregón, Venustiano Carranza, and Emiliano Zapata. A famous photograph shows Zapata and Villa taking turns trying out Díaz's presidential chair in Mexico City. The decade that followed is referred to as the Mexican Revolution. Around 2 million Mexicans died for the cause. Drastic reforms occurred in this period, and the surge of vitality and progress from this exciting, if turbulent, time has inspired Mexicans to the present. Succeeding presidents have invoked the spirit of the Revolution, which lives in the hearts and minds of Mexicans as though it happened yesterday.

BEYOND THE REVOLUTION   The decades from the beginning of the Revolution in 1911 to stabilization in the 1940s and 1950s were tumultuous. While great strides were made during these years in distributing land to the peasant populations, irrigation, development of mineral resources, and the establishment of education, health, and sanitation programs, the tremendous economic pressure Mexico faced from its own internal problems and the world depression of the 1930s did little for

[Porfirio Díaz] looks what he is—a Man of Iron, the most forceful character in Mexico. Whatever was done in the 16th century was the work of Cortez . . . who was responsible for everything but the climate. Whatever is effected in Mexico today is the work of Porfirio Díaz.

—Stanton Davis Kirkham, *Mexican Trails* (1909)

political stability. From 1911 to 1940 16 men were president of Mexico. Some stayed in power a year or less.

One of the most significant leaders of the period, and the longest-lasting, was Lázaro Cárdenas (1934–40). He helped diminish the role of Mexico's military in national politics by dismantling the machine of General Plutarco Calles and exiling him from the country. He is remembered fondly as a president who listened to and cared about commoners. He made good on a number of the Revolution's promises, distributing nearly 50 million acres of land, primarily to *ejidos,* or communal farming groups; pouring money into education; and encouraging organized labor. And in one of his most memorable and controversial decisions, he nationalized Mexico's oil industry in 1938, sending foreign oil companies packing. Although Mexicans still view this act with great pride—the government stood up for Mexican labor—it did considerable damage to Mexico's standing with the international business community.

Despite many steps foward during the Cárdenas era, jobs could not keep pace with population growth, and with foreign investors shy of Mexico, and the world mired in the Great Depression, the Cárdenas era ended in 1940 with the nation in dark economic circumstances.

From the 1930s through the 1970s, socialism had a strong voice in Mexico; its impact was most marked in the state's attempts to run the country's businesses—not just oil, but railroads, mining, utilities, hotels, motion pictures, the telephone company, supermarkets, etc.

Miguel Alemán Valdés, president from 1946 to 1952, continued progress by building dams, improving highways and railways, encouraging trade, and building the Ciudad Universitario (University City) in Mexico City, home of Mexico's national university. Americans began to invest in Mexico again. Yet problems remained, many of which still plague the country today: The country's booming population created unemployment, wages of the common people were appallingly low, and Alemán's administration was plagued by corruption and graft.

In 1970, Luis Echeverría came to power, followed in 1976 by José López Portillo. During their presidencies there emerged a studied coolness in relations with the United States and an activist role in international affairs. This period also saw an increase in charges of large-scale corruption in the upper echelons of Mexican society. The corruption, though endemic to the system, was encouraged by the river of money from the rise in oil prices. When oil income skyrocketed, Mexican borrowing and spending did likewise. The reduction of oil prices in the 1980s left Mexico with an enormous foreign bank debt and serious infrastructure deficiencies.

The country inherited by President Miguel de la Madríd Hurtado in 1982 was one without King Oil, and with new challenges to build agriculture, cut expenditures, tame corruption, and keep creditors at bay. He began the process of privatizing government-held businesses (airlines, hotels, banks, etc.) and led the country into membership in GATT (the General Agreement on Tariffs and Trade), an important preparation for entering NAFTA (the North American Free Trade Agreement), which was accomplished during his successor's presidency. Nevertheless, soaring inflation of 200% faced Carlos Salinas de Gortari as he took office in 1989. Salinas's accomplishments included decreasing inflation to 15% annually by adeptly gaining the necessary agreement of industry and labor leaders to hold wages and prices; continuing the privitization of government-held businesses called the *pacto;* and leading the country into NAFTA, which over a 15-year period would reduce trade barriers and allow business to flourish more freely between Mexico, the United States, and Canada. During Salinas's 6-year term Mexico's world position as a country poised for great prosperity strengthened, and Mexican public opinion held his administration in high esteem. But a cloud arose over the country towards the end of the Salinas era when disgruntled Maya Indians staged an armed uprising after the NAFTA agreement was signed, and assassins' bullets felled both the PRI presidential candidate and the head of the PRI party. The presidential elections, while automated for the first time and more honest than previous ones, were still marred by allegations of corruption. Still, these incidents failed to dampen Mexico's hope for continued progress when Ernesto Zedillo assumed office in December 1994.

TOWARD THE FUTURE   From the time of the Revolution to the present, political parties and their roles have changed tremendously in Mexico. Although one political party, the **Partido Revolucionario Institucional** (PRI, called "el pree") has been in control under that name since 1946, opposition to it has become increasingly vocal and effective in recent years. In the beginning, the forerunner of the PRI, the Partido Revolucionario Mexicano, established by Lázaro Cárdenas, had four equal constituent groups—popular, agrarian, labor, and the military. At the risk of greatly oversimplifying a complex history and attendant issues, the widespread perception that the party is out of touch with the common Mexican, and its current problems retaining leadership, are the result of a change in focus away from those groups. The PRI today is heavily backed by, and in turn run by, business and industry leaders.

The crisis in Chiapas has become a focal point for many of the nation's problems. Opposition parties such as the **Partido Accion Nacional** (PAN) had taken up the cause of the seemingly disenfranchised masses, but no one had spoken for or paid much attention to Mexico's millions of poor indigenous people for some time. And on New Year's Day in 1994, when militant Maya Indians attacked Chiapan towns, killing many, attention was drawn to the plight of neglected indigenous groups and others in rural society, which the PRI-led government seemed to relegate to the bottom of the agenda. These groups are still clamoring for land they never received after the Revolution. That population growth has outstripped the availability of distributable land and that Mexico needs large-scale, modern agribusiness to keep up with the country's food needs are realities not understood by the millions of rural Mexicans who depend on their small family-run fields to feed themselves. President Carlos Salinas de Gortari's bold, controversial decision in the early 1990s to allow sale of *ejido* land may reflect Mexico's 21st-century needs, but it is at odds with firmly entrenched farm- and land-use traditions born before the 16th-century conquest. These issues of agrarian reform and the lack of other basics of life (roads, electricity, running water, education, health care, and more) are being raised in areas besides Chiapas, most notably Oaxaca, Chihuahua, Guerrero, and Michoacán. This is a grave and festering problem, made all the more serious now that Mexico is reeling from the devaluation of the peso.

The surprise decision to devalue the currency threw domestic and international confidence in Mexico into turmoil. The peso had already been in a fairly rapid, but controlled, daily devaluation process just prior to the government intervention, and it had been obvious for at least 3 years that a devaluation was overdue. But the Zedillo government erred in not involving industry and labor in the decision, in shocking the population with an overnight devaluation, and in not anticipating national and international repercussions. Within 3 months of the devaluation the peso lost half its value, reducing Mexico's buying power by 50%. After the government issued its harsh economic recovery program, interest rates on credit cards and loans (which have variable, not fixed rates in Mexico), soared 80% to 140%. Overnight the cost of gasoline increased 35% and gas and electricity 20%. As a partial solution, a $40 million loan package offered by the United States to ease the peso crisis uses Mexico's sacred petroleum revenue as collateral—a staggering blow to Mexico's national pride. The effect so far has been a loudly expressed lack of confidence in Zedillo and in the PRI, a dramatically slowed and cautious international investment climate, and a feeling among the citizenry of betrayal by the government. Responsibility for paying for governmental mismanagement of the economy has been shifted to ordinary Mexican citizens who were blindsided by this unexpected financial burden. Ordinary costs of daily living exceed the ability of average people to pay; businesses are closing and jobs are being eliminated.

Meanwhile as the effects of the peso crisis worsened, the Chiapan rebels threatened another uprising, the volcano Popocatepetl began spitting smoke and flames, and inflation predictions of 45% to 60% were heard. Former president Carlos Salinas de Gortari's brother was jailed and accused of involvement in the assassination of their brother-in-law, the head of the PRI party. Carlos Salinas de Gortari and his family left Mexico quickly for the United States, after Salinas threatened a hunger strike unless his name was cleared regarding the assassination of his brother-in-law, and after he spoke publicly (an unheard-of breach of conduct by a past president) against the present government's handling of the peso crisis.

It seems incredulous that a country so poised for prosperity should career backwards so rapidly, and that such an admired and trusted president should so quickly fall from grace—because the people's trust and hopes in government under Salinas were so high, the betrayal is particularly bitter. However, as grim as all this seems, using Mexico's history just this century as a rule, the country bounces back from adversity to become even stronger. A strong popular will to progress undergirds the Mexican spirit, and despite recent sobering events, the country still bustles with commercial activity. Meanwhile, as long as inflation doesn't outpace the effect of the devaluation, the country is quite a bargain; even a year after the devaluation, prices are still better than they've been since 1985.

Economically, Mexico, though still a third world country, is by no means a poor country. Only about a sixth of the economy is in agriculture. Mining is still fairly important. Gold, silver, and many other important minerals are still mined, but the big industry today is oil. Mexico is also well industrialized, manufacturing everything from textiles and food products to cassette tapes and automobiles.

3 Margaritas, Tortillas & *Mole:* Food & Drink in Mexico

Mexican food served in the United States or almost anywhere else in the world is almost never truly Mexican. The farther you get from the source the more the authenticity is lost in translation. True Mexican food usually isn't fiery hot, for example; hot spices are added from sauces and garnishes at the table.

While there are certain staples like tortillas and beans that appear almost universally around the country, Mexican food and drink varies considerably from region to region; even the beans and tortillas will sidestep the usual in different locales.

MEALS & RESTAURANTS *A LA MEXICANA*

BREAKFAST Traditionally, businesspeople in Mexico may start their day with a cup of coffee or *atole* and a piece of sweet bread just before heading for work around 8am; they won't sit down for a real breakfast until around 10 or 11am, when restaurants fill with men (usually) eating hearty breakfasts that may look more like lunch with steak, eggs, beans, and tortillas. Things are slowly changing as some executives are beginning to favor an earlier breakfast hour, beginning between 7 and 8am, during which business and the morning meal are combined.

Foreigners searching for an early breakfast will often find that nothing gets going in restaurants until around 9am; however, markets are bustling by 7am (they are great places to get an early breakfast) and the capital's hotel restaurants often open as early as 7am to accommodate business travelers and those leaving on early flights. If you like to stoke the fires first thing, you might also bring your own portable coffee pot and coffee and buy bakery goodies the night before to make breakfast yourself.

LUNCH The main meal of the day, lunch, has traditionally been a 2- to 3-hour break, occurring between 1 and 5pm. But in the capital at least an abbreviated midday break is beginning to take hold. Short or long, the typical Mexican lunch begins with soup, then rice, then a main course with beans and tortillas and a bit of vegetable, and lastly dessert and coffee. But here too you'll see one-plate meals and fast food beginning to encroach on the multicourse meal. Workers return to their jobs until 7 or 8pm.

DINNER The evening meal is taken late, usually around 9 or 10pm. Although you may see many Mexicans eating in restaurants at night, big evening meals aren't traditional; a typical meal at home would be a light one with leftovers from breakfast or lunch, perhaps soup or tortillas and jam, or a little meat and rice.

RESTAURANT TIPS & ETIQUETTE Some of the foreigner's greatest frustrations in Mexico occur in restaurants, when they need to hail and retain the waiter or get their check. To summon the waiter, waive or raise your hand, but don't motion with your index finger, a demeaning gesture that may even cause the waiter to ignore you. To gesture someone to them, Mexicans will stand up, extend an arm straight out at shoulder level, and make a straight-armed, downward, diving motion with their hand cupped. A more discreet version, good to use when seated, has the elbow bent and perpendicular to the shoulder; with hand cupped, make a quick, diving motion out a bit from the armpit. (Both of these motions may make you feel silly until you practice. The latter one looks rather like the motion Americans make to signify "be still" or "shut up.")

If the waiter arrives to take your order before you are ready, you may have trouble getting him again. Once an order is in, however, the food usually arrives in steady sequence. Frequently, just before you've finished, when your plate is nearly empty, the waiter appears out of nowhere to whisk it away—unwary diners have seen their plates disappear midbite.

Finding your waiter when you're ready for the check can also be difficult. While waiters may hover too much while you're dining, they tend to disappear entirely by meal's end. It's considered rude for the waiter to bring the check before it's requested, so you have to ask for it, sometimes more than once. (To find a missing waiter, get up as if to leave and scrape the chairs loudly; if that fails, you'll probably find him chatting in the kitchen.) If you want the check and the waiter is simply across the room, a smile and a scribbling motion into the palm of your hand will send the message. In many budget restaurants, waiters don't clear the table of finished plates or soft-drink bottles because they use them to figure the tab. Always double-check the addition.

FOOD AROUND THE COUNTRY

You won't have to confine yourself to Mexican food during a visit to Mexico—you'll find restaurants that prepare world-class French, Italian, Swiss, German, and other international cuisines. But you can also delve into the variety of Mexico's traditional foods, which derive from pre-Hispanic, Spanish, and French cuisines. At its best Mexican food is among the most delicious in the world. Visitors can fairly easily find hearty, filling meals on a budget, but finding truly delicious food is not so easy—one positive is that some of the country's best food is found in small inexpensive restaurants where regional specialties are made to please discerning locals. Explanations of specific dishes are found in the appendix.

Recipes such as mole poblano—developed by nuns during colonial times to please priests and visiting dignitaries—have become part of the national patrimony, but the basics of Mexico's cuisine have endured since pre-Hispanic times. Corn, considered holy, was the foundation staple food of pre-Hispanic peoples. These people used corn leaves to bake and wrap food and ground corn to make the *atole* drink in many flavors (bitter, picante, or sweet) as well as tortillas and tamales (stuffed with meat).

When the Spanish arrived they found a bounty of edibles never seen in the Old World, including turkey, chocolate, tomatoes, squash, beans, avocados, peanuts, and vanilla (in addition to corn). All of these ingredients were integral parts of pre-Hispanic foods, and remain at the heart of today's Mexican cooking. Also central to the Indian peoples' cuisines were chiles, nopal cactus, amaranth, eggs of ants, turtles and iguanas, corn and maguey worms, bee and fly larvae, flowers of the maguey and squash, grasshoppers, jumiles (similar to stinkbugs), armadillos, rattlesnakes, hairless dogs, deer, squirrels, monkeys, rats, frogs, ducks, parrots, quail, shrimp, fish, crabs, and crawfish. Exotic fruits such as sapodilla, guava, mamey, chirimoya, and pitahuayas rounded out the diet. Some of these are mainstream foods today, and others are considered delicacies and may be seen on specialty menus.

But much of what we consider Mexican food wouldn't exist without the contributions of the Spanish. They introduced sugarcane, cattle, sheep, wheat, grapes, barley, and rice. The French influence is best seen in the extensive variety of baked goods available in the capital.

MEXICO'S REGIONAL CUISINES   Tamales are a traditional food all around Mexico, but there are many regional differences. In Mexico City you can often find the traditional Oaxaca tamales, which are steamed in a banana leaf. The *zacahuil* of coastal Veracruz is the size of a pig's leg (that's what's in the center) and is pit-baked in a banana leaf; it can be sampled from street vendors on Sunday at the Lagunilla market.

Tortillas, another Mexican basic, are also not made or used equally. In northern Mexico flour tortillas are served more often than corn tortillas. Blue corn tortillas, once a market food, have found their way to gourmet tables throughout the country. Tortillas are fried and used as a garnish in tortilla and Tarascan soup. Filled with meat they become, of course, tacos. A tortilla stuffed, rolled, or covered in a sauce

Tequila!!!

Perhaps looking to distract themselves from the cares of conquest, the first waves of Spanish colonists in Mexico fiddled around with *pulque* (*pool*-kay), a mildly intoxicating drink popular among indigenous peoples. They hit upon a stronger drink in the late 16th century when Cenobio Sauza distilled his first bottle of a special hooch in Tequila, Jalisco—thus was born an 80-proof potation now consumed the world over, which can truly be called the "spirit" of Mexico.

True tequila is made only from the sweet sap at the heart of the blue *agave* (ah-*gah*-veh) plant, grown in the states of Jalisco, Nayarit, and Michoacán. The laborious process by which tequila is produced involves roasting the enormous agave heart (it can weigh 100 lb. or more) in a pit; the cooked heart is then pulped and the juice distilled. It is double distilled before it is bottled.

The basic tequila is *blanco,* or white. Many "gold" tequilas are just *blanco* with a little artificial coloring; the true golds are always *reposado,* or "rested" at least 6 months. The aging process does lend tequilas a light-gold tint. Also available, at the super-premium end of the market, are *añejo* tequilas, which must be aged at least 2 years.

A similar but less-refined drink is *mescal;* it is made from one of the other 400 varieties of agave. It's mescal, not tequila, that comes with a worm in the bottom of the bottle. Pulque, which comes from yet another agave, is still produced.

The hoary old ritual for drinking tequila, dating back long before margaritas began hogging the spotlight, is to put a dash of salt in your left hand, a shot glass of tequila before you in the middle, and a nice fresh slice of lime on your right—consume them from left to right, in bang-bang-bang fashion. This is a bracing combination—I dare you to do it without falling into unconscious mimicry of Jack Nicholson having a snort in *Easy Rider.* (It should be noted that reckless repetition of this procedure has felled many a tourist onto barroom floors.)

In the 1940s, when Margarita Sames concocted the original tequila-based "margarita" drink, she entertained friends with it in her Acapulco home. She never imagined that sunsets from Anchorage to Argentina would one day be celebrated with the tasty lime-laden cocktail, and sipped from big, long-stemmed glasses named especially for her drink. The concoction became so popular that bartenders far and wide laid claim to its creation, but Sames's story is the most believable. Sames made her drink with tequila, fresh-squeezed lime juice, and Cointreau, a French liqueur made with the skins of both bitter and sweet oranges. The particulars can change, but these three categories of ingredient—real tequila, lime juice, and orange-flavored liqueur—are the holy trinity of margarita making.

Here are a few variations you can work into your bartending. There are a lot of tequilas available beyond the usual Cuervo and Sauza varieties. Herradura is another big-name brand, perhaps the best of these. If your liquor store is enlightened they may be able to procure lesser-known brands; you can also, of course, add a special bottle of tequila to your shopping list for each trip you make south of the border. As far as liqueur goes, these days most people use triple sec instead of

and garnished results in an enchilada. A tortilla filled with cheese and lightly fried is a quesadilla. Rolled into a narrow tube stuffed with chicken, then deep fried, it becomes a flauta. Leftover tortillas cut in wedges and crispy fried are called totopos and used to scoop beans and guacamole salad. Yesterday's tortillas mixed with eggs,

Cointreau—both are orange-based liqueurs, but Cointreau is considerably more expensive. If you're using an expensive premium tequila, try the Cointreau—it's delicious. If you're using triple sec, don't buy one of the bargain-basement varieties—it's just not the real stuff. Marie Brizard, Bols, and DeKuyper all make good triple secs. Another substitute for triple sec is Grand Marnier, a top-shelf orange- and cognac-flavored liqueur—it may sound odd, but the cognac flavor lends an interesting character to a margarita. And finally, while traditionalists will tell you there's no substitute for fresh-squeezed lime juice, it can be nearly impossible to procure a decent supply of juicy, ripe limes—the fruit is notorious for inconsistent quality. One solution is to use fresh-squeezed lemon juice; the flavors are nearly indistinguishable in the context of the cocktail, and lemons are much more consistent. Another is to use a bottled lime juice, but if you do, get Rose's Lime Juice—it's just better than any of the other brands.

The proportions of the cocktail are 2 parts tequila, 1 part liqueur, and 1 1/2 parts lime juice. Purists will tell you that there's only one way to mix a margarita (in a shaker with fairly coarse chunks of ice) and only two ways to serve it (either "on the rocks" into a kosher salt–rimmed hurricane glass or "straight up" strained from the shaker into a salt-rimmed martini- or champagne-style glass). But why let an ideologue impinge on your fun? If you want to use a blender for frozen margaritas, knock yourself out—just use less expensive brands of tequila and triple sec, as the Slurpee effect will dilute the flavors of the spirits. Or add some fresh fruit—strawberries, raspberries, ripe peaches, and kiwis all are delicious additions to a frozen margarita. All the squabbles over minor additives, salt or no salt, or who actually created the drink aside, three cheers to the margarita itself: so refreshingly smooth it goes down as agreeably as lemonade on a summer day . . . just watch out for that sneaky wallop—Mike Tyson's got nothing on it for knockout power.

In Chapala, Jalisco, a widow (in Spanish, *viuda*) invented a spicy orange juice–based drink as a tequila chaser and bottled it under the La Viuda label, which is made in Chapala and sold countrywide. Along came Bloody Mary–style tequila drinks and many more including the tequila sunrise, which blends tequila, orange juice, and a splash of grenadine into a cocktail that looks as promising as a tropical sunrise.

Tequila is making inroads into new territory these days—as a flavoring in food in everything from banana nut bread, cookies, and jalapeño jelly, to salsa, pot roast, baked chicken, and stuffed peppers. If this revolution takes hold the way margaritas did, we could soon see tequila beside wine on the cook's list of pantry staples. Tequila-flavored dishes are already beginning to appear on menus of fine restaurants in Mexico.

At least four books are available that expound at length the versatility of Mexico's most famous liquor: *Tequila: The Spirit of Mexico* by Lucinda Hutson (Ten Speed Press, 1994); *The Tequila Cook Book* by Lynn Nusom (Golden West Publishers, 1994); *Tomás' Tequila Book* by Don and Alice Hutson and Dianne Goss (Pasquale Publishing, 1992); and *The Tequila Book* by Ann Walker (Chronicle Books, 1994).

chicken, peppers, and other spices are called chilaquiles. Small fried corn tortillas are delicious with ceviche, or when topped with fresh lettuce, tomatoes, sauce, onions, and chicken they become tostadas. Each region has a variation of these tortilla-based dishes and most can be found in Mexico City.

Since a variety of Mexico's cuisines appear on menus all over the country, it's useful to know some of the best to try.

Puebla is known for the many dishes created by colonial-era nuns, among them traditional *mole poblano* (a rich sauce with more than 20 ingredients served over turkey), the eggnoglike *rompope,* and *bunuelos* (a kind of puff pastry dipped in sugar). Puebla is also known for its Mexican-style barbecue, lamb mixiotes (cooked in spicy sauce and wrapped in maguey paper), and *tinga* (a delicious beef stew). *Chiles enogada,* the national dish of Mexico, was created in Puebla in honor of Emperor Agustín Iturbide. The national colors of red, white, and green appear in this dish, in which large green poblano peppers are stuffed with spicy beef, topped with white almond sauce, and sprinkled with red pomegranate seeds. It's served around Independence Day in September.

Tamales wrapped in banana leaves and a number of different mole sauces are hallmarks of **Oaxacan** cuisine.

The **Yucatán** is noted for its rich (but not *picante*) sauces and pit-baked meat. Mild but flavorful achiote-based paste is one of the main flavorings for Yucatecan sauces.

The states of **Guerrero, Nayarit,** and **Jalisco** produce *pozole,* a soup of hominy and chicken or pork made in a clear broth or one from tomatoes or green chiles (depending on the state), and topped with a variety of garnishes.

Michoacán comes forth with a triangular-shaped tamal called *corunda,* and *uchepo,* a rectangular tamal that is either sweet or has meat inside. The state is also known for its soups, among them the delicious *Tarascan* soup, made with a bean-broth base.

And **Veracruz,** of course, is famous for seafood dishes, especially red snapper Veracruz-style, smothered in tomatoes, onions, garlic, and olives.

DISTINCTIVE MEXICAN DRINKS

Though Mexico grows flavorful **coffee** in Chiapas, Veracruz, and Oaxaca, a jar of instant coffee is often all that's offered, especially in budget restaurants. Decaffeinated coffee appears on some menus, but often it's the instant variety, even in the best restaurants.

Specialty drinks are almost as varied as the food in Mexico. **Tequila** comes from the blue agave grown near Guadalajara and it's the intoxicating ingredient in the famed margarita. Hot *ponche* (punch) is found often at festivals and is usually made with fresh fruit and spiked with tequila or rum.

Domestic wine and beer are excellent choices in Mexico, and in the past have been cheaper than any imported variety. However, NAFTA has lowered trade barriers against U.S.-made alcoholic drinks, and prices for them are becoming lower as well.

Baja California and the region around Querétaro is prime grape growing land for Mexico's **wine** production. Excellent **beer** is produced in Monterrey, the Yucatán, and Veracruz. The best *pulque,* a pre-Hispanic drink derived from the juice of the maguey plant, supposedly comes from Hidalgo State. Mexicans prefer freshly fermented pulque and generally avoid the canned variety, saying it's just not the real thing. Visitors to the capital can sample it at restaurants around Garibaldi Square. Delicious **fruit-flavored waters** appear on tables countrywide; they are made from hibiscus flowers, ground rice and melon seeds, watermelon, and other fresh fruits. Be sure to ask if they are made with purified water. **Sangria** is a spicy tomato-, orange juice-, and pepper-based chaser for tequila shots—not the sweet red wine with fruit in it that Americans are used to.

Though the rich, eggnoglike *rompope* was invented in Puebla, now other regions such as San Juan de los Lagos, Jalisco, produce it. It's sold in liquor and grocery stores countrywide.

4 Recommended Books

There are an endless number of books written on the history, culture, and archaeology of Mexico and Central America. I have listed those I especially enjoyed.

HISTORY   Dennis Tedlock produced an elegant translation of the *Popul Vuh,* a collection of ancient Maya mythological tales (Simon & Schuster, 1985). *A Short History of Mexico* (Doubleday, 1962) by J. Patrick McHenry is a concise historical account. A remarkably readable and thorough college textbook is *The Course of Mexican History* (Oxford University Press, 1987) by Michael C. Meyer and William L. Sherman. Bernal Díaz's *The Conquest of New Spain* (Shoe String, 1988) is the famous story of the Mexican Conquest written by Cortés's lieutenant. *The Crown of Mexico* (Holt, Rinehart & Winston, 1971) by Joan Haslip, a biography of Maximilian and Carlota, reads like a novel. Eric Wolf's *Sons of the Shaking Earth* (University of Chicago Press) is the best single-volume introduction to Mexican history and culture that I know. *Ancient Mexico; An Overview* (University of New Mexico Press, 1985) by Jaime Litvak, is a short, very readable history of pre-Hispanic Mexico.

The Wind That Swept Mexico (University of Texas Press, 1971) by Anita Brenner, is a classic illustrated account of the Mexican Revolution. Early this century Charles Flandrau wrote the classic *Viva Mexico: A Traveller's Account of Life in Mexico* (Eland Books, 1985), a blunt and humorous description of Mexico. Jonathan Kandell's *La Capital, Biography of Mexico City* (Random House, 1988) is assiduously researched, yet wonderfully readable.

Life in Mexico: Letters of Fanny Calderón de la Barca (Doubleday, 1966), edited and annotated by Howard T. Fisher and Marion Hall Fisher, is as lively and entertaining today as when it first appeared in 1843, but the editor's illustrated and annotated update makes it even more contemporary. Scottish-born Fanny was married to the Spanish ambassador to Mexico, and the letters are the accounts of her experiences. *My Heart Lies South* by Elizabeth Borton de Treviño (1953) is a humorous, tender, and insightful autobiographical account of the life of an American woman married to a Mexican in Monterrey; it begins in the 1930s.

Several modern writers have attempted to view Mexican culture through the lens of history. Harry A. Franck's *Trailing Cortés Through Mexico* by Frederick A. Stokes (1935), and Mathew J. Bruccoli's *Reconquest of Mexico* (Vanguard Press, 1974) pursue the Conquest route of Cortés, interweaving history with the customs of rural and city life of this century.

CONTEMPORARY MEXICAN LIFE   *Five Families* (Basic Books, 1979) and *Children of Sanchez* (Random House, 1979), both by Oscar Lewis, are sociological studies written in the late 1950s about typical Mexican families. Irene Nicholson's *Mexican and Central American Mythology* (Peter Bedrick Books, 1983) is a concise illustrated book that simplifies the subject.

A good but controversial all-around introduction to contemporary Mexico and its people is *Distant Neighbors: A Portrait of the Mexicans* (Random House, 1984) by Alan Riding. In a more personal vein is Patrick Oster's *The Mexicans: A Personal Portrait of the Mexican People* (HarperCollins, 1989), a reporter's insightful account of ordinary Mexican people. A book with valuable insights into the Mexican character is *The Labyrinth of Solitude* (Grove Press, 1985) by Octavio Paz. The best single source of information on Mexican music, dance, and mythology is Frances Toor's *A Treasury of Mexican Folkways* (Crown, 1967).

Anyone going to San Cristóbal de las Casas, Chiapas, should first read *Living Maya* (Harry N. Abrams, 1987) by Walter F. Morris, with excellent photographs by Jeffrey J. Foxx, all about the Maya living today in the state of Chiapas. Peter Canby's *The Heart of the Sky: Travels Among the Maya* (Kodansha International, 1994) takes readers on a rare but rugged journey as he searches to understand the real issues facing the Maya of Mexico and Guatemala today. For some fascinating background on northern Mexico and the Copper Canyon, read *Unknown Mexico* (Dover Press, 1987) by Carl Lumholtz, an intrepid writer and photographer around the turn of the century.

PRE-HISPANIC MEXICO   Anyone heading for Yucatán should first read the wonderfully entertaining accounts of travel in that region by the 19th-century traveler, New York lawyer, and amateur archaeologist John L. Stephens. His book *Incidents of Travel in Central America, Chiapas and Yucatán,* and also the account of his second trip, *Incidents of Travel in Yucatán,* have been reprinted by Dover complete with Frederick Catherwood's original illustrations. Dover has also released Diego de Landa's *Yucatán Before and After the Conquest* (Dover, 1978), written in the 1560s. Friar Diego's account is a detailed description of Maya daily life, much of which has remained the same from his time until today. Another must is *The Maya* (Thames and Hudson, 1987) by Michael Coe, which is helpful in relating to the different Maya periods. *A Forest of Kings: The Untold Story of the Ancient Maya* (William Morrow, 1990) by Linda Schele and David Freidel, uses the written history of Maya hieroglyphs to tell the dynastic history of selected Maya sites. You'll never view the sky the same after reading *Maya Cosmos: Three Thousand Years on the Shaman's Path* (William Morrow, 1993) by David Freidel, Linda Schele, and Joy Parker, whose personal insights and scholarly work take us along a very readable path into the amazing sky-centered world of the Maya. (*The Blood of Kings: Dynasty and Ritual in Maya Art* (George Braziller, 1986) by Linda Schele and Mary Ellen Miller, is a pioneer work and unlocks the bloody history of the Maya. The most comprehensive guide to Maya ruins is Joyce Kelly's *An Archaeological Guide to Mexico's Yucatán Peninsula* (University of Oklahoma, 1993).

Michael Coe's *Mexico: From the Olmecs to the Aztecs* (Thames and Hudson, 1994), takes us through the latest discoveries and theories regarding Mexico's ancient Indian cultures (but excludes the Maya which are covered in his other book *The Maya,* mentioned above). For the latest on the mysterious Olmec culture don't miss *The Olmec World: Ritual and Rulership* (The Art Museum, Princeton University and Harry N. Abrahms, 1996), the splendid catalog of a major exhibition of privately owned Olmec art in the United States. Major Olmec scholars in the United States provided essays on current theories about Mexico's little-studied "mother culture."

Several ficitionalized accounts of Aztec life have been written. These include Gary Jenning's *Aztec* (Avon, 1981), a superbly researched and colorfully written account of Aztec life before and after the Conquest. Equally revealing is *The Luck of Huemac,* by Daniel Peters (Random House, 1981), a compelling novel about four generations of an Aztec family between the years 1428 and 1520.

ART & ARCHITECTURE   A book that tells the story of the Indians' "painted books" is *The Mexican Codices and Their Extraordinary History* (Ediciones Lara, 1985) by María Sten. *Mexico Splendors of Thirty Centuries* (Metropolitan Museum of Art, 1990), the catalog of the 1991 traveling exhibition, is a wonderful resource on Mexico's art from 1500 B.C. through the 1950s. Another superb catalog, *Images of Mexico: The Contribution of Mexico to 20th Century Art* (Dallas Museum of Art, 1987) is a fabulously illustrated and detailed account of Mexican art gathered from collections around the world. Elizabeth Wilder Weismann's *Art and Time in Mexico: From the Conquest to the Revolution* (HarperCollins, 1985), illustrated with 351 photographs, covers Mexican religious, public, and private architecture with excellent photos and text. *Casa Mexicana* (Stewart, Tabori & Chang, 1989) by Tim Street-Porter, takes readers through the interiors of some of Mexico's finest homes-turned-museums or public buildings and private homes using color photographs. *Mexican Interiors* (Architectural Book Publishing Co., 1962) by Verna Cook Shipway and Warren Shipway, uses black-and-white photographs to highlight architectural details from homes all over Mexico.

FOLK ART Chloè Sayer's *Costumes of Mexico* (University of Texas Press, 1985) is a beautifully illustrated and written work. *Mexican Masks* (University of Texas Press, 1980) by Donald Cordry, based on the author's collection and travels, remains the definitive work on Mexican masks. Cordry's *Mexican Indian Costumes* (University of Texas Press, 1968) is another classic on the subject. Carlos Espejel wrote both *Mexican Folk Ceramics* and *Mexican Folk Crafts* (Editorial Blume, 1975 and 1978), two comprehensive books that explore crafts state by state. *Folk Treasures of Mexico* (Harry N. Abrams, 1990) by Marion Oettinger, curator of Folk and Latin American Art at the San Antonio Museum of Art, is the fascinating illustrated story behind the 3,000-piece Mexican folk-art collection amassed by Nelson Rockefeller over a 50-year period, and also includes much information about individual folk artists. The fantastically colorful sculpted animals and figures of Oaxaca's wood-carvers is the subject of *Oaxacan Wood Carving* (Chronicle Books, 1993), by Shepard Barbash and photographed by Vicki Ragan. It is both a finely illustrated exposition of colorful work from wood-carvers in Oaxaca and an insightful glimpse of the rural communities where the artists live.

NATURE *A Naturalist's Mexico* (Texas A&M University Press, 1992), by Roland H. Wauer, is a fabulous guide to birding in Mexico. *A Hiker's Guide to Mexico's Natural History* (Mountaineers, 1995), by Jom Conrad, covers Mexican flora and fauna and tells how to find the easy-to-reach and out-of-the-way spots he describes. Most comprehensive of all the birding guide books is *A Guide to the Birds of Mexico and North Central America* (Oxford University Press, 1995), by Steve N. Ottowell and Sophie Webb, an encyclopedic volume with hundreds of color illustrations. *Peterson Field Guides: Mexican Birds* (Houghton Mifflin), by Roger Tory Peterson and Edward L. Chalif, is an excellent guide to the country's birds. *Birds of the Yucatán* (Amigos de Sian Ka'an) has color illustrations and descriptions of 100 birds found primarily in the Yucatán peninsula. *A Guide to Mexican Mammals and Reptiles* (Minutiae Mexicana), by Norman Pelham Wright and Dr. Bernardo Villa Ramírez, is a small but useful guide to some of the country's wildlife.

2

Planning a Trip to Southern Pacific Mexico

Before any trip, you need to do a bit of advance planning. When should I go? What's the best way to get there? How much will this trip cost? And can I catch a festival during my visit? I'll answer these and other questions for you in this chapter.

1 Visitor Information, Entry Requirements & Money

SOURCES OF INFORMATION

The **Mexico Hotline** (☎ 800/44-MEXICO in the U.S.) is a good source for very general informational brochures on the country and for answers to the most commonly asked questions. If you have a fax, Mexico's Ministry of Tourism also offers **FaxMeMexico** (☎ 503/385-9282). Call, provide them with a fax number, and select from a variety of topics—from accommodations (the service lists 400 hotels) to shopping, dining, sports, sightseeing, festivals, and nightlife. They'll then fax you the materials you're interested in.

The **U.S. Department of State** (☎ 202/647-5225 for travel information, ☎ 202/647-9225 for bulletin board information), offers a **Consular Information Sheet** on Mexico, with a compilation of safety, medical, driving, and general travel information gleaned from reports by official U.S. State Department offices in Mexico. You can also request the Consular Information Sheet (☎ 202/647-2000) by fax. The **Center for Disease Control hot line** (☎ 404/332-4559), is another source for medical information affecting travelers to Mexico and elsewhere.

MEXICAN GOVERNMENT TOURIST OFFICES   Mexico has tourist offices throughout the world, including the following:

United States: 70 E. Lake St., Suite 1413, Chicago, IL 60601 (☎ 312/565-2778); 5075 Westheimer, Suite 975-West Houston, TX 77056 (☎ 713/629-1611); 10100 Santa Monica Blvd., Suite 224, Los Angeles, CA 90067 (☎ 310/203-8191); 2333 Ponce de Leon Blvd., Suite 710, Coral Gables, FL 33134 (☎ 305/443-9160); 405 Park Ave., Suite 1401, New York, NY 10022 (☎ 212/838-2947); and the Mexican Embassy Tourism Delegate, 1911 Pennsylvania Ave. NW, Washington, DC 20006 (☎ 202/728-1750).

Canada: One Place Ville-Marie, Suite 1526, Montréal, PQ H3B 2B5 (☎ **514/ 871-1052**); 2 Bloor St. W., Suite 1801, Toronto, ON M4W 3E2 (☎ **416/ 925-1876**); 99 W. Hastings, no. 1610, Vancouver, British Columbia V6C 2W2 (☎ **604/669-3498**).

Europe: Weisenhüttenplatz 26, D 6000 Frankfurt-am-Main 1, Germany (☎ **49/ 69-25-3413**); 60-61 Trafalgar Sq., London WC2 N5DS, United Kingdom (☎ **171/ 734-1058**); Calle de Velázquez 126, 28006 Madrid, Spain (☎ **341/261-1827**); 4 rue Notre-Dame-des-Victoires, 75002 Paris, France (☎ **331/4020-0734**); and via Barberini 3, 00187 Rome, Italy (☎ **396/482-7160**).

Asia: 2.15.1 Nagato-Cho, Chiyoda-Ku, Tokyo 100, Japan (☎ **813/580-2962**).

STATE TOURISM DEVELOPMENT OFFICES   Two Mexican states have tourism and trade development offices in the United States: **Casa Guerrero State Promotion Office,** 5075 Westheimer, Suite 980 W., Houston, TX 77056 (☎ **713/ 552-0930;** fax 713/552-0207); **Casa Nuevo León State Promotion Office,** 100 W. Houston St., Suite 1400, San Antonio, TX 78205 (☎ **210/225-0732;** fax 210/ 225-0736).

OTHER SOURCES   The following newsletters may be of interest to readers: *Mexico Meanderings,* P.O. Box 33057, Austin, TX 78764, aimed at readers who travel to off-the-beaten-track destinations by car, bus, or train (six to eight pages, photographs, published six times annually, subscription $18); *Travel Mexico,* Apdo. Postal 6-1007, 06600 Mexico, D.F., from the publishers of the *Traveler's Guide to Mexico,* the book frequently found in hotel rooms in Mexico, covers a variety of topics from archaeological news to hotel packages, new resorts and hotels, and the economy (six times annually, subscription $18).

For other newsletters, see "For Seniors" under "Tips for Travelers with Special Needs," below.

ENTRY REQUIREMENTS

DOCUMENTS   All travelers to Mexico are required to present **proof of citizenship,** such as an original birth certificate with a raised seal, a valid passport, or naturalization papers. Those using a birth certificate should also have a current photo identification such as a driver's license. And those whose last name on the birth certificate is different from their current name (women using a married name, for example) should also bring a photo identification card *and* legal proof of the name change such as the *original* marriage license or certificate (I'm not kidding). This proof of citizenship may also be requested when you want to reenter either the United States or Mexico. Note that photocopies are *not* acceptable.

You must also carry a **Mexican Tourist Permit,** which is issued free of charge by Mexican border officials after proof of citizenship is accepted. The Tourist Permit is more important than a passport in Mexico, so guard it carefully. If you lose it, you may not be permitted to leave the country until you can replace it—a bureaucratic hassle that takes several days to a week at least. (If you do lose your Tourist Permit, get a police report from local authorities indicating that your documents were stolen; having one *might* lessen the hassle of exiting the country without all your identification.)

A Tourist Permit can be issued for up to 180 days, and although your stay south of the border may be shorter than that, you should ask for the maximum time, just in case. Sometimes officials don't ask—they just stamp a time limit, so be sure to say "six months" (or at least twice as long as you intend to stay). If you should decide to extend your stay, you'll eliminate hassle by not needing to renew your papers.

This is especially important for people who take a car into Mexico. Additional documentation is required for driving a personal vehicle in Mexico (see "By Car" under "Getting There," below).

Note that children under age 18 traveling without parents or with only one parent must have a notarized letter from the absent parent or parents authorizing the travel.

Lost Documents   To replace a **lost passport,** contact your embassy or nearest consular agent (see "Fast Facts: Mexico," below). You must establish a record of your citizenship and also fill out a form requesting another Mexican Tourist Permit. Without the **Tourist Permit** you can't leave the country, and without an affidavit affirming your passport request and citizenship, you may have hassles at customs when you get home. So it's important to clear everything up *before* trying to leave. Mexican customs may, however, accept the police report of the loss of the Tourist Permit and allow you to leave.

CUSTOMS ALLOWANCES   When you enter Mexico, customs officials will be tolerant as long as you have no illegal drugs or firearms. You're allowed to bring in two cartons of cigarettes, or 50 cigars, plus a kilogram (2.2 lb.) of smoking tobacco; the liquor allowance is two bottles of anything, wine or hard liquor; you are also allowed 12 rolls of film.

When reentering the United States, federal law allows you to bring in duty-free up to $400 in purchases every 30 days. The first $1,000 over the $400 allowance is taxed at 10%. You may bring in a carton (200) of cigarettes or 50 cigars or 2 kilograms (4.4 lb.) of smoking tobacco, plus 1 liter of an alcoholic beverage (wine, beer, or spirits).

Canadian citizens are allowed $20 in purchases after a 24-hour absence from the country or $100 after a stay of 48 hours or more.

Going through Customs   Mexican customs inspection has been streamlined. At most points of entry tourists are requested to punch a button in front of what looks like a traffic signal, which alternates on touch between red and green signals. A green light means you go through without inspection; a red light means your luggage or car may be inspected briefly or thoroughly. I've been seeing more red lights these days; seems the government is stepping up their inspections.

MONEY

CASH/CURRENCY   In 1993, the Mexican government dropped three zeroes from its currency. The new currency is called the *Nuevo Peso,* or New Peso. The purpose was to simplify accounting; all those zeroes were becoming too difficult to manage. Old Peso notes were valid through 1996. Paper currency comes in denominations of 10, 20, 50, and 100 New Pesos. Coins come in denominations of 1, 2, 5, and 10 pesos and 20 and 50 *centavos* (100 centavos make one New Peso). The coins are somewhat confusing because different denominations have a similar appearance. You may still see some prices written with *N* or *NP* beside them, which refer to New Pesos. Currently the U.S. dollar equals around NP$7.50; at that rate an item costing NP$5, for example, would be equivalent to U.S. 67¢.

These changes are likely to cause confusion among U.S. and Canadian travelers to Mexico in several ways. Before the New Peso was instituted, merchants and others skipped the small change, but now they don't. Small change (a peso or less than a peso) is often unavailable, so cashiers often offer gum or candy to make up the difference. Centavos will appear on restaurant bills and credit cards, but are paid differently depending on if you pay in cash or by credit card. On restaurant bills that you pay in cash, for example, the centavos will be rounded up or down to the nearest five centavos. Credit-card bills, however, will show the exact amount (not rounded), and will have *N* written before the amount to denote that the bill is in New Pesos. Be sure to double-check any credit-card vouchers to be sure the *N* or *NP* appears on the total line.

Getting change continues to be a problem in Mexico. Small-denomination bills and coins are hard to come by, so start collecting them early in your trip and continue as you travel. Shopkeepers everywhere seem to always be out of change and small bills; that's doubly true in a market.

Note: The dollar sign ($) is used to indicate pesos in Mexico. To avoid confusion, I will use the dollar sign in this book *only* to denote U.S. currency.

Only dollar prices are listed in this book; they are a more reliable indication than peso prices. Many establishments dealing with tourists quote prices in dollars. To avoid confusion, they use the abbreviations "Dlls." for dollars and "m.n." (*moneda nacional*—national currency) for pesos.

Every effort has been made to provide the most accurate and up-to-date information in this guide, but price changes are inevitable.

EXCHANGING MONEY   The December 1994 devaluation of the peso has had varied meanings for tourists. First, the rate of exchange fluctuates daily, so be careful not to exchange too much of your currency at once. Don't forget, however, to allow enough money to carry you over a weekend or Mexican holiday, when banks are closed. Cash can sometimes be difficult to exchange because counterfeit U.S. dollars have been circulating recently in Mexico; merchants and banks are wary, and many, especially in small towns, refuse to accept dollars in cash. In general, avoid carrying the U.S. $100 bill, the one most commonly counterfeited. Since small bills and coins in pesos are hard to come by in Mexico, the U.S. $1 bill is very useful for tipping.

Bottom line on exchanging money of all kinds: It pays to ask first and shop around. Banks in Mexico often give a less favorable rate of exchange than the official daily rate, and hotels usually exchange less favorably than do banks. Exchange houses are generally more convenient than banks since they have more locations and longer hours, and the rate of exchange may be the same as a bank or slightly lower. Personal checks may be cashed but not without weeks of delay—a bank will wait for your check to clear before giving you your money. Canadian dollars seem to be most easily exchanged for pesos at branches of Banamex and Bancomer.

Note: Before leaving a bank or exchange house window, always count your change in front of the teller before the next client steps up.

Banks are open Monday through Friday from 9am to 1:30pm; a few banks in large cities offer extended afternoon hours. Most banks won't exchange money until 10am, when they receive the day's official rate. Large airports have currency-exchange counters that often stay open whenever flights are arriving or departing. Don't go for the first one you see in an airport—there's usually more than one and you'll often find a better exchange rate farther along the concourse.

TRAVELER'S CHECKS   Traveler's checks are readily accepted nearly everywhere, but they can be difficult to cash on a weekend or holiday or in an out-of-the-way place. Their best value is in replacement in case of theft. I usually arrive in Mexico with half of my money in cash (in $1, $20, and $50 bills) and half in traveler's checks ($20 and $50 denominations). Mexican banks sometimes pay more for traveler's checks than for dollars in cash, but in some places *casas de cambio* (exchange houses) pay more for cash than for traveler's checks. Additionally, some but not all banks charge a service fee to exchange either traveler's checks or dollars.

CREDIT CARDS & ATMS   You'll be able to charge some hotel and restaurant bills, almost all airline tickets, and many store purchases on your credit cards. You can get cash advances of several hundred dollars on your card, but there may be a wait of 20 minutes to 2 hours. You can't charge gasoline purchases in Mexico.

Visa ("Bancomer" in Mexico), MasterCard ("Carnet" in Mexico), and, less widely, American Express are the most accepted cards. The Bancomer bank, with branches throughout the country, has inaugurated a system of **automatic teller machines (ATMs)** linked to Visa International's network. If you are a Visa customer, you may be able to get peso cash from one of the Bancomer ATMs.

ATM machines are also associated with other banks and may work with your own bank ATM. There's usually a $200 limit per transaction. Two cautions about using automatic teller machines are in order: First, though ATMs are located next to banks, or in a bank lobby, use the same precautions you would at home—don't use one at night, or on a lonely street, etc.; second, don't depend on them totally for your extra cash—you might not always have access to one, and you'll be out of luck if the machine eats your card.

BRIBES & SCAMS

You will probably find yourself in situations in Mexico where bribes—called *propinas* (tips) or *mordidas* (bites)—are expected, or where con artists are working their trade. Here's how to deal with them.

BRIBES   Extortion, of course, exists everywhere in the world, but in Mexico as in other developing countries, the tolls are smaller and collected more often.

Border officials appear to be slipping back into the petty-extortion habit they largely shed during the administration of President Salinas de Gortari. Just so you're prepared, here are a few hints based on my experiences.

First rule: even if you speak Spanish, don't say a word of it to Mexican officials. This allows you to appear to be innocent, even dumb, all the while understanding every word. Some border officials will do what they're supposed to do (stamp your passport or birth certificate and perhaps lightly inspect your luggage) and then wave you on through. If you don't offer a tip of a few dollars to the man who inspects your car (if you're driving), he may ask for it, as in "Give me a tip (*propina*)." I usually ignore this request, but you'll have to decide for yourself based on your circumstances at the time, especially if the official decides a complete search of your belongings is suddenly in order. If you're charged for the stamping or inspection, (for example, the inspector says "One dollar"), followed by an outstretched hand, ask for a receipt (*recibo;* "ray-*see*-bow"). If he says there's no receipt, don't pay the bribe. By then he's probably already nonchalantly waved you ahead anyway, the quicker to hit up the next unsuspecting victim. You can also simply ignore the request or pretend not to understand it, and move on.

Officials don't ask for bribes from everybody. Travelers dressed in a formal suit and tie, wearing pitch-black sunglasses and a scowl, are rarely asked to pay a bribe. Those who are dressed for vacation fun or seem good-natured and accommodating are targets. Whatever you do, avoid impoliteness, and absolutely *never* insult a Latin American official! When an official's sense of machismo is roused, he can and will throw the book at you, and you may be in trouble. Stand your ground, but do it politely.

How do I know when paying a bribe would be better than fighting it? Here are a couple of scenarios: A driving rain is drenching the world outside and the scowling border guard orders everyone out of the vehicle to unpack belongings for inspection—in the rain. Cut your losses and offer a bribe. You're stopped for a traffic infraction that you did or didn't commit, and the policeman keeps inspecting your car documents, your driver's license, or your Tourist Permit, finding things "wrong." If you're in a hurry, offer a bribe. If you're not, offer to follow him to the station. He'll probably not want to do that, and will find some way to save face—your credentials are all right after all—and move on. You must allow him to save face.

How much should I offer? Usually $3 to $5 or the equivalent in pesos will do the trick. There's supposedly a number to report irregularities with customs officials (toll free 91-800/00148 in Mexico). Your call will go to the office of the Comptroller and Adminstrative Development Secretariat (SECODAM). It's worth a try. But be sure you have some basic information, such as the name of the person who wanted a bribe or was rude, and the place, time, and day of the event.

SCAMS As you travel in Mexico, you may encounter several types of scams. The **distraction scam** is found frequently on the Mexico City subway, or on crowded buses, but it can happen on a busy city street, at a market or festival, or anywhere. Someone in front of you on the subway or street drops to the ground searching for something. You're mildly distracted as you manage to get around the person in the way, probably with people crowding you from behind. By the time you're beyond the distraction, a hand has already found its way to your wallet—even when it's stowed in a front-facing fanny pack or your front pants pocket. As a variation, an impeccably dressed man or woman tells you that you've got a foreign substance, like white powder or a wet paintlike substance, on the back of your nice jacket. He (usually it's a male, but sometimes it's a "married couple") spends a long time helping you remove the stain with his nicely pressed handkerchief. Your thanks are so profuse for this kind assistance to you, the foreigner, that you don't realize until later that your wallet is missing. A variation of this one, starring the impeccably dressed local again, occurs in hotel lobbies: He or she strikes up a conversation with you, and while your head is turned, your purse, bag, or packages disappear. Or the lobby is filled with well-dressed people and you turn your attention away from your belongings for a second, and the next thing you know a well-dressed someone with straight-faced aplomb has disappeared with your purse or valise on his or her arm. If you catch the villain, he or she will feign mortification switching quickly to indignant anger while proclaiming that the object looked just like his or hers. Another variation is the unaccompanied, frightened or perhaps lost child, who takes your hand for safety on the subway. Who would deny a child a hand—right? Meanwhile the child, or an accomplice, manages to plunder your pockets. Needless to say, these people are really slick and outwardly unsuspicious looking.

More and more in Mexico City I'm confronted with the **"I've just been robbed and lost everything" scam.** A distraught person appearing to be in wide-eyed shock and on the verge of tears approaches you and says, "Someone just stole my purse!" (Or vehicle, or wallet, etc.) "Can you give me money to take a bus home." Then it turns out he or she lives in Tijuana or some other distant city and the pesos required for the trip are substantial. Often the perpetrator of this one has hungry, poorly dressed children in tow, and maybe a hopeless-faced or teary-eyed wife as well. Or well-dressed, innocent-looking teenagers accompany the truthful-sounding con artist, and you think "These people are middle class and educated—how can this be a scam?" And of course, they'll need food money, because the trip takes several days. Then, naturally they've got to pay for transportation to the bus station. It really tugs at your heart strings. I usually say I've just run out of money myself and they quickly move on to the next target.

Because hotel desk clerks are usually so helpful, I hesitate to mention the **lost objects scam** for fear of tainting them all. But here's how it works. You "lose" your wallet after cashing money at the desk, or you leave something valuable such as a purse or camera in the lobby. You report it. The clerk has it, but instead of telling you he does, he says he will see what he can do; meanwhile, he suggests you offer a high reward. This scam has all kinds of variations. In one story a reader wrote about, a desk clerk in Los Mochis was in cahoots with a bystander in the lobby who lifted the reader's wallet in the elevator.

Another scam readers have mentioned might be called the **infraction scam.** Officials, or men presenting themselves as officials, demand money for some supposed infraction. Never get into a car with them. I avoided one begun by a bona fide policeman-on-the-take in Chetumal when my traveling companion feigned illness and began writhing, moaning, and pretending to have the dry heaves. It was more than the policeman could handle.

Legal and necessary car searches by military personnel looking for drugs are mentioned elsewhere in this book. Every now and then, however, there are police-controlled illegal roadblocks where motorists are forced to pay before continuing on their way.

Along these lines, if you are stopped by the police, I also suggest you avoid handing your driver's license to a policeman. Hold it so that it can be read but don't give it up.

Then there's the **taxi ticket scam.** This usually happens at taxi ticket booths in airports and bus stations. You're vulnerable because you may be a new arrival to the country and not yet have your peso legs, your Spanish may not be up to par, or you're preoccupied with getting where you're going. You give the ticket seller a 50-peso bill and the seller returns change for 20 pesos. I'll say this elsewhere: *Count your change before leaving the booth!* Better yet, when you hand the seller the bill, say out loud the amount of the ticket and the amount of the bill and say *cambio* (*kahm*-bee-oh) which means change.

The **shoeshine scam** is an old trick, used most often in Mexico City. Here's how it works. A tourist agrees to a shine for, say, 15 pesos. When the work is complete, the vendor says "That'll be 50 pesos" or $15 dollars, and insists that the shocked tourist misunderstood. A big brouhaha ensues involving bystanders who side with the shoeshine vendor. The object is to get the bewildered tourist to succumb to the howling crowd and embarrassing scene and fork over the money. A variation of the scam has the vendor saying the price quoted is per shoe. To avoid this scam, ask around about the price of a shine, and when the vendor quotes his price, write it down and show it to him *before* the shine.

Similar to the shoeshine scam because of the pronunciation of numbers is the *dos* **(two) and** *doce* **(twelve) scam.** Usually taxi drivers work this one. You ask how much and he holds up two fingers or says "dos." You think the ride costs two pesos. At drop off he says "That'll be two U.S. dollars," looking at you as though you're especially stupid to think he'd ever accept two pesos. Or he says "dos" (pronounced "dohs") pesos but when you get to your destination he says "doce" (pronounced "*doh*-say") pesos. Or he says "doce," which you understand to refer to pesos, and then he wants 12 *dollars* before you depart. The same confusion can cause an uproar over *tres* ("trays") which means three and *trece* ("*tray*-say"), meaning thirteen, *quince* ("*keen*-say"), which means fifteen, and *quinientos* ("*keen*-ee-ehn-tohs"), the word for five hundred, or *cuatro* ("*kwah*-troh"), which means four and *catorce* ("kah-*tohr*-say") which means fourteen.

Tourists are suckered daily into the **iguana scam,** especially in Puerto Vallarta and nearby Yelapa beach. Someone, often a child, strolls by carrying a huge iguana and says "Wanna take my peekchur?" Photo-happy tourists seize the opportunity. Just as the camera is angled properly, the holder of the iguana says (more like mumbles) "One dollar." That means a dollar per shot! Sometimes they wait until the shutter clicks to mention money.

Although you should be aware of such hazards and how to deal with them, I log thousands of miles and many months in Mexico each year without serious incident, and I feel safer there than at home in the United States. So I must reiterate that you are more likely to meet kind and helpful Mexicans than you are to encounter those who've mastered thievery and deceit. And as you can see by these scams, Mexicans with bad intentions prefer to use stealth and wit more than an outright holdup to take your possessions. (See also "Emergencies" under "Fast Facts: Mexico" and "Safety" under "Health, Safety & Insurance," later in this chapter).

2 When to Go

THE CLIMATE

Pacific Mexico offers one of the world's most perfect winter climates—dry and balmy with temperatures ranging from the 80s by day to the 60s at night. From Puerto Vallarta south you can swim year-round. In summer the area becomes warm and rainy.

HOLIDAYS

On national holidays, banks, stores, and businesses are closed; hotels fill up quickly; and transportation is crowded. Mexico celebrates the following national holidays: **January 1,** New Year's Day; **February 5,** Constitution Day; **March 21,** Birthday of Benito Juárez; March through April (movable), **Holy Week** (Good Friday–Easter Sunday); **May 1,** Labor Day; **May 5,** Battle of Puebla, 1862 (Cinco de Mayo); **September 1,** President's Message to Congress; **September 16,** Independence Day; **October 12,** Day of the Race (Columbus Day in the U.S.); **November 1 and 2,** All Saints' and All Souls' days (Day of the Dead); **November 20,** Anniversary of the Mexican Revolution; **December 11 and 12,** Feast Day of the Virgin of Guadalupe (Mexico's patron saint); **December 24 and 25,** Christmas Eve and Christmas Day.

MEXICO CALENDAR OF EVENTS

January
- **Three Kings Day.** Commemorates the Three Kings' bringing of gifts to the Christ Child. On this day the Three Kings "bring" gifts to children. January 6.

February
- **Candlemas.** On January 6, Rosca de Reyes, a round cake with a hole in the middle, is baked with a tiny doll inside representing the Christ Child. Whoever gets the slice with the doll must give a party on February 2.
- **Ash Wednesday.** The start of Lent and time of abstinence. It's a day of reverence nationwide, but some towns honor it with folk dancing and fairs. Movable date.

March–April
- **Benito Juárez's Birthday.** Small hometown celebrations countrywide, especially in Juárez's birthplace—Guelatao, Oaxaca.
- ✪ **Holy Week.** Celebrates the last week in the life of Christ from Good Friday through Easter Sunday with somber religious processions almost nightly,

spoofing of Judas, and reenactments of specific biblical events, plus food and craft fairs. Among the Tarahumara in the Copper Canyon, celebrations have pre-Hispanic overtones. Businesses close and Mexicans travel far and wide during this week.

Where: Special in Taxco. **When:** March or April. **How:** Reserve early with a deposit. Airline seats on flights into and out of the country will be reserved months in advance. Buses to these towns or to almost anywhere in Mexico will be full, so try arriving on the Wednesday or Thursday before Good Friday. Easter Sunday is quiet.

May

- **Labor Day.** Workers' parades countrywide and everything closes. May 1.
- **Holy Cross Day,** Día de la Santa Cruz. Workers place crosses on top of unfinished buildings and celebrate with food, bands, folk dancing, and fireworks around the work sites. May 3.
- **Cinco de Mayo.** A national holiday that celebrates the defeat of the French at the Battle of Puebla. May 5.
- **Feast of San Isidro.** The patron saint of farmers is honored with a blessing of seeds and work animals. May 15.

June

- **Navy Day.** Celebrated by all port cities. June 1.
- ✪ **Corpus Christi.** Honors the Body of Christ—the Eucharist—with religious processions, masses, and food. Celebrated nationwide. Variable date, 66 days after Easter.
- **St. Peter's Day,** Día de San Pedro. Celebrated wherever St. Peter is the patron saint and honors anyone named Pedro or Peter. June 29.

July

- **Virgin of Carmen.** A nationally celebrated religious festival centered in churches nationwide. July 16.
- **St. James Day,** Día de Santiago. Observed countrywide wherever St. James is the patron saint and for anyone named Jaime or James or any village with Santiago in its name. Rodeos, fireworks, dancing, and food. July 25.

August

- ✪ **Assumption of the Virgin Mary.** Celebrated throughout the country with special masses and in some places with processions. Streets are carpeted in flower petals and colored sawdust. At midnight on the 15th a statue of the Virgin is carried through the streets; the 16th is a running of the bulls. On August 15 in Santa Clara del Cobre, near Pátzcuaro, Our Lady of Santa Clara de Asis and the Virgen de la Sagrado Patrona are honored with a parade of floats, dancers on the main square, and an exposition of regional crafts, especially copper. August 15–16.

September

- **Independence Day.** Celebrates Mexico's independence from Spain. A day of parades, picnics, and family reunions throughout the country. At 11pm on September 15 the president of Mexico gives the famous independence *grito* (shout) from the National Palace in Mexico City. At least half a million people are crowded into the Zócalo, and the rest of the country watches the event on television. September 16 (parade day).

October

- **Cervantino Festival.** Begun in the 1970s as a cultural event bringing performing artists from all over the world to Guanajuato, a picturesque village northeast of

Mexico City. Now the artists travel all over the republic after appearing in Guanajuato. Check local calendars for appearances. Early to mid-October.

- **Feast of San Francisco de Asis.** Anyone named Frances, Francis, or Francisco and towns whose patron saint is Francisco celebrate with barbecue parties, regional dancing, and religious observances. October 4.
- **Día de la Raza,** Day of the Race, or Columbus Day (the day Columbus landed in America). Commemorates the fusion of the Spanish and Mexican peoples. October 12.

November

✪ **Day of the Dead.** What's commonly called the Day of the Dead is actually 2 days, All Saints' Day, honoring saints and deceased children, and All Souls' Day, honoring deceased adults. Relatives gather at cemeteries countrywide, carrying candles and food, often spending the night beside graves of loved ones. Weeks before, bakers begin producing bread formed in the shape of mummies or round loaves decorated with bread "bones." Decorated sugar skulls emblazoned with glittery names are sold everywhere. Many days ahead, homes and churches erect special altars laden with Day of the Dead bread, fruit, flowers, candles, and favorite foods and photographs of saints and of the deceased. On the 2 nights of the Day of the Dead, children dress in costumes and masks, often carrying mock coffins through the streets and pumpkin lanterns into which they expect money will be dropped. Cemeteries around Oaxaca City are well known for their solemn vigils and some for their carnival-like atmosphere. November 1–2.

- **Revolution Day.** Commemorates the start of the Mexican Revolution in 1910 with parades, speeches, rodeos, and patriotic events. November 20.

December

✪ **Feast of the Virgin of Guadalupe.** Throughout the country the Patroness of Mexico is honored with religious processions, street fairs, dancing, fireworks, and masses. The Virgin of Guadalupe appeared to a young man, Juan Diego, in December 1531 on a hill near Mexico City. He convinced the bishop that the apparition had appeared by revealing his cloak, upon which the Virgin was emblazoned. It's customary for children to dress up as Juan Diego, wearing mustaches and red bandanas. Every village celebrates this day, often with processions of children carrying banners of the Virgin and with *charreadas* (rodeos), bicycle races, dancing, and fireworks. December 12.

- **Christmas Posadas.** On each of the 12 nights before Christmas it's customary to reenact the Holy Family's search for an inn, with door-to-door candlelit processions in cities and villages nationwide. Taxco is one of the best places in Mexico to witness this tradition.
- **Christmas.** Mexicans extend this celebration and leave their jobs often beginning two weeks before Christmas all the way through New Year's. Many businesses close, and resorts and hotels fill up. On December 23 there are significant celebrations. Querétaro has a huge parade. In Oaxaca it's the "Night of the Radishes," with displays of huge carved radishes, as well as elaborate figures made of corn husks and dried flowers. In the evening of December 24 in Oaxaca, processions culminate on the central plaza.
- **New Year's Eve.** As in the United States, New Year's Eve in Mexico is the time to gather for private parties and to explode fireworks and sound noisemakers. Places with special festivities include Santa Clara del Cobre, with its candlelit procession of Christs, and Tlacolula near Oaxaca, with commemorative mock battles for good luck in the new year.

3 Outdoor Sports, Adventure Travel & Wilderness Trips

Mexico has numerous **golf** courses, especially in the resort areas. **Tennis, racquet-ball, squash, waterskiing, surfing, bicycling,** and **horseback riding** are all sports visitors can enjoy in Mexico. **Mountain and volcano climbing** is a rugged sport where you'll meet like-minded folks from around the world.

Mexico is behind the times with regard to ecological adventure and wilderness travel. As a result, most of the national parks and nature reserves are understaffed and/or not staffed by knowledgeable people. Most companies offering this kind of travel are U.S. operated, with trips led by specialists. The following companies offer a variety of off-the-beaten-path travel experiences:

Intercontinental Adventures, Georgia 120-9 (A), 03810 Mexico, D. F. (☎ 5/536-3700; fax 5/669-0086) under the leadership of Augustine Arroyo offers a new tour covering the original **route of Cortés,** though unlike Cortés and his henchmen, you're not on horseback or foot. Highlights include the ruins of Zempoala; the cities of Veracruz (where you learn the local dance "danzon"), Jalapa and the excellent Museo de Antropologia there, Puebla, Tlaxcala, and Mexico City; river rafting (if you desire); plus cultural experiences in food, history, and literature along the way. Trips can be customized.

Mexico Sportsman, 202 Milam Bldg., San Antonio, TX 78205 (☎ 210/212-4567; fax 210/212-4568) is sportfishing central for anyone interested in advance arrangements for fishing in Cancún, Cozumel, Puerto Vallarta, Ixtapa/Zihuatanejo, Cabo San Lucas, or Mazatlán. The company offers complete information from the cost (nothing hidden) to the length of a fishing trip, type of boat, line and tackle used, and whether or not bait, drinks, and lunch are included. Prices are as good as you'll get on site in Mexico.

Mountain Travel Sobek, 6420 Fairmount Ave., El Cerrito, CA 94530 (☎ 510/527-8100 or 800/227-2384), leads groups into the Copper Canyon and kayaking in the Sea of Cortez.

Other Americas, 2333 Sunset Blvd., Houston, TX 77005 (☎ 713/526-6175; fax 713/526-3551), combines photography instruction, culture, language, and adventure travel into colorful, experience-packed trips. Led by well-known photographer Goeff Winningham (head of the Rice University photography program), small groups of between 5 and 18 participants journey off the beaten path to very unusual festivals and events for one-of-a-kind experiences in Mexico.

Trek America, P. O. Box 189 Rockaway, NJ 07866 (☎ 201/983-1144 or 800/221-0596 in the U.S.; fax 201/983-8551) organizes lengthy, active trips that combine trekking and hiking with van transportation and camping in the Yucatán, Chiapas, Oaxaca, the Copper Canyon, and Mexico's Pacific Coast, and touching on Mexico City and Guadalajara.

Victor Emanuel Tours, P.O. Box 33008, Austin, TX 78764 (☎ 512/328-5221 or 800/328-VENT), is an established leader in birding and natural-history tours.

Wings, Inc., P.O. Box 31930, Tucson, AZ 85751 (☎ 602/749-1967; e-mail: Wings@rtd.com), has a wide assortment of trips, including birding in Oaxaca, Chiapas, Colima, and Jalisco.

Zapotec Tours, 2334 W. Lawrence Ave., Suite 219, Chicago, IL 60625 (☎ 312/973-2444 or, outside Ill., 800/44-Oaxaca in the U.S.), offers a variety of tours to Oaxaca City and the Oaxaca coast (including Puerto Escondido and Huatulco), and two specialty trips: Day of the Dead in Oaxaca, and the chocolate route in the states of Tabasco and Oaxaca. Coastal trips emphasize nature. In Oaxaca City, tours focus on the immediate area with visits to weavers, potters, and markets. They are also the U.S. contact for several hotels in Oaxaca City and for the Oaxaca state route of **AeroMorelos airlines** (serving the Oaxaca coast and Oaxaca City). Call them for information, but all reservations must be made through a travel agent.

4 Learning Vacations

SPANISH LESSONS   A dozen towns south of the border are famous for their Spanish-language programs. Besides specific mention later in this book of language schools in towns mentioned below, the Mexican Government Tourist Offices may also have information about schools in Cuernavaca. Go any time of year—you needn't really wait for a "semester" or course year to start. It's best to begin on a Monday, however.

Don't expect the best and latest in terms of language texts and materials; many are well out-of-date. Teachers tend to be underpaid and perhaps undertrained but very friendly and extremely patient.

The **National Registration Center for Studies Abroad (NRCSA),** 823 N. Second St., Milwaukee, WI 53203 (☎ **414/278-0631**), has a catalog ($5) of schools in Mexico. They will register you at the school of your choice, arrange for room and board with a Mexican family, and make your airline reservations. Charge for their service is reflected in a fee that's included in the price quoted to you for the course you select.

HOMESTAYS   Living with a Mexican family is another way to learn Spanish. Family stays can be particularly inexpensive, so you should get more than your money's worth in terms of interaction and language practice.

Spanish-language schools frequently provide lists of families who offer rooms to students. Often the experience is just like being part of the family.

World Learning, Inc., The U.S. Experiment in International Living, Kipling Road, P.O. Box 676, Brattleboro, VT 05302-0676 (☎ **802/257-7751;** fax 802/258-3248), offers a wide range of international experiences ranging from accredited programs to homestays and Elderhostel affiliation.

5 Health, Safety & Insurance

STAYING HEALTHY

Of course, the very best way to avoid illness or to mitigate its effects is to make sure you're in top health when you travel and that you don't overdo it.

Important note: Antibiotics and other drugs that you'd need a prescription to buy in the States are sold over-the-counter in Mexican pharmacies, but Mexican pharmacies don't have the common over-the-counter sinus or allergy remedies we're accustomed to finding easily. If you're prone to this trouble, bring your own supply of pills.

COMMON AILMENTS   It's a rare person indeed who doesn't experience some degree of gastric upheaval when traveling; see the box on Moctezuma's Revenge for tips on preventing and dealing with **traveler's diarrhea.**

Altitude sickness is another problem travelers experience; Mexico City is at an elevation of more than 7,000 feet, as are a number of other central Mexican cities. At high elevations it takes about 10 days to acquire the extra red blood corpuscles you need to adjust to the scarcity of oxygen.

Ay Caramba! Moctezuma's Revenge

Turista, or Moctezuma's revenge, are the names given to the persistent diarrhea, often accompanied by fever, nausea, and vomiting, that attacks so many travelers to Mexico. Doctors, who call it travelers' diarrhea, say it's not caused by just one "bug," or factor, but by a combination of consuming different food and water, upsetting your schedule, being overtired, and experiencing the stresses of travel. Being tired and careless about food and drink is a sure ticket to turista. A good high-potency (or "therapeutic") vitamin supplement, and even extra vitamin C, is a help; yogurt is good for healthy digestion and is becoming much more available in Mexico than in the past.

Preventing Turista: The U.S. Public Health Service recommends the following measures for prevention of travelers' diarrhea:

• *Drink only purified water.* This means tea, coffee, and other beverages made with boiled water; canned or bottled carbonated beverages and water; beer and wine; or water you yourself have brought to a rolling boil or otherwise purified. Avoid ice, which may be made with untreated water. However, most restaurants with a large tourist clientele use only purified water and ice.

• *Choose food carefully.* In general, avoid salads, uncooked vegetables, and unpasteurized milk or milk byproducts (including cheese). Choose food that is freshly cooked and still hot. Peel fruit yourself. Don't eat undercooked meat, fish, or shellfish.

The Public Health Service does not recommend you take any medicines as preventatives. All the applicable medicines can have nasty side effects if taken for

---

Altitude sickness results from the relative lack of oxygen and the decrease in barometric pressure that characterizes high elevations (over 5,000 ft./1,500m). Symptoms include shortness of breath, fatigue, headache, and even nausea.

Take it easy for the first few days after you arrive at a high elevation. Drink extra fluids but avoid alcohol. If you have heart or lung problems, talk to your doctor before going above 8,000 feet.

Mosquitoes and gnats are prevalent along the coast. Insect repellent (*rapellante contra insectos*) is a must, and it's not always available in Mexico. If you're sensitive to bites, pick up some antihistamine cream from a drugstore at home. Rubbed on a fresh mosquito bite, the cream keeps the swelling down and reduces the itch.

Though they proliferate in the deserts, most readers won't ever see a scorpion (*alacrán*). If you are stung, go to a doctor.

MORE SERIOUS DISEASES   You shouldn't be overly concerned about tropical diseases if you stay on the normal tourist routes and don't eat street food. However, both dengue fever and cholera have appeared in Mexico in recent years. Talk to your doctor, or a medical specialist in tropical diseases, about any precautions you should take. You can also get medical bulletins from the U.S. State Department and the Center for Disease Control (see "Sources of Information," above). You can protect yourself by taking some simple precautions. Watch what you eat and drink; don't swim in stagnant water (ponds, slow-moving rivers, and Yucatecan *cenotes,* or wells); avoid mosquito bites by covering up, using powerful repellent, sleeping under mosquito netting, and staying away from places that seem to have a lot of mosquitoes.

several weeks. In addition, something so simple as clean hands can go a long way toward preventing turista. I carry packages of antiseptic towelettes for those times when wash facilities aren't available and to avoid using a communal bar of soap—a real germ carrier.

How to Get Well: If you get sick, there are lots of medicines available in Mexico that can harm more than help. Ask your doctor before you leave home what medicine he or she recommends for travelers' diarrhea.

The Public Health Service guidelines are the following: If there are three or more loose stools in an 8-hour period, especially with other symptoms (such as nausea, vomiting, abdominal cramps, and fever), see a doctor.

The first thing to do is go to bed and don't move until the condition runs its course. Traveling makes it last longer. Drink lots of liquids: Tea without milk or sugar or the Mexican *té de manzanilla* (chamomile tea) is best. Eat only *pan tostada* (dry toast). Keep to this diet for at least 24 hours, and you'll be well over the worst of it. If you fool yourself into thinking a plate of enchiladas can't hurt or beer or liquor will kill the germs, you'll have a total relapse.

The Public Health Service advises that you be especially careful to replace fluids and electrolytes (potassium, sodium, and the like) during a bout of diarrhea. Do this by drinking Pedialyte, a rehydration solution available at most Mexican pharmacies, or glasses of fruit juice (high in potassium) with honey and a pinch of salt added, or you can also try a glass of boiled pure water with a quarter teaspoon of sodium bicarbonate (baking soda) added.

The most dangerous areas seem to be on Mexico's west coast, away from the big resorts (which are relatively safe).

EMERGENCY EVACUATION   For extreme medical emergencies there's a service from the United States that will fly people to American hospitals: **Air-Evac,** a 24-hour air ambulance (☎ **800/854-2569** in the U.S. or call collect: ☎ **510/786-1592**). You can also contact the service in Guadalajara (☎ **3/616-9616** or 91-800/90345).

SAFETY

Boisterous drunks aside, I've never had trouble of any kind in Mexico, and seldom feel suspicious of anyone or any situation. You will probably feel physically safer in most Mexican cities and villages than in any comparable place at home.

Crime, however, is more of a problem in Mexico than it used to be. Be smart, be careful, take all the normal precautions you'd take to deter pickpockets and muggers traveling to any large American city, for example.

Keep a photocopy of your credit cards, driver's license, and passport or birth certificate in a separate place from where you're keeping the originals. (In case you lose, or are relieved of, the originals, these copies will make replacement easier). Use hotel security boxes or in-room safes for your passport and other valuables.

Keep your things with you on the less responsible village buses and some second-class buses on country routes.

And, of course, *never* carry a package back to the States for an acquaintance or a stranger.

The Traveler's Toolbox

There are a few miscellaneous gadgets and sundries that come in handy time and again in Mexico: a rain poncho for those seasonable and unseasonable rains; arm, waist, or leg money pouches; a washcloth, or better yet, a face sponge (which dries quickly)—you'll rarely find washcloths in a budget-category hotel room, and many first class hotels don't furnish cloths either; a basin plug (it's packaged by that name), for all those plugless sinks; a small plastic bag can double as a plug in a pinch; inflatable hangers and a stretch clothesline; a luggage cart saves much effort and tip money—buy a sturdy, steel one with at least 4-inch wheels that can take the beating of cobblestone streets, stairs, and curbs; a heat immersion coil, plastic cup, and spoon for preparing coffee, tea, and instant soup; a small flashlight for those generator-operated places with no lights after 10pm and archaeological sites with dark interiors; and a combination pocketknife for peeling fruit, fixing cameras and eyeglasses, and opening *cervezas* and bottles of wine.

See "Sources of Information" at the beginning of this chapter for details on how to contact the U.S. State Department for their latest advisories. At press time their advice cautions particularly about robberies and murders on Highway 15 and the adjacent toll highway, from the U.S. border on down the Pacific Coast.

Lastly I urge you not to let these cautionary statements deter you from traveling in Mexico. Were I to write a similar section about travel in the United States, it would take several pages. Mexico is a wonderful country, and your good experiences with its people and culture will far outweigh any negative incidents. I eagerly return there year after year.

INSURANCE

HEALTH/ACCIDENT/LOSS   Even the most careful of us can experience the Murphy's Law of travel—you discover you've lost your wallet, your passport, your airline ticket, or your Tourist Permit. Always keep a photocopy of these documents in your luggage—it makes replacing them easier. To be reimbursed for insured items once you return, you'll need to report the loss to the Mexican police and get a written report. If you don't speak Spanish, take along someone who does. If you lose official documents, you'll need to contact both Mexican and U.S. officials in Mexico before you leave the country.

Health Care Abroad, Wallach and Co. Inc., 107 W. Federal St. (P.O. Box 480), Middleburg, VA 22117 (☎ **540/687-3166** or 800/237-6615), and **World Access,** 6600 W. Broad St., Richmond, VA 23230 (☎ **804/285-3300** or 800/628-4908), offer medical and accident insurance as well as coverage for luggage loss and trip cancellation. Always read the fine print on the policy to be sure that you're getting the coverage you want.

6 Tips for Travelers with Special Needs

FOR SENIORS   Mexico is a popular country for retirees—for decades, North Americans have been living indefinitely in Mexico by returning to the border and recrossing with a new tourist card every six months. Recently, but not uniformly at every border crossing, Mexico has begun to crack down on this practice by refusing readmittance to someone they remember just crossed over. So if you've been in Mexico for six months and haven't decided on permanent residency yet, and want to return immediately for another stay on a Tourist Permit, you'll have to exercise caution about where and when you recross.

Cuernavaca and Oaxaca are popular places for long-term stays.

The following newsletters are written for prospective retirees: *AIM,* Apdo. Postal 31–70, 45050 Guadalajara, Jalisco, Mexico, is a well-written, candid, and very informative newsletter on retirement in Mexico. Recent issues evaluated retirement in Puerto Angel, Puerto Escondido and Huatulco, Oaxaca, and Taxco, among other places. Subscriptions cost $16 to the United States and $19 to Canada. Back issues are three for $5.

FOR SINGLES   Mexico may be an old favorite for romantic honeymoons, but it's also a great place to travel on your own without really being or feeling alone. Although offering an identical room rate regardless of single or double occupancy is slowly becoming a trend in Mexico, most of the hotels mentioned in this book still offer singles at lower rates.

Mexicans are very friendly, and it's easy to meet other foreigners. Acapulco and Huatulco can have so many twosomes as to leave single travelers feeling as though an appendage is missing, but places like Zihuatanejo, Ixtapa, Puerto Angel, and Puerto Escondido are great places to go on your own.

If you don't like the idea of traveling alone, then try **Travel Companion Exchange,** P.O. Box 833, Amityville, NY 11701 (☎ **516/454-0880;** fax 516/454-0170), which brings prospective travelers together. Members complete a profile, then place an anonymous listing of their travel interests in the newsletter. Prospective traveling companions then make contact through the Exchange. Membership costs $99 for six months or $159 for a year.

For Women   As a frequent female visitor to Mexico, mostly traveling alone, I can tell you firsthand that I feel safer traveling in Mexico than in the United States. Mexicans are very warm and welcoming people, and I'm not afraid to be friendly wherever I go. But I use the same commonsense precautions I use traveling anywhere else in the world—I'm alert to what's going on around me.

Mexicans in general, and men in particular, are nosy about single travelers, especially women. They want to know with whom you're traveling, whether you're married or have a boyfriend, and how many children you have. My advice to anyone asked these details by taxi drivers or other people with whom you don't want to become friendly is to make up a set of answers (regardless of the truth): "I'm married, traveling with friends, and I have three children."

If you're a divorcee, revealing such may send out the wrong message about availability. Drunks are a particular nuisance to the lone female traveler. Don't try to be polite—just leave or duck into a public place.

Generally lone women will feel comfortable going to a hotel lobby bar, yet are asking for trouble by going into a pulquería or cantina. In restaurants, as a general rule, single women are offered the worst table and service. You'll have to be vocal about your preference and insist on service. Don't tip if service is bad.

For Men   I'm not sure why, but non-Spanish-speaking foreign men seem to be special targets for scams and pickpockets. So if you fit this description, whether traveling alone or in a pair, exercise special vigilance.

FOR FAMILIES   Mexicans travel extensively in their country with their families, so your child will feel very welcome. Hotels will often arrange for a baby-sitter. Several hotels in the middling-to-luxury range have small playgrounds and pools for children and hire caretakers on weekends to oversee them. Few budget hotels offer these amenities.

Before leaving, you should check with your doctor to get advice on medications to take along. Bring along a supply just to be sure. Disposable diapers cost about the same in Mexico but are of poorer quality. Gerber's baby foods are sold in many stores. Dry cereals, powdered formulas, baby bottles, and purified water are all easily available in midsize and large cities.

Cribs, however, may present a problem. Except for the largest and most luxurious hotels, few Mexican hotels provide cribs. However, rollaway beds to accommodate children staying in the room with parents are often available. Likewise, child seats or high chairs at restaurants are rare.

Many of the hotels I mention, even in noncoastal regions, have swimming pools, which can be a treat at the end of a day of traveling with a child who has had it with sightseeing.

FOR PEOPLE WITH DISABILITIES   Travelers who are unable to walk or who are in wheelchairs or on crutches discover quickly that Mexico is one giant obstacle course. Beginning at the airport on arrival, you may encounter steep stairs before finding a well-hidden elevator or escalator—if one exists. Airlines will often arrange wheelchair assistance to the baggage area for passengers. Porters are generally available to help with luggage at airports and large bus stations, once you've cleared baggage claim.

In addition, escalators (there aren't many in the country) are often not operating. Few handicapped-equipped rest rooms exist, or when one is available, access to it may be via a narrow passage that won't accommodate a wheelchair or someone on crutches. Many deluxe hotels (the most expensive) now have rooms with baths for the handicapped and handicapped access to the hotel. Those traveling on a budget should stick with one-story hotels or those with elevators. Even so, there will probably still be obstacles somewhere. Stairs without handrails abound in Mexico. Intracity bus drivers generally don't bother with the courtesy step on boarding or disembarking. On city buses, the height between the street and the bus step can require considerable force to board. Generally speaking, no matter where you are, someone will lend a hand, although you may have to ask for it.

Few airports offer the luxury of boarding an airplane from the waiting room. You either descend stairs to a bus that ferries you to the waiting plane that's boarded by climbing stairs, or you walk across the airport tarmac to your plane and ascend the stairs. Deplaning offers the same in reverse.

7 Getting There

BY PLANE

The airline situation in Mexico is changing rapidly, with many new regional carriers offering scheduled service to areas previously not served. In addition to regularly scheduled service, charter service direct from U.S. cities to resorts is making Mexico more accessible from the United States.

THE MAJOR INTERNATIONAL AIRLINES   The main airlines operating direct or nonstop flights from the United States to points in Mexico include **Aero California** (☎ 800/237-6225), **Aeroméxico** (☎ 800/237-6639), **Air France** (☎ 800/237-2747), **Alaska Airlines** (☎ 800/426-0333), **American** (☎ 800/433-7300), **Continental** (☎ 800/231-0856), **Lacsa** (☎ 800/225-2272), **Mexicana** (☎ 800/531-7921), **Northwest** (☎ 800/225-2525), **United** (☎ 800/241-6522), and **USAir** (☎ 800/428-4322).

Southwest Airlines (☎ 800/435-9792) serves the U.S. border. The main departure points in the United States for international airlines are Chicago, Dallas/Fort Worth, Denver, Houston, Los Angeles, Miami, New Orleans, New York, Orlando, Philadelphia, Raleigh/Durham, San Antonio, San Francisco, Seattle, Toronto, Tucson, and Washington, D.C.

Excursion and package plans proliferate, especially in the off-season. A good travel agent will be able to give you all the latest schedules, details, and prices, but you may have to investigate the details of the plans to see if they are real deals. You'll also have to sleuth regional airlines for yourself (see "By Plane" under "Getting Around," below), since most travel agents don't have that information.

Important note for those bound for Oaxaca: For points inside the state of Oaxaca only—Oaxaca City, Puerto Escondido, and Puerto Angel—contact Zapotec Tours (☎ 312/973-2444 or, outside Ill., 800/44-Oaxaca in the U.S.), and **Aerovias Oaxaqueñas** (☎ 951/6-3824 in Oaxaca).

CHARTERS   Charter service is growing, especially during winter months and usually is sold as a package combination of air and hotel. Charter airlines, however, may sell air packages only, without hotel. Check your local paper for seasonal charters.

Well known **tour companies** operating charters include **Club America Vacations, Apple Vacations,** and **Friendly Holidays.** You can make arrangements with these companies through your travel agent.

PACKAGE TOURS   Package tours offer some of the best values to the coastal resorts, especially during high season—from December until after Easter. Off-season packages can be real bargains. However, to know for sure if the package will save you money, you must price the package yourself by calling the airline for round-trip flight costs and the hotel for rates. Add in the cost of transfers to and from the airport (which packages usually include) and see if it's a deal.

Packages are usually per person, and single travelers pay a supplement. In the high season a package may be the only way of getting to certain places in Mexico because wholesalers have all the airline seats. The cheapest package rates will be those in hotels in the lower range, always without as many amenities as higher-priced hotels. You can still use the public areas and beaches of more costly hotels without being a guest.

Travel agents have information on specific packages.

BY CAR

Driving is certainly not the cheapest way to get to Mexico, but it is the best way to see the country. Even so, you may think twice about taking your own car south of the border once you've pondered Mexico's many bureaucratic requirements for doing so.

In 1994, Mexico's Ministry of Tourism published its own *Official Guide: Traveling to Mexico by Car.* Unfortunately its information can be inconsistent, unclear, or inaccurate. Of possible use, however, is the list it includes of the times at which you'll find government officials on-duty at border crossings to review your car documents and issue Temporary Car Importation Permits. To get a copy, inquire at a branch of the regional Mexican Government Tourism Office.

It's wise to check and double-check all the requirements before setting out for a driving tour of Mexico. Read through the rest of this section, and then address any additional questions you have or confirm the current rules by calling your nearest Mexican consulate, Mexican Government Tourist Office, AAA, or Sanborn's (☎ 800/222-0185 in the U.S.). To check on road conditions, or to get help with any travel emergency while in the country, there's a 24-hour number (toll free **91-800/9-0329** in Mexico) that you can call. Another 24-hour help number (☎ **5/250-0123** or 5/250-0151) is in Mexico City. Both numbers are supposed to be staffed by English-speaking operators.

In addition, check with the U.S. State Department (see "Sources of Information" at the beginning of this chapter) for their warnings about areas where driving the highways can be dangerous. Their current warnings regarding crime and highway travel are under "Safety," above.

CAR DOCUMENTS   To drive a personal car into Mexico, you'll need a Temporary Car Importation Permit, granted upon completion of a long and strictly required list of documents (see below). The permit can be obtained either through Banco del Ejército (*Banjercito*) officials, who have a desk, booth, or office at the Mexican Customs (*Aduana*) building after you cross the border into Mexico. You can obtain the permit before you travel through Sanborn's Insurance and the American Automobile Association (AAA), each of which maintains border offices in Texas, New Mexico, Arizona, and California. These companies may charge a fee for this service, but it will be worth it to avoid the uncertain prospect of traveling all the way to the border without proper documents for crossing. However, even if you go through Sanborn's or AAA, your credentials *may* be reviewed again by Mexican officials at the border—you must have them all with you since they are still subject to questions of validity.

The following requirements for border crossing were accurate at press time:

- *A valid driver's license,* issued outside of Mexico.
- *Current, original car registration and a copy of the original title certificate.* If the registration or title is in more than one name and not all the named people are traveling with you, then a notarized letter from the absent person(s) authorizing use of the vehicle for the trip is required; have it ready just in case. The car registration and your credit card (see below) must be in the same name.
- *An original notarized letter from the lien or lease holder,* if your registration shows a lien or lease, giving you permission to take the vehicle into Mexico.
- *A valid international major credit card.* Using only your credit card, you are required to pay a $12 car-importation fee. The credit card must be in the same name as the car registration.

    Note: Those without credit cards will forego the $12 importation fee and instead will be required to post a cash bond based on the value of the car. The rules and procedures are complicated (and expensive), so contact AAA or Sanborn's for details.
- A signed declaration promising to return to your country of origin with the vehicle. This form is provided by AAA or Sanborn's before you go or by Banjercito officials at the border. There's no charge. The form does not stipulate that you return through the same border entry you came through on your way south.

You must carry your Temporary Car Importation Permit, Tourist Permit, and, if you purchased it, your proof of Mexican car insurance in the car at all times.

Important reminder: Someone else may drive the car, but the person (or relative of the person) whose name appears on the Car Importation Permit must *always* be in the car at the same time. (If stopped by police, a nonregistered family-member driver, driving without the registered driver, must be prepared to prove familial relationship to the registered driver.) Violation of this rule makes the car subject to impoundment and the driver to imprisonment and/or a fine.

Only under certain circumstances will the driver of the car be allowed to leave the country without the car. If it's undrivable, you can leave it at a mechanic's shop if you get a letter to that effect from the mechanic and present it to the nearest Secretaria de Hacienda y Credito Público (a Treasury Department official) for further documentation, which you then present to a Banjercito official upon leaving the country. Then you must return personally to retrieve the car. If the driver of the car has to leave the country without the car due to an emergency, the car must be put under Customs seal at the airport and the driver's Tourist Permit must be stamped to that effect. There may be storage fees. If the car is wrecked or stolen, your Mexican insurance adjuster will provide the necessary paperwork for presentation to Hacienda officials.

If you receive your documentation at the border (rather than through Sanborn's or AAA), Mexican border officials will make two copies of everything and charge you for the copies.

The Temporary Car Importation Permit papers will be issued for six months and the Tourist Permit is usually issued for 180 days, but they might stamp it for half that, so check. It's a good idea also to overestimate the time you'll spend in Mexico, so that if something unforeseen happens and you have to—or want to—stay longer, you'll have avoided the long hassle of getting your papers renewed.

Important note: Whatever you do, don't overstay either permit. Doing so invites heavy fines and/or confiscation of your vehicle, which will not be returned. Remember also that six months does not necessarily work out to be 180 days—be sure that you return before whichever expiration date comes first.

Other documentation is required for an individual's permit to enter Mexico—see "Entry Requirements," above.

MEXICAN AUTO INSURANCE   Although auto insurance is not legally required in Mexico, driving without it is foolish. U.S. insurance is invalid in Mexico; to be insured there, you must purchase Mexican insurance. Any party involved in an accident who has no insurance is automatically sent to jail and his or her car is impounded until all claims are settled. This is true even if you just drive across the border to spend the day, and it may be true even if you're injured.

I always buy my car insurance through **Sanborn's Mexico Insurance,** P.O. Box 310, Dept. FR, 2009 S. 10th, McAllen, TX 78505-0310 (☎ **210/686-0711** or 800/222-0158 in the U.S.; fax 210/686-0732). The company has offices at all of the border crossings in the United States. Their policies cost the same as the competition's do, but you get legal coverage (attorney and bail bonds if needed) and a detailed mile-by-mile guide to your proposed route—to me, this last part is the kicker. With the ongoing changes in Mexico's highway system it's inevitable that your log will occasionally be a bit outdated, but for the most part having it is like having a knowledgeable friend in the car telling you how to get in and out of town, where to buy gas (and which stations to avoid), what the highway conditions are, and what scams you need to watch out for. It's especially helpful in remote places. Most of Sanborn's border offices are open Monday through Friday, and a few are staffed on Saturday and Sunday. You can purchase your auto liability and collision coverage by phone in advance and have it waiting at a 24-hour location if you are crossing when the office is closed. The annual insurance includes a type of evacuation assistance in case of emergency, and emergency evacuation insurance for shorter policies is available for a small daily fee. They also offer a medical policy.

AAA auto club also sells insurance.

All agencies selling Mexican insurance will show you a full table of current rates and recommend the coverage they think is adequate. The policies are written along lines similar to those north of the border, with the following exception: The contents of your vehicle aren't covered. It's no longer necessary to overestimate the amount of time you plan to be in Mexico because it's now possible to get your policy term lengthened by fax from the insurer. However, if you are staying longer than 48 days, it's more economical to buy a nonrefundable annual policy. For example, Sanborn's Insurance quotes a car (registered to an individual, not a business) with a value of $10,000 can be insured for $137.82 for two weeks or $73.91 for one week. An annual policy for a car valued between $10,000 and $15,000 would be a reduced rate of $519 which you get by joining Sanborn's Amigo Club for $40. (The Amigo Club membership offers hotel discounts, emergency air ambulance, and a newsletter.) Be sure the policy you buy will pay for repairs in either the United States or Mexico and will pay out in dollars, not pesos.

PREPARING YOUR CAR   Check the condition of your car thoroughly before you cross the border. Parts made in Mexico may be inferior, but service generally is quite good and relatively inexpensive. Carry a spare radiator hose and belts for the engine fan and air conditioner. Be sure your car is in tune to handle Mexican gasoline. Also, can your tires last a few thousand miles on Mexican roads?

Don't forget a flashlight and a tire gauge—Mexican filling stations generally have air to fill tires but no gauge to check the pressure. When I drive into Mexico, I always bring along a combination gauge/air compressor sold at U.S. automotive stores that plugs into the car cigarette lighter, making it a simple procedure to check the tires every morning and pump them up at the same time.

Not that many Mexican cars comply, but Mexican law requires that every car have **seat belts** and a **fire extinguisher.** Be prepared!

CROSSING THE BORDER WITH YOUR CAR   After you cross the border into Mexico from the United States and you've stopped to get your Tourist Card and Car Permit, somewhere between 12 and 16 miles down the road you'll come to a Mexican customs post. In the past all motorists had to stop and present travel documents and possibly have their cars inspected. Now there is a new system under which some motorists are stopped at random for inspection. All car papers are examined, however, so you must stop. If the light is green, go on through; if it's red, stop for inspection. In the Baja Peninsula the procedures may differ slightly—first you get your Tourist Permit, then further down the road you may or may not be stopped for the car inspection.

RETURNING TO THE U.S. WITH YOUR CAR   The car papers you obtained when you entered Mexico *must* be returned when you cross back with your car or at some point within the time limit of 180 days. (You can cross as many times as you wish within the 180 days.) If the documents aren't returned, heavy fines are imposed ($250 for each 15 days late), and your car may be impounded and confiscated or you may be jailed if you return to Mexico. You can only return the car documents to a Banjercito official on duty at the Mexican Customs (*Aduana*) building *before* you cross back into the United States. Some border cities have Banjercito officials on duty 24 hours a day, but others do not; some also do not have Sunday hours. On the U.S. side customs agents may or may not inspect your car from stem to stern.

8 Getting Around

An important note: If your travel schedule depends on an important connection, say a plane trip between points, or a ferry or bus connection, use the telephone numbers in this book or other information resources mentioned here and find out if the connection you are depending on is still available. Although I've done my best to provide accurate information, transportation schedules can and do change.

BY PLANE

To fly from point to point within Mexico, you'll rely on Mexican airlines. Mexico has two privately owned large national carriers: **Mexicana** (☎ **800/531-7921** in the U.S.) and **Aeroméxico** (☎ **800/237-6639** in the U.S.), in addition to several up-and-coming regional carriers. Mexicana and Aeroméxico both offer extensive connections to the United States as well as within Mexico.

Several of the new regional carriers are operated by or can be booked through Mexicana or Aeroméxico. Regional carriers are **Aero Caribe** (see Mexicana), **Aerolitoral** (see Aeroméxico), **Aero Monterrey** (see Mexicana), **Aero Morelos** (☎ **73/17-5588** in Cuernavaca; fax 73/17-2320).

Important note for those bound for Oaxaca: For points inside the state of Oaxaca only—Oaxaca City, Puerto Escondido, and Puerto Angel—contact Zapotec Tours (☎ **312/973-2444** or, outside Ill., 800/44-Oaxaca in the U.S.), and **Aerovias Oaxaqueñas** (☎ **951/6-3824** in Oaxaca).

The regional carriers are expensive, but they go to places that are difficult to reach. In each applicable section of this book, I've mentioned regional carriers with all pertinent telephone numbers.

Because major airlines can book some regional carriers, read your ticket carefully to see if your connecting flight is on one of these smaller carriers—they may leave from a different airport or check in at a different counter.

AIRPORT TAXES   Mexico charges an airport tax on all departures. Passengers leaving the country on an international departure pay $12 in cash—dollars or the peso equivalent. (That tax is usually included in your ticket.) Each domestic departure you make within Mexico costs around $6, unless you're on a connecting flight and have already paid at the start of the flight; you shouldn't be charged again if you have to change planes for a connecting flight.

RECONFIRMING FLIGHTS   Although airlines in Mexico say it's not necessary to reconfirm a flight, I always do. Aeroméxico seems particularly prone to cancelling confirmed reservations. Also, be aware that airlines routinely overbook. To avoid getting bumped, check in for an international flight the required hour and a half in advance of travel.

BY BUS

Except for the Baja and Yucatán peninsulas, where bus service is not as well developed as in other parts of the country, Mexican buses are frequent, readily accessible, and can get you to almost anywhere you want to go. Buses are an excellent way to get around, and they're often the only way to get from large cities to other nearby cities and small villages. Ticket agents can be quite brusque or indifferent, especially if there's a line; in general, however, people are willing to help, so never hesitate to ask questions if you're confused about anything. *Important Note:* There's little English spoken at bus stations, so come prepared with your destination written down, then double-check the departure several times just to make sure you get to the right departing lane on time.

Dozens of Mexican companies operate large, air-conditioned, Greyhound-type buses between most cities. Travel class is generally labeled first, second, and deluxe, referred to by a variety of names—*plus, de lujo, ejecutivo, primera plus,* and so on. The deluxe buses often have fewer seats than regular buses, show video movies en route, are air-conditioned, and have few stops; some have complimentary refreshments. Many run express from origin to final destination. They are well worth the few dollars more you'll pay than you would for first-class buses. First-class buses may get there as fast as a deluxe bus, but without the comfort; they may also have many stops.

Second-class buses have many stops and cost only slightly less than first-class or deluxe buses. In rural areas, buses are often of the school-bus variety, with lots of local color.

Whenever possible, it's best to buy your reserved-seat ticket, often via a computerized system, a day in advance on many long-distance routes and especially before holidays. Schedules are fairly dependable, so be at the terminal on time for departure.

Many Mexican cities have replaced the bewildering array of tiny private company offices scattered all over town with new central bus stations, much like sophisticated airport terminals.

Keep in mind that routes and times change, and as there is no central directory of schedules for the whole country, current information must be obtained from local bus stations.

For long trips, *always* carry food, water, toilet paper, and a sweater (in case the air-conditioning is too strong).

A Safety Precaution: The U.S. State Department notes that bandits target long-distance buses traveling at night, but there have also been daylight robberies as well. I've always avoided overnight buses, primarily because they usually must negotiate mountain roads in the dark, which I prefer not to risk. (See "Sources of Information," above, for contact info, and "Safety" in "Health, Safety & Insurance," above, for specific areas of caution.)

See the Appendix for a list of helpful bus terms in Spanish.

BY CAR

Most Mexican roads are not up to U.S. standards of smoothness, hardness, width of curve, grade of hill, or safety marking. Never drive at night if you can avoid it—the roads aren't good enough; the trucks, carts, pedestrians, and bicycles usually have no lights; and you can hit potholes, animals, rocks, dead ends, or bridges out with no warning. Enough said!

You will also have to get used to the "spirited" style of Mexican driving, which sometimes seems to ask superhuman vision and reflexes from drivers. Be prepared for new procedures, as when a truck driver flips on his left-turn signal when there's not a crossroad for miles. He's probably telling you the road's clear ahead for you to pass—after all, he's in a better position to see than you are. It's difficult to know, however, whether he really means that he intends to pull over on the left-hand shoulder. Another strange custom decides who crosses a one-lane bridge first when two cars approach from opposite directions—the first car to flash its headlights has right of way. Still another custom that's very important to respect is how to make a left turn. Never turn left by stopping in the middle of a highway with your left signal on. Instead, pull off the highway onto the right shoulder, wait for traffic to clear, then proceed across the road. Other driving exasperations include following trucks without mufflers and pollution-control devices for miles. Under these conditions, drop back and be patient, take a side road, or stop for a break when you feel tense or tired.

GASOLINE   There's one government-owned brand of gas and one gasoline station name throughout the country—**Pemex** (Petroleras Mexicanas). Each station has a franchise owner who buys everything from Pemex. There are two types of gas in Mexico: *nova,* an 82-octane leaded gas, and *magna sin,* an 87-octane unleaded gas. Magna sin is sold from brilliantly colored pumps and costs around $1.15 a gallon; nova costs slightly less. In Mexico, fuel and oil are sold by the liter, which is slightly more than a quart (40 liters equals about $10\frac{1}{2}$ gallons). Nova is readily available. Magna sin is now available in most areas of Mexico, along major highways, and in the larger cities. Plan ahead; fill up every chance you get, and keep your tank topped off. *Important Note:* No credit cards are accepted for gas purchases.

Here's what to do when you have to fuel up. First rule is to keep your eyes on the pump meters as your tank is being filled. Check that the pump is turned back to zero, go to your fuel filler cap and unlock it yourself, and watch the pump and the attendant as the gas goes in. Though many service-station attendants are honest, many are not. It's better to ask for a specific peso amount rather than saying "full." This is because the attendants tend to overfill, splashing gas on the car and anything within range.

As there are always lines at the gas pumps, attendants often finish fueling one vehicle, turn the pump back quickly (or don't turn it back at all), and start on another vehicle. You've got to be looking at the pump when the fueling is finished because it may show the amount you owe for only a few seconds. This "quick draw" from car to car is another good reason to ask for a certain peso amount of gas. If you've asked for a certain amount, the attendant can't charge you more for it. (Just for convenience's sake, I'll note that, at the current exchange rate, the $10 fill-up you'd ask for at home would be approximately 70 ("say-*ten*-tah") pesos in Mexico. (See the Appendix for pronunciation of other useful round numbers.)

Once the fueling is complete, let the attendant check the oil or radiator or put air in the tires. Do only one thing at a time, be with him as he does it, and don't let him rush you. Get into these habits, or it'll cost you.

If you get oil, make sure the can that is tipped into your engine is a full one. If in doubt, have the attendant check the dipstick again after the oil has supposedly been put in. Check your change and, again, don't let them rush you. Check that your locking gas cap is back in place.

DRIVING RULES   If you park illegally or commit some other infraction and are not around to discuss it, police are authorized to remove your license plates (*placas*). You must then trundle over to the police station and pay a fine to get them back. Mexican car-rental agencies have begun to weld the license tag to the tag frame; you may want to devise a method of your own to make the tags more difficult to remove. Theoretically, this may encourage a policeman to move on to another set of tags, one easier to confiscate. On the other hand, he could get his hackles up and decide to have your car towed. To weld or not to weld is up to you.

Be attentive to road signs. A drawing of a row of little bumps means there are speed bumps (*topes*) across the road to force you to reduce speed while driving through towns or villages. Slow down when coming to a village whether you see the sign or not—sometimes they install the bumps but not the sign!

Mexican roads are never as well marked as you'd like—when you see a highway route sign, take note and make sure you're on the right road. Don't count on plenty of notice of where to turn, even on major interchanges; more often than not, the directional sign appears without prior notice exactly at the spot where you need to make a decision. Common road signs include these:

Camino en Reparación	Road Repairs
Conserva Su Derecha	Keep Right
Cuidado con el Ganado, el Tren	Watch Out for Cattle, Trains
Curva Peligrosa	Dangerous Curve
Derrumbes	Falling Rocks
Deslave	Caved-in Roadbed
Despacio	Slow
Desviación	Detour

Disminuya Su Velocidad	Slow Down
Entronque	Highway Junction
Escuela	School (Zone)
Grava Suelta	Loose Gravel
Hombres Trabajando	Men Working
No Hay Paso	Road Closed
Peligro	Danger
Puente Angosto	Narrow Bridge
Raya Continua	Continuous (Solid) White Line
Tramo en Reparación	Road Under Construction
Un Solo Carril a 100m	One-Lane Road 100 Meters Ahead
Zone Escolar	School Zone

TOLL ROADS   Mexico charges among the highest tolls in the world to use its network of new toll roads. As a result they are comparatively little used. Generally speaking, using the toll roads will cut your travel time between destinations. The old roads, on which no tolls are charged, are generally in good condition but overall mean longer trips—they tend to be mountainous and clotted with slow-moving trucks.

MAPS   Guia Roji, AAA, and International Travel Map Productions have good maps to Mexico. In Mexico, maps are sold at large drugstores like Sanborn's, at bookstores, and in hotel gift shops.

BREAKDOWNS   Your best guide to repair shops is the Yellow Pages. For specific makes and shops that repair them, look under "Automoviles y Camiones: Talleres de Reparación y Servicio"; auto-parts stores are listed under "Refacciones y Accesorios para Automoviles." On the road, often the sign of a mechanic simply says TALLER MECÁNICO.

I've found that the Ford and Volkswagen dealerships in Mexico give prompt, courteous attention to my car problems, and prices for repairs are, in general, much lower than those in the United States or Canada. I suspect other big-name dealerships give similar satisfactory service. Often they will begin work on your car right away and make repairs in just a few hours, sometimes minutes. Hondas are now manufactured in Mexico, so those parts will become more available.

If your car breaks down on the road, help might already be on the way. Radio-equipped green repair trucks manned by uniformed English-speaking officers patrol the major highways during daylight hours to aid motorists in trouble. These **"Green Angels"** will perform minor repairs and adjustments for free, but you pay for parts and materials.

MINOR ACCIDENTS   When possible, many Mexicans drive away from minor accidents to avoid hassles with police. If the police arrive while the involved persons are still at the scene, everyone may be locked in jail until blame is assessed. In any case you have to settle up immediately, which may take days of red tape. Foreigners who don't speak fluent Spanish are at a distinct disadvantage when trying to explain their side of the event. Three steps may help the foreigner who doesn't wish to do as the Mexicans do: If you're in your own car, notify your Mexican insurance company, whose job it is to intervene on your behalf. If you're in a rental car, notify the rental company immediately and ask how to contact the nearest adjuster. (You did buy insurance with the rental—right?) Finally, if all else fails, ask to contact the nearest Green Angel, who may be able to explain to officials that you are covered by insurance.

See also "Mexican Auto Insurance" in "By Car" under "Getting There," above.

PARKING When you park your car on the street, lock it up and leave nothing within view inside (day or night). I use guarded parking lots, especially at night, to avoid vandalism and break-ins. This way you also avoid parking violations. When pay lots are not available, small boys usually offer to watch your car for you—tip them well on your return.

CAR RENTALS With some trepidation I wander into the subject of car-rental rules, which change often in Mexico. The best prices are obtained by reserving your car a week in advance in the United States. Mexico City and most other large Mexican cities have rental offices representing the various big firms and some local ones. You'll find rental desks at airports, all major hotels, and many travel agencies. The large firms like Avis, Hertz, National, and Budget have rental offices on main streets as well. Renting a car during a major holiday may prove difficult if all the cars are booked or not returned on time. If possible plan your arrival before the anticipated rush of travelers to avoid being stranded without a vehicle.

I don't recommend renting a car in Mexico City for 1-day excursions from the city. It can be a real hassle, and parking is also a problem.

Cars are easy to rent if you have a credit card (American Express, Visa, MasterCard, and the like), are 25 or over, and have a valid driver's license and passport with you. Without a credit card you must leave a cash deposit, usually a big one. Rent-here/leave-there arrangements are usually simple to make but very costly.

Costs Don't underestimate the cost of renting a car. Unfortunately, the devaluation of the peso has not resulted in lower car-rental costs in Mexico. When I checked recently for rental on May 15 (after Easter when rates go down) the basic cost of a 1-day rental of a Volkswagen Beetle, with unlimited mileage (but before 15% tax and $15 daily insurance) was $44 in Cancún, $45 in Mexico City, $38 in Puerto Vallarta, $45 in Oaxaca, and $25 in Mérida. Renting by the week gives you a lower daily rate. Avis was offering a basic 7-day weekly rate for a VW Beetle (without tax or insurance) of $180 in Cancún and Puerto Vallarta, $150 in Mérida, and $216 in Mexico City.

So you can see that it makes a difference where you rent, for how long, and when. If you have a choice of renting in Mérida and driving to Cancún, you might save more money than if you rent in Cancún. Mileage-added rates can run the bill up considerably. Car-rental companies usually write up a credit-card charge in U.S. dollars. *Important Tip:* Take advantage of Avis's prepay offer. You *prepay* the daily rental by credit card before you go and receive a considerable discount. Under this plan, you pay tax and insurance in Mexico. As an example, working through Avis here in the States, I recently prepaid a week's use of a VW Beetle in Cancún for $167 (before tax and insurance), which averages $23.86 daily. If I had chosen to pay in Cancún *after* using the car, the weekly rate would have been $267, or $38.14 daily (before tax and insurance).

Rental Confirmation Make your reservation directly with the car-rental company. Write down your confirmation number and request that a copy of the confirmation be mailed to you (rent at least a week in advance so the confirmation has time to reach you). Present that confirmation slip when you appear to collect your car. If you're dealing with a U.S. company, the confirmation must be honored, even if the company has to upgrade you to another class of car—don't allow them to send you to another agency. The rental confirmation will also display the agreed-on price, which protects you from being charged more in case there is a price change before you arrive. Insist on the rate printed on the confirmation slip.

Deductibles Be careful—deductibles vary greatly; some are as high as $2,500, which comes out of your pocket immediately in case of car damage. Hertz's deductible is $1,000 on a VW Beetle; Avis's deductible is $500 for the same car. You will be asked to sign two separate credit-card vouchers, one for the insurance, which is torn up on your return if there's no damage to the car, and one for the rental. Don't fail to get information about deductibles.

Insurance Many credit-card companies offer their cardholders free rental-car insurance. *Don't use it in Mexico,* for several reasons. Even though insurance policies that specifically cover rental cars are supposedly optional in Mexico, there may be major consequences if you don't have one. First, if you buy insurance, you pay only the deductible, which limits your liability. Second, if you have an accident or your car is vandalized or stolen and you don't have insurance, you'll have to pay for everything before you can leave the rental-car office. This includes the full value of the car if it is unrepairable—a determination made only by the rental-car company. While your credit card may eventually pay your costs, you will have to lay out the money in the meantime. Third, if an accident occurs, everyone may wind up in jail until guilt is determined, and if you are the guilty party, you may not be released from jail until restitution is paid in full to the rental-car owners and to injured persons—made doubly difficult if you have no rental-car insurance. Fourth, if you elect to use your credit-card insurance anyway, the rental company may ask you to leave them with a cash bond, or a credit-card voucher with a high amount filled in.

Insurance is offered in two parts. **Collision and damage** insurance covers your car and others if the accident is your fault, and **personal accident** insurance covers you and anyone in your car. I always take both.

Damage Always inspect your car carefully, and mark all problem areas using this checklist:

- Hubcaps
- Windshield (for nicks and cracks)
- Tire tread
- Body (for dents, nicks, etc.)
- Fenders (for dents, etc.)
- Muffler (is it smashed?)
- Trim (loose or damaged?)
- Head and taillights
- Fire extinguisher (it should be under the driver's seat, as required by law)
- Spare tire and tools (in the trunk)
- Seat belts (required by law)
- Gas cap
- Outside mirror
- Floor mats

Note every damaged or missing area, no matter how minute, on your rental agreement or you will be charged for all missing or damaged parts, including missing car tags, should the police confiscate your tags for a parking infraction (which is very costly). I can't stress enough how important it is to check your car carefully. A tiny nick in a windshield can grow the length of the glass while in your care, and you'll be charged for the whole windshield if you didn't note the nick at the time of rental. Car companies have attempted to rent me cars with bald tires and tires with bulges; a car with a license plate that would expire before I returned the car; and cars with missing trim, floor mats, or fire extinguishers. They've also attempted to charge me for dings that were on the auto when I rented it, which they were unable to do because the dings were marked on the agreement.

Fine Print Read the fine print on the back of your rental agreement and note that insurance is invalid if you have an accident while driving on an unpaved road.

Trouble Number One last detail to see to before starting out with a rental car: Be sure you know the rental company's trouble number. Get the direct number to the agency where you rented the car and write down its office hours. The large firms have toll-free numbers, but they may not be well staffed on weekends.

Problems, Perils, Deals At present, I find the best prices are through Avis, and that's the company I use; generally I am a satisfied customer, though I sometimes have to dig in my heels and insist on proper service. I have had even more difficult problems with other agencies. I have encountered certain kinds of situations within the past four years that could occur with any company. These problems have included an attempt to push me off to a no-name company rather than upgrade me to a more expensive car when a VW Beetle wasn't available; poorly staffed offices with no extra cars, parts, or mechanics in case of a breakdown. Since potential problems are varied, I'd rather deal with a company based in the States so at least I have recourse if I am not satisfied.

Signing the Rental Agreement Once you've agreed on everything, the rental clerk will tally the bill before you leave and you will sign an open credit-card voucher that will be filled in when you return the car, and a credit-card voucher for the amount of the deductible which will be used only if there is damage. Read the agreement and double-check all the addition. The time to catch mistakes is before you leave, not when you return.

Picking Up/Returning the Car When you rent the car, you agree to pick it up at a certain time and return it at a certain time. If you're late in picking it up or if you cancel the reservation, there are usually penalties—ask what they are when you make the reservation. If you return the car more than an hour late, an expensive hourly rate kicks in. Also, you must return the car with the same amount of gas in the tank it had when you drove out. If you don't, the charge added to your bill for the difference is much more than for gas bought at a public station.

BY RV

Touring Mexico by recreational vehicle (RV) is a popular way of seeing the country. Many hotels have hookups. RV parks, while not as plentiful as those in the United States, are available throughout the country.

BY FERRY

Ferries connect Baja California at La Paz and Santa Rosalía with the mainland at Topolobampo and Mazatlán. In the Yucatán, ferries also take passengers between Puerto Juárez and Isla Mujeres, Playa Linda and Isla Mujeres, and Playa del Carmen and Cozumel.

BY HITCHHIKING

You see Mexicans hitching rides (for example, at crossroads after getting off a bus), but as a general rule hitchhiking isn't done. It's especially unwise for foreigners, who may be thought to carry large amounts of cash.

FAST FACTS: Mexico

Abbreviations   Dept. = apartments; Apdo. = post office box; Av. = Avenida; Calz. = Calzada (boulevard). "C" on faucets stands for *caliente* (hot), and "F" stands for *fría* (cold). PB (*planta baja*) means ground floor.

Business Hours   In general, Mexican businesses in larger cities are open between 9am and 7pm; in smaller towns many close between 2 and 4pm. Most are closed on Sunday. Bank hours are Monday through Friday from 9 or 9:30am to 1pm. A few banks in large cities have extended hours.

Camera/Film   Buying a camera can be inconvenient in Mexico, but there are cheap, imported models available. Film costs about the same as that in the United States. Take full advantage of your 12-roll film allowance by bringing 36-exposure rolls. Also bring extra batteries: AA batteries are generally available, but AAA and small disk batteries for cameras and watches are rare. A few places in resort areas advertise color film developing, but it might be cheaper to wait until you get home.

Important note about camera use: Tourists wishing to use a video or still camera at any archaeological site in Mexico and at many museums operated by the Instituto de Historia y Antropología (INAH) may be required to pay $8.50 per video camera and/or still camera in their possession at each site or museum visited. (In some museums camera use is not permitted.) If you want to use either kind of camera or both, the fee must be paid for each piece of equipment. When you pay the fee, your camera will be tagged and you are permitted to use the equipment. Watchmen are often posted to see that untagged cameras are not used. Such fees are noted in the listings for specific sites and museums.

It's courteous to ask permission before photographing anyone. In some areas, such as around San Cristóbal de las Casas, Chiapas, there are other restrictions on photographing people and villages. Such restrictions are noted in specific cities, towns, and sites.

Cigarettes   Cigarettes are much cheaper in Mexico than in the United States, even U.S. brands, if you buy them at a grocery or drugstore and not a hotel tobacco shop.

Doctors/Dentists   Every embassy and consulate is prepared to recommend local doctors and dentists with good training and modern equipment; some of the doctors and dentists even speak English. See the list of embassies and consulates under "Embassies/Consulates," below, and remember that at the larger ones, a duty officer is on call at all times. Hotels with a large foreign clientele are often prepared to recommend English-speaking doctors. Almost all first-class hotels in Mexico have a doctor on call.

Drug Laws   Briefly, don't use or possess illegal drugs in Mexico. Mexicans have no tolerance for drug users, and jail is their solution, with very little hope of getting out until the sentence (usually a long one) is completed or heavy fines or bribes are paid. (*Important Note:* It isn't uncommon to be befriended by a fellow user, only to be turned in by that "friend"—he's collected a bounty for turning you in. It's a no-win situation!) Bring prescription drugs in their original containers. If possible, pack a copy of the original prescription with the generic name of the drug.

I don't need to go into detail about the penalties for illegal drug possession upon return to the United States. Customs officials are also on the lookout for diet drugs sold in Mexico, possession of which could also land you in a U.S. jail because they are illegal here. If you buy antibiotics over the counter (which you can do in Mexico)—say, for a sinus infection—and still have some left, you probably won't be hassled by U.S. customs.

Drugstores   Drugstores (*farmacías*) will sell you just about anything you want, with or without a prescription. However, over-the-counter medicines such as aspirin, decongestants, or antihistamines are rarely sold. Most drugstores are open Monday through Saturday from 8am to 8pm. If you need to buy medicines after normal hours, ask for the *farmacía de turno*—pharmacies take turns staying open during off-hours. Find any drugstore, and in its window may be a card showing the schedule of which drugstore will be open at what time.

Electricity   The electrical system in Mexico is 110 volts, 60 cycles, as in the United States and Canada. However, in reality it may cycle more slowly and overheat your appliances. To compensate, select a medium or low speed for hairdryers and curling irons though they may still overheat. Older hotels still have electrical outlets for flat two-prong plugs; you'll need an adapter for using any modern electrical apparatus that has an enlarged end on one prong or that has three prongs to insert. Many first-class and deluxe hotels have the three-holed outlets (*trifacicos* in Spanish). Those that don't may loan adapters, but to be sure, it's always better to carry your own.

Embassies/Consulates   They provide valuable lists of doctors and lawyers, as well as regulations concerning marriages in Mexico. Contrary to popular belief, your embassy cannot get you out of a Mexican jail, provide postal or banking services, or fly you home when you run out of money. Consular officers can provide you with advice on most matters and problems, however. Most countries have a representative embassy in Mexico City and many have consular offices or representatives in the provinces.

The Embassy of **Australia** in Mexico City is at Jaime Balmes 11, Plaza Polanco, Torre B (☎ 5/395-9988 or 5/566-3053); it's open Monday through Friday from 8am to 1pm.

The Embassy of **Canada** in Mexico City is at Schiller 529, in Polanco (☎ 5/724-7900); it's open Monday through Friday from 9am to 1pm and 2 to 5pm (at other times the name of a duty officer is posted on the embassy door). In Acapulco, the Canadian consulate is in the Hotel Club del Sol, Costera Miguel Alemán, at the corner of Reyes Católicos (☎ 74/85-6621); it's open Monday through Friday from 8am to 3pm.

The Embassy of **New Zealand** in Mexico City is at Homero 229, 8th floor (☎ 5/250-5999 or 5/250-5777); it's open Monday through Thursday from 9am to 2pm and 3 to 5pm and Friday from 9am to 2pm.

The Embassy of the **United Kingdom** in Mexico City is at Lerma 71, at Río Sena (☎ 5/207-2569 or 5/207-2593); it's open Monday through Friday from 9am to 2pm. There are honorary consuls in the following cities: Acapulco, Hotel Las Brisas, Carretera Escénica (☎ 74/84-6605 or 74/84-1580); Ciudad Juárez, Calle Fresno 185 (☎ 16/7-5791); Guadalajara, Paulino Navarro 1165 (☎ 3/611-1678); Mérida, Calle 58 no. 450 (☎ 99/28-6152 or 99/28-3962); Monterrey, Privada de Tamazunchale 104 (☎ 83/78-2565); Oaxaca, Ev. Hidalgo 817 (☎ 951/6-5600); Tampico, 2 de Enero 102-A-Sur (☎ 12/12-9784 or 12/12-9817); Tijuana, Blv. Salinas 1500 (☎ 66/81-7323); and Veracruz, Emparan 200 PB (☎ 29/31-0955).

The Embassy of the **United States** in Mexico City is next to the Hotel María Isabel Sheraton at Paseo de la Reforma 305, at the corner of Río Danubio (☎ 5/211-0042). There are U.S. Consulates General in Ciudad Juárez, López Mateos 924-N (☎ 16/13-4048); Guadalajara, Progreso 175 (☎ 3/625-2998); Monterrey, Av. Constitución 411 Poniente (☎ 83/45-2120); and Tijuana, Tapachula 96

(☎ **66/81-7400**). There are U.S. Consulates in Hermosillo, Av. Monterrey 141 (☎ **621/7-2375**); Matamoros, Av. Primera 2002 (☎ **88/12-4402**); Mérida, Paseo Montejo 453 (☎ **99/25-6366**); Nuevo Laredo, Calle Allende 3330 (☎ **871/ 4-0512**); In addition, Consular Agencies are in Acapulco (☎ **74/85-6600** or 74/ 5-7207); Cabo San Lucas (☎ **114/3-3566**); Cancún (☎ **98/84-2411** or 98/ 84-6399); Mazatlán (☎ **69/13-4444**, ext. 285); Oaxaca (☎ **951/4-3054**); Puerto Vallarta (☎ **322/2-0069**); San Luis Potosí (☎ **481/2-1528**); San Miguel de Allende (☎ **465/2-2357** or 465/2-0068); Tampico (☎ **12/13-2217**); and Veracruz (☎ **29/31-5821**).

Emergencies　The 24-hour Tourist Help Line in Mexico City is 5/250-0151.

Legal Aid　International Legal Defense Counsel, 111 S. 15th St., 24th Floor, Packard Building, Philadelphia, PA 19102 (☎ **215/977-9982**), is a law firm specializing in legal difficulties of Americans abroad. See also "Embassies/Consulates" and "Emergencies," above.

Mail　Mail service south of the border tends to be slow and undependable—though it is improving. If you're on a two-week vacation, it's not a bad idea to buy and mail your postcards in the arrivals lounge at the airport to give them maximum time to get home before you do.

For the most reliable and convenient mail service, have your letters sent to you c/o the American Express offices in major cities, which will receive and forward mail for you if you are one of its clients (a travel-club card or an American Express traveler's check is proof). They charge a fee if you wish to have your mail forwarded.

If you don't use American Express, have your mail sent to you care of Lista de Correos (General Delivery), followed by the Mexican city, state, and country. In Mexican post offices there may actually be a "lista" posted near the Lista de Correos window bearing the names of all those for whom mail has been received. If there's no list, ask and show them your passport so they can riffle through and look for your letters. If the city has more than one office, you'll have to go to the central post office—not a branch—to get your mail. By the way, in many post offices they return mail to the sender if it has been there for more than 10 days. Make sure people don't send you letters too early.

In major Mexican cities there are also branches of such U.S. express mail companies as UPS, Federal Express, and DHL, as well as private mail boxes such as Mail Boxes Etc.

Newspapers/Magazines　Two English-language newspapers *The News,* and *The Times* are published in Mexico City, and carry world news and commentaries, plus a calendar of the day's events including concerts, art shows, and plays. Newspaper kiosks in larger Mexican cities will carry a selection of English-language magazines.

Pets　Taking a pet into Mexico entails a lot of red tape. Consult the Mexican Government Tourist Office nearest you (see "Visitor Information, Entry Requirements & Money," above, in this chapter).

Police　Police in general in Mexico are to be suspected rather than trusted; however, you'll find many who are quite honest, and helpful with directions, even going so far as to lead you where you want to go.

Rest Rooms　The best bet in Mexico is to use rest rooms in restaurants and hotel public areas. Always carry your own toilet paper and hand soap, neither of which is in great supply in Mexican rest rooms. Public facilities, usually near the central market, vary in cleanliness and usually have an attendant who charges a few pesos for toilet use and a few squares of toilet paper. Pemex gas stations have improved the maintenance of their rest rooms along major highways. No matter where you are, even if the toilet flushes with paper, there'll be a waste basket for paper disposal. Many people come from homes without plumbing and are not accustomed to toilets that will take paper, so they'll throw used paper on the floor rather than put it in the toilet; thus, you'll see the basket no matter what quality of place you are in. On the other hand, the water pressure in many establishments is so low that paper won't go down. Thus the disposal basket again—which can be a disgusting sight. But better that than on the floor. There's often a sign telling you whether or not to flush paper.

Taxes   There's a 15% IVA tax on goods and services in most of Mexico, and it's supposed to be included in the posted price. This tax is 10% in Cancún, Cozumel, and Los Cabos.

Telephone/Fax   Telephone area codes are gradually being changed all over the country. The change may affect the area code and first digit or only the area code. Some cities are even adding exchanges and changing whole numbers. Often a personal or business telephone number will be changed without notification to the subscriber. Telephone courtesy messages announcing a phone number change are nonexistent in Mexico. You can try operator assistance for difficult-to-reach numbers, but often the phone company doesn't inform its operators of recent changes. People who have fax machines often turn them off when their offices are closed. Many fax numbers are also regular telephone numbers; you have to ask whoever answers your call for the fax tone *(Por favor darme el tono por fax)*. Telephone etiquette in Mexico does not prompt the answerer to offer to take a message or to have someone return your call; you'll have to make these suggestions yourself. In addition, etiquette doesn't necessarily demand that a business answer its phone by saying its name; often you'll have to ask if you have the right place.

Time   Central standard time prevails throughout most of Mexico. The west-coast states of Sonora, Sinaloa, and parts of Nayarit are on mountain standard time. The state of Baja California Norte is on Pacific time, but Baja California Sur is on mountain time. Though adoption of **Daylight Savings Time** was announced at least twice before, and didn't happen, beginning in October 1996, it will occur—by presidential decree.

Water   Most hotels have decanters or bottles of purified water in the rooms, and the better hotels have either purified water from regular taps or special taps marked *agua purificada.* In the resort areas, especially the Yucatán, hoteliers are beginning to charge for in-room bottled water. If the water in your room is an expensive imported variety such as Evian, for sure there's an extra charge for using it. Virtually any hotel, restaurant, or bar will bring you purified water if you specifically request it, but you'll usually be charged for it. Bottled purified water is sold widely at drugstores and grocery stores.

3 Mexico's Southern Pacific Beach Resorts

The southern part of Mexico's Pacific coast encompasses its oldest resort, Acapulco; its newest, the Bahías de Huatulco (Bays of Huatulco); and its best pair, modern Ixtapa and its neighbor, Zihuatanejo, a centuries-old oceanfront fishing village. Between Acapulco and Huatulco lie the small laid-back coastal villages of Puerto Escondido and Puerto Angel, both of which front beautiful bays.

Only a 4-hour drive north of Acapulco, the resort city of Ixtapa opened in the mid-1970s beside the seaside village of Zihuatanejo. Here you can experience the best of Mexico—sophisticated high-rise hotels in Ixtapa alongside the colorful village of Zihuatanejo—and you'll pay less overall for a vacation than you would in Acapulco.

Acapulco, on the other hand, has historical glamour. The largest and most colorful resort of them all, Acapulco caught the world's attention in the late 1930s when Hollywood stars began arriving. Behind them came a groundswell of tourists, and the city became internationally known as the place to see and be seen. It has retained this exciting edge even into the mid-1990s. South of Acapulco, the Bahías de Huatulco megaproject began in 1986 when the first of nine planned bays opened on an undeveloped portion of Oaxaca's coast.

This chapter encompasses two states, Guerrero and Oaxaca, both of which contain stunning coastlines and lush mountainous terrain. Outside the urban centers, roads are few, and both states are still poor despite decades of tourism.

EXPLORING THE SOUTHERN PACIFIC COAST

Most people traveling to this part of Mexico have sun, surf, and sand firmly entrenched in their imaginations, and tend to camp themselves in a single destination and relax. Each of these beach towns—from Ixtapa and Zihuatanejo in the north to Acapulco and on through the Oaxacan resorts of Puerto Escondido and Huatulco—stands alone as a holiday resort worth enjoying for a few days, or for a week or more. If you've got a little more time and some wanderlust, several of the coastal resorts covered in this chapter could be combined into a single peripatetic trip.

Each has a distinct personality—your choices range from a city that offers every luxury to sleepy towns offering only basic-but-charming seaside relaxation.

Acapulco City offers the best airline connections, the broadest range of all-night entertainment, some very sophisticated dining, and a wide range of accommodations, from hillside villas and luxury resort hotels to modest inns on the beach and in Old Acapulco. Beaches are wide, clean, and numerous, but the ocean is polluted—though cleaner than in the past. It's a good launching pad for side trips to colonial Taxco (Mexico's "Silver Capital"), only 2¹/₂ hours away using the toll road, and to Ixtapa/Zihuatanejo. The latter offers all that Acapulco has but on a smaller, newer, less hectic scale, plus excellent beaches and clean ocean waters. Since the two are only a 4- to 5-hour drive apart, many people fly into Acapulco (where air service is better), spend a few days there, and go on to Ixtapa/Zihuatanejo by bus or rental car.

Puerto Escondido is a 6-hour drive south of Acapulco on coastal Highway 200. Most people don't drive or take a bus from Acapulco to Puerto Escondido, though that's easy enough to do. Usually Puerto Escondido, noted for its surfing waves, laid-back beachside village, inexpensive inns, and nearby nature excursions, is a destination on its own. But many travelers combine it with a trip to or from the inland city of Oaxaca. The two are six hours apart by serpentine highway, or less than an hour by air.

The small village of Puerto Angel, only 50 miles south of Puerto Escondido or 30 miles north of the Bays of Huatulco, could be a day-trip from either of those destinations, or a quiet place to vacation for several days providing you aren't big on nightlife and grand hotels of which there are none in Puerto Angel. A couple of hotels serve very good food, and there are beachside restaurants serving fresh fish, but otherwise dining is limited. However, visiting nearly unoccupied beaches near Puerto Angel can be a prime activity.

Huatulco, 80 miles south of Puerto Escondido, with its 18-hole golf course and a few resort hotels, was built to appeal to the luxury traveler. Besides golf, boat tours of the nine Huatulco Bays, and a couple of nature excursions that are actually nearer Puerto Escondido, there's not a lot to do. But the setting is beautiful and relaxing. The few budget-priced hotels in Huatulco cost more than budget hotels of similar quality almost anywhere on the Pacific coast.

1 Zihuatanejo & Ixtapa

360 miles SW of Mexico City, 353 miles SE of Manzanillo, 158 miles NW of Acapulco

Zihuatanejo, a picturesque, authentically Mexican oceanside village, complements Ixtapa, a tranquil, sophisticated oceanfront resort created in 1976. With the explosion of population from 4,000 in 1976 to 85,000 today, the pleasing pair is also developing some of the vibrancy of Puerto Vallarta, including excellent restaurants, shopping, and nightlife. In comparison to both Puerto Vallarta and Acapulco, food and lodging are still reasonably priced—if you know where to look. Ixtapa is my favorite of all Mexico's planned resorts, primarily because it has retained its tranquility while offering the visitor a taste of both village life and modern Mexico.

ESSENTIALS
GETTING THERE & DEPARTING

BY PLANE   See Chapter 2, "Planning a Trip to Southern Pacific Mexico," for information on flying to Ixtapa/Zihuatanejo from the United States and Canada. Here are the local numbers of some international carriers: **Aeroméxico, ☎ 755/4-2018,** 755/4-2022, or 755/4-2019; **Mexicana, ☎ 755/3-2208,** 755/3-2209, or 755/4-2227; **Northwest, ☎ 5/202-4444** in Mexico City.

Ask your travel agent about **charter flights,** which are becoming the most efficient and least expensive way to get here.

If you're flying in from elsewhere in Mexico, **Mexicana** has nonstop or direct flights from Guadalajara and Mexico City, and **Aeroméxico** flies in from Mexico City.

Taxis are the only option for returning to the airport from town and charge around $5.50 to $10 one way.

BY BUS   There are two bus terminals in Zihuatanejo: the **Central de Autobuses,** from which most lines operate, and the **Estrella de Oro station,** on Paseo del Palmar near the market and within walking distance of downtown hotels.

At the **Central de Autobuses,** several companies offer service to Acapulco and other cities, including first-class **Estrella Blanca** (☎ 755/4-3478) and second-class **Flecha Roja** (☎ 755/4-3477 or 755/4-3483). Estrella Blanca's buses are air-conditioned—most of the time—and depart for Acapulco hourly from 6am to 10pm; the cost is $8.50 one way. Keep in mind, however, that the Estrella Blanca station in Acapulco is far from the hotels I've recommended in that city and means a costly taxi ride on arrival. Flecha Roja buses to Acapulco run every hour or so; these stop in Zihuatanejo and take on passengers as space permits. En route they stop frequently and take longer to reach Acapulco so choose them only if there's no other way. Buses depart from **Frontera** to Puerto Escondido and Huatulco daily at 6:30 and 9pm.

To go north to Manzanillo or Puerto Vallarta, you must buy a ticket for Lázaro Cárdenas (Estrella Blanca has service every 30 min.) and change buses there.

First-class **Estrella de Oro** (☎ 755/4-2175) runs five first-class and three deluxe daily buses to Acapulco between 7am and 10pm. You can purchase advance tickets with seat assignments in Ixtapa at **Turismo Caleta** in the La Puerta shopping center next to the tourism office (☎ 755/3-0044; fax 755/3-2024). In Acapulco the Estrella de Oro station is near many budget hotels.

The trip from Mexico City to Zihuatanejo takes five hours (bypassing Acapulco); from Acapulco, four to five hours. From Zihuatanejo, it's six to seven hours to Manzanillo, and an additional six to Puerto Vallarta, which doesn't include time spent waiting for buses.

BY CAR   From Mexico City, the shortest route is to take Highway 15 to Toluca, then Highway 130/134 the rest of the way, though on the latter highway gas stations are few and far between. The other route is Highway 95D (four lanes) to Iguala, then Highway 51 west to Highway 134.

From Acapulco or Manzanillo, the only choice is the coastal highway, Highway 200. The ocean views along the winding, mountain-edged drive from Manzanillo can be spectacular.

Motorists' advisory: Motorists planning to follow Highway 200 northwest up the coast from Ixtapa or Zihuatanejo toward Lázaro Cárdenas and Manzanillo should be aware of reports of car and motorist hijackings on that route, especially around Playa Azul. Before heading in that direction, ask locals and the tourism office about the status of the route when you are there, and don't drive at night. According to tourism officials, police patrols of the highway have been increased and the number of crime incidents has decreased dramatically.

ORIENTATION

ARRIVING BY PLANE   The Ixtapa-Zihuatanejo airport is 15 minutes (about 7 miles) south of Zihuatanejo. **Transportes Terrestres** minivans (or colectivos) transport travelers to hotels in Zihuatanejo for $3.75, to Ixtapa for $5, and to Club Med

Zihuatanejo & Ixtapa Area

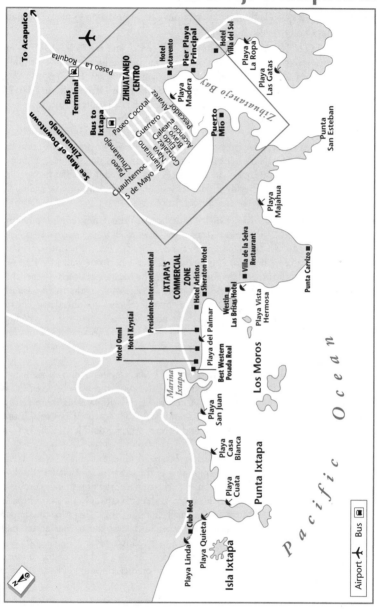

To Acapulco

See Map of Downtown Zihuatanejo

Paseo La Roquita

Bus Terminal

Bus to Ixtapa

ZIHUATANEJO CENTRO

Hotel Sotavento

Pier Playa Principal

Hotel Villa del Sol

Playa La Ropa

Playa Las Gatas

Playa Madera

Paseo Cocotal

Pescador Alvarez

Ascencio

Bravo

Galeana

Guerrero

Gonzalez

Nava

Ejido

Altamirano

Paseo Zihuatanejo

Cuauhtemoc

5 de Mayo

Zihuatanejo Bay

Puerto Mío

Punta San Esteban

Playa Majahua

IXTAPA'S COMMERCIAL ZONE

Presidente-Intercontinental

Hotel Aristos

Sheraton Hotel

Villa de la Selva Restaurant

Westin

Las Brisas Hotel

Playa Vista Hermosa

Punta Carrizo

Hotel Omni

Hotel Krystal

Playa del Palmar

Best Western Posada Real

Marina Ixtapa

Los Moros

Playa San Juan

Playa Casa Blanca

Playa Cuata

Punta Ixtapa

Club Med

Playa Linda

Playa Quieta

Isla Ixtapa

Pacific Ocean

Airport ✈ Bus ◼

2-0008

---

for $5.75; colectivo tickets are sold just outside the baggage-claim area. A taxi will cost $14 to Zihuatanejo, $17 to Ixtapa, and $20 to Club Med.

ARRIVING BY BUS In Zihuatanejo, the **Estrella de Oro bus station,** on Paseo del Palmar at Morelos, is a few blocks beyond the market and is within walking distance of some of the downtown hotels I have suggested. The clean, warehouselike **Central de Autobuses,** the main terminal where all other buses converge, is a mile or so farther out, opposite the Pemex gas station and IMSS Hospital on Paseo

Zihuatanejo at Paseo la Boquita. A taxi from either bus station to most Zihuatanejo hotels costs $1.60; continuing to Ixtapa costs $5 or so.

INFORMATION   The **State Tourism Office** (☎ and fax **755/3-1967**) is in La Puerta shopping center in Ixtapa across from the Presidente Inter-Continental Hotel; it's open Monday through Friday from 9am to 2pm and 4 to 7pm and on Saturday from 9am to 2pm. The **Zihuatanejo Tourism Office** (☎ and fax **755/4-2001,** ext. 120) is on the main square by the basketball court at Álvarez; it's open Monday through Friday from 9am to 3pm and 6 to 8pm.

Time-share booths in both towns formerly masqueraded as information booths, but the State of Guerrero clamped down on their deceptive practices. Booths must be clearly marked by their business names and cannot carry signs claiming to be tourist information centers. Time-share employees must wear uniforms and may not leave their stands to accost passersby. If you encounter any problems or false claims from the time-share operators, contact the tourist office.

CITY LAYOUT   The fishing village and resort of **Zihuatanejo** spreads out around the beautiful Bay of Zihuatanejo, framed by downtown to the north and a beautiful long beach and the Sierra foothills to the east. Beaches line the perimeter and boats bob at anchor. The heart of Zihuatanejo is the waterfront walkway **Paseo del Pescador** (also called the **Malecón**), bordering the Municipal Beach. Rather than a plaza as in most Mexican villages, Zihuatanejo's centerpiece is the **town basketball court,** which fronts the beach; I use it as a point of reference for directions. The main thoroughfare for cars, however, is **Juan Álvarez,** a block behind the Malecón. Sections of several of the main streets are designated as *zona peatonal* (pedestrian zone blocked off to cars). The area is zigzagged and seems to block parts of streets haphazardly.

A cement-and-sand **walkway** runs from the Malecón in downtown Zihuatanejo along the water to Playa Madera, making it much easier to walk between the two points. The walkway is lit at night. Access to Playa la Ropa is via the main road, **Camino a Playa la Ropa,** about a half-hour walk from downtown. A road is under construction between Playa La Ropa and Playa Las Gatas; until it's finished the only access is by boat.

A good highway connects "Zihua" to **Ixtapa,** 4 miles to the northwest. The 18-hole Ixtapa Golf Club marks the beginning of the inland side of Ixtapa. Tall hotels line Ixtapa's wide beach, **Playa Palmar,** against a backdrop of lush palm groves and mountains. It's accessed by the main street, **Bulevar Ixtapa.** On the opposite side of the main boulevard lies a huge area of small shopping plazas (many of the shops are air-conditioned) and restaurants. At the far end of Bulevar Ixtapa, **Marina Ixtapa** has opened with excellent restaurants, private yacht slips, and an 18-hole golf course. Condominiums and private homes surround the marina and golf course, and more developments are rising in the hillsides past the marina en route to Playa Quieta and Playa Linda.

GETTING AROUND   A **shuttle bus** goes back and forth between Zihuatanejo and Ixtapa every 10 or 15 minutes from 5am to 11pm daily, charging about 50¢ one way. In Zihuatanejo it stops near the corner of Morelos/Paseo Zihuatanejo and Juárez, about three blocks north of the market. In Ixtapa it makes numerous stops along Bulevar Ixtapa. A taxi from one town to the other costs about $4 one way; from midnight to 5am rates increase by 50% (agree on a price before getting into a cab).

Special note: The highway leading from Zihuatanejo to Ixtapa widens and narrows in odd ways—keep your eyes on the white line or you'll end up in a parking lot or on a side street paralleling the highway. Going out of town toward Acapulco, the outside lane ends without warning, sending unwary drivers into a graveled area before the lane picks up again farther on. Surprise speed-control bumps (*topes*) dot the thoroughfare and appear on other streets as well—keep your eyes peeled. Most of the *topes* on the highway from Zihuatanejo to Acapulco have been removed, thus speeding up the trip.

Street signs are becoming more common in Zihuatanejo, and good signs lead you in and out of both towns. However, both locations have an area called the Zona Hotelera (Hotel Zone), so if you're trying to reach Ixtapa's hotel zone, you may be confused by signs in Zihuatanejo pointing to that village's own hotel zone.

FAST FACTS: ZIHUATANEJO & IXTAPA

American Express   The main office is in the Westin Hotel (☎ 755/3-0853; fax 755/3-1206).

Area Code   The telephone area code changed in 1995 from 753 to 755.

Banks   Ixtapa has only one bank, Bancomer, in the La Puerta Centro shopping center. Zihuatanejo has four banks, but the most centrally located is Banamex, Cuauhtémoc 4. Banks change money from 10am to noon on weekdays.

Climate   Summer is hot and humid, though tempered by the sea breezes and brief showers; September is the wettest month.

Gasoline   There's a busy Pemex station in Zihuatanejo by the Central Camionera on the highway leading to Acapulco and the airport and another near the airport entrance.

FUN ON & OFF THE BEACH

The **Museo Arqueología de la Costa Grande,** near Guerrero at the east end of Paseo del Pescador, traces the history of the Costa Grande (comprising the area from Acapulco to Ixtapa/Zihuatanejo) from its significance in pre-Hispanic times, when it was known as Cihuatlán and was marked by cultural transition, through the colonial era. Most of the museum's pottery and stone artifacts show evidence of extensive trade with other far-off cultures and regions, including the Toltec and Teotihuacán cultures near Mexico City; the Olmec culture on both the Pacific and Gulf coasts; and areas known today as the states of Nayarit, Michoacán, and San Luis Potosí. Some items are from a site found several years ago near the airport. Among the tribute items indigenous groups from this area paid the Aztecs were cotton *tilmas* (capes) and *cacao* (chocolate). The museum is well done and worth the half an hour or less it takes to stroll through; information is given in Spanish. Admission is $1, and it's open Tuesday through Sunday from 10am to 5pm.

THE BEACHES

In Zihuatanejo

At Zihuatanejo's town beach, **Playa Municipal,** the local fishermen pull their colorful boats up onto the sand. Small shops and restaurants line the waterfront, making this a great spot for people watching and for absorbing the flavor of daily village life. This beach is protected from the main surge of the Pacific.

Besides the peaceful Playa Municipal, Zihuatanejo has three other beaches (*playas*): Madera, La Ropa, and Las Gatas. **Playa Madera,** just east of Playa Municipal, is open to the surf but generally tranquil. Many attractive budget lodgings overlook this area from the hillside.

South of Playa Madera is Zihuatanejo's largest and most beautiful beach, **Playa La Ropa,** a long sweep of sand with a great view of the sunset. Some lovely, small hotels and restaurants nestle into the hills, and palm groves edge the shoreline.

Although it's also open to the Pacific surge, the waves are usually gentle. A taxi from town costs $2.

Playa Las Gatas, a pretty, secluded beach can be seen across the bay from Playa Ropa and Zihuatanejo. The small coral reef just offshore makes it a good spot for snorkeling and diving. The open-air seafood restaurants on this beach also make it an appealing lunch spot for a splurge. Small launches with shade run to Las Gatas from the Zihuatanejo town pier, a 10-minute trip; the captains will take you across whenever you ask between 8am and 4pm, and the round-trip fare is $2.75. Usually the last boat back leaves Las Gatas at 4:30pm; be sure to double-check! Snorkeling and water-sports gear can be rented at the beach.

In Ixtapa

Ixtapa's main beach, **Playa Palmar,** is a lovely white-sand arc edging the hotel zone, with dramatic rock formations silhouetted in the sea. The surf here can be rough; use caution and never swim when a red flag is posted.

Several of the nicest beaches in the area are essentially closed to the public as lavish resort developments rise and claim them. **Playa Quieta,** on the mainland across from Isla Ixtapa, is largely claimed by the all-inclusive Club Med and Qualton Club. The remaining piece of beach used to be the launching point for the boats to the Isla Ixtapa, but it is gradually being taken over by a private development. Now, the Isla Ixtapa–bound boats leave from the jetty on **Playa Linda,** about 8 miles north of Ixtapa. Water taxis here ferry passengers to Isla Ixtapa for about $3 round-trip. Playa Linda is the primary out-of-town beach, with water-sports equipment and horse rental available. **Playa las Cuatas,** a pretty beach and cove a few miles north of Ixtapa, and **Playa Majahua,** an isolated beach just west of Zihuatanejo, are both being transformed into large resort complexes. You may be able to reach them by boat, but you won't be able to get there by land as the building continues. Lovely **Playa Vista Hermosa** is framed by striking rock formations and bordered by the Westin Brisas Hotel high on the hill.

WATER SPORTS & BOAT TRIPS

Probably the most popular boat trip is to **Isla Ixtapa** for snorkeling and lunch at El Marlin restaurant. Though you can book this outing as a tour through local travel agencies, you can also go on your own from Zihuatanejo by following the directions to Playa Linda above and taking a boat from there. Boats leave at 11:30am for Isla Ixtapa and return around 4pm. Along the way, you'll pass dramatic rock formations and the Los Moros de Los Péricos islands, known for the great variety of birds that nest on the rocky points jutting out into the blue Pacific. On Isla Ixtapa you'll find good snorkeling and a nature trail through an unfenced area with a few birds and animals. Snorkeling, diving, and other water-sports gear is available for rent on the island. Be sure to catch the last water taxi back at 4pm—and be sure to double-check that time.

Separate day-trips to **Los Moros de Los Péricos Islands** for **bird watching** can usually be arranged through local travel agencies, though it would probably be less expensive to rent a boat with a guide at Playa Linda. The islands are offshore from Ixtapa's main beach.

Sunset cruises on the trimaran *TriStar,* arranged through **Yates del Sol** (☎ 755/4-3589), depart from the town pier at Puerto Mío. The sunset cruise costs $40 and includes an open bar. An all-day trip to Isla Ixtapa on this yacht begins at 10:30am, costs $60, and includes an open bar and lunch. Schedules, along with special trips, vary, so call for current information and about special trips.

Downtown Zihuatanejo

To Ixtapa

Main Bus Terminal

Avenida Morelos

Paseo Zihuatanejo

Tres Estrellas Bus Terminal

Paseo del Palmar

I. Altamirano

Cuáuhtémoc

Avenida Nava

Benito

C. González

Market

Kioto   Plaza

Camino a la playa la Ropa

Vicente Guerrero

Juárez

Ejido

Galeana

Paseo de la Boquita

Canal

5 de Mayo

Calle Adelita

Calle Mateos

Las Salinas

N. Bravo

Pedro Ascencio

Avenida Ramírez

Museo Archeologica

J.N. Alvarez

Paseo del Pescador

Playa Municipal

Playa Municipal

Playa La Ropa

Muelle Pier

Bahía de Zihuatanejo

Punta Godomia

Playa Las Gatas

Bus   Post Office ⊠

2-0009

Fishing trips can be arranged with the boat cooperative at the Zihuatanejo town pier (☎ 755/4-2056) and cost $100 to $250, depending on the size of the boat, how long the trip lasts, and other factors (though most trips last 6 hours). The cost is higher for a trip arranged through a local travel agency; the least expensive trips are on small launches called *pangas;* most have shade. Both small-game and deep-sea fishing are offered, and the fishing here rivals that found in Mazatlán or Baja. Trips that combine fishing with a visit to near-deserted ocean beaches that extend for miles along the coast from Zihuatanejo can also be arranged. Sportfishing packages including air transportation and hotels can be arranged through **Mexico Sportsman,** 202 Milam Bldg., San Antonio, TX 78205 (☎ 210/212-4567; fax 210/212-4568). San Lushinsky at **Ixtapa Sportfishing Charters,** 33 Olde Mill Run, Stroudsburg, PA 18360 (☎ 717/424-8323; fax 717/424-1016) is another fishing outfitter.

Boating and fishing expeditions from the new **Marina Ixtapa,** a bit north of the Ixtapa hotel zone, can also be arranged.

Sailboats, windsurfers, and other water-sports equipment rentals are usually available at various stands on Playa la Ropa, Playa las Gatas, Isla Ixtapa, and at the main beach, Playa Palmar, in Ixtapa. **Parasailing** is also available at La Ropa and Palmar. **Kayaks** are available for rent at the **Zihuatanejo Scuba Center** (see below), hotels in Ixtapa, and some water-sports operations on Playa La Ropa. The rate is about $5 per hour.

Scuba-diving trips are arranged through the **Zihuatanejo Scuba Center,** on Cuauhtémoc 3 (☎ and fax **755/4-2147**). Fees start at around $65 for two dives, including all equipment and lunch. Marine biologist and dive instructor Juan Barnard speaks excellent English and is very knowledgeable about the area, which has nearly 30 different dive sites, including walls and caves. Diving is done year-round, though the water is clearest May through December, when there is 100-foot visibility or better. The nearest decompression chamber is in Acapulco, though local divers are hopeful that the one in Zihuatanejo will be repaired soon. Advance reservations for dives are advised during Christmas and Easter.

Surfing is good at Petacalco Beach north of Ixtapa.

LAND SPORTS & ACTIVITIES

In Ixtapa, the **Club de Golf Ixtapa** (☎ **755/3-1062** or 755/3-1163) has an 18-hole course designed by Robert Trent Jones, Jr. Bring your own clubs or rent them here. The greens fee is $50; caddies cost $17; and electric carts cost $33. Call for reservations. The **Marina Ixtapa Golf Course** (☎ **755/3-1410;** fax 755/3-0825), designed by Robert von Hagge, has 18 challenging holes. The greens fee is $55 with cart, or $45 without cart. Call for reservations.

To polish your **tennis** serve in Zihuatanejo, try the **Hotel Villa del Sol** at Playa la Ropa (☎ **755/4-2239** or 755/4-3239). In Ixtapa, the **Club de Golf Ixtapa** (☎ **755/3-1062** or 755/3-1163) and the **Marina Ixtapa Golf Course** (☎ **755/ 3-1410;** fax 755/3-0825) both have courts that are lit at night and both rent equipment. Fees are $7 per hour, $10 per hour at night. Call for reservations. In addition, the **Dorado Pacífico** and several other hotels on the main beach of Ixtapa have courts.

For **horseback riding, Rancho Playa Linda** (☎ **755/4-3085**) offers guided trail rides from the Playa Linda beach (about 8 miles north of Ixtapa). Guided rides begin at 8:30, 9:45, and 11am and 3:30 and 5pm. Groups of three or more riders can arrange their own tour, which is especially nice a little later in the evening for sunset (though you'll need mosquito repellent in the evening). Riders can choose to go along the beach to the mouth of the river and back through coconut plantations or stay along the beach for the whole ride (which usually lasts 1 to 1¹/₂ hours). The fee is $20. Travel agencies in either town can arrange your trip but will charge a bit more for transportation. Reservations are suggested in the high season.

A **countryside tour** of fishing villages, coconut and mango plantations, and the Barra de Potosí Lagoon, which is 14 miles south of Zihuatanejo and known for its tropical birds, is available through local travel agencies for $25 to $30. The tour typically lasts 5¹/₂ hours and includes lunch and time for swimming.

For **off-the-beaten-track tours,** contact Alex León Pineda, the knowledgeable owner of **Fw4 Tours** in the Los Patios Center in Ixtapa (☎ **755/3-1442;** fax 755/ 3-2014). His countryside tour goes to coconut and banana plantations, small villages where brick makers work in the traditional fashion and residents live in palm thatch huts, and to the beach at La Saladita, where fishermen and the tour clients prepare a lunch of fresh lobster, dorado, or snapper. When I last visited, Fw4 Tours was in the process of putting together a cultural tour to include the town of Petatlán and the small archaeological site of La Chole.

SHOPPING
ZIHUATANEJO

Like other resorts in Mexico, Zihuatanejo has its quota of T-shirt and souvenir shops. But it's becoming a better place to buy Mexican crafts, folk art, and jewelry. The **artisan's market** on Calle Cinco de Mayo is a good place to start a shopping spree before moving on to specialty shops. The **municipal market** on Avenida Benito Juárez (about five blocks inland from the waterfront) is also good, especially the stands specializing in huaraches, hammocks, and baskets. The market area sprawls over several blocks and is well worth an early morning visit. Spreading inland from the waterfront three or four blocks are numerous small shops worth exploring. Besides the places listed below, check out **Alberto's** at Cuauhtémoc 15 and **Ruby's** at Cuauhtémoc 7 for jewelry.

Shops are generally open Monday through Saturday from 10am to 2pm and 4 to 8pm; many of the better shops close on Sunday, but some smaller souvenir stands stay open, though hours vary.

Boutique D'Xochitl
Ejido at Cuauhtémoc. ☎ **755/4-2131.**

This is my favorite place to pick up light crinkle cotton clothing that's perfect for tropical climes. Hours are Monday through Saturday from 9am to 9pm, Sunday from 2 to 9pm.

Casa Marina
Paseo del Pescador 9. ☎ **755/4-2373.**

This small complex extends from the waterfront to Álvarez near Cinco de Mayo and houses four shops, each specializing in handcrafted wares from Mexico and Guatemala. Items include handsome rugs, textiles, masks, papier-mâché, colorful wood carvings, and silver jewelry. Café Marina, the small coffee shop in the complex, has shelves and shelves of used paperback books in several languages for sale. It's open daily from 9am to 9pm during the high season and from 10am to 2pm and 4 to 8pm during the rest of the year.

Coco Cabaña Collectibles
Guerrero and Álvarez. ☎ **755/4-2518.**

Located next to Coconuts Restaurant, this gorgeous shop is crammed with carefully selected crafts and folk art from all over the country, including fine Oaxaca wood carvings. Owner Pat Cummings once ran a gallery in New York, and the inventory reveals her discriminating eye. If you purchase something, she'll cash your dollars at the going rate. It's opposite the Hotel Citali and is open Monday through Saturday from 10am to 2pm and 6 to 10pm; it's closed during September and October.

Galería Maya
Bravo 31. ☎ **755/4-3606.**

This small folk-art store is packed with Guatemalan jackets, *santos,* silver, painted wooden fish from Guerrero, tin mirror frames, masks, lacquered gourds, rain sticks, and embroidered T-shirts. It's open Monday through Saturday from 10am to 2pm and 6 to 9pm.

Mueblart

Álvarez 13-B. ☎ **755/3-2530.**

You'll wish you owned a nearby beach house after browsing through this handsome collection of handcrafted furniture; or you can simply ship your purchases back home if you'd like. Smaller items include wooden and gourd masks and wicker baskets in bright colors. The store is across the street from the Hotel Avila. It's open Monday through Saturday from 11am to 2:30pm and 5 to 9pm.

IXTAPA

Shopping gets better in Ixtapa every year as several fine folk art shops become established. There are several plazas with air-conditioned shops carrying fashionable resort wear and contemporary art, as well as T-shirts and jewelry. Brand-name sportswear is sold at shops that include **Ferroni, Bye-Bye, Aca Joe,** and **Navale.** All of these shops are within the same area on Bulevar Ixtapa, across from the beachside hotels, and most are open from 9am to 2pm and 4 to 9pm, including Sundays.

La Fuente

Los Patios Center on Bulevar Ixtapa. ☎ **755/3-0812.**

This terrific shop carries gorgeous talavera pottery, wicker tables in the form of jaguars, handblown glassware, masks, tin mirrors and frames, and wood and papier-mâché miniatures. It's open daily from 9am to 2pm and 4 to 9pm.

Mic-Mac

La Puerta Center on Bulevar Ixtapa. ☎ **755/3-1733.**

The owners of La Fuente created a second shop featuring embroidered and appliquéd clothing from Guatemala and Mexico, textile wall hangings, and ceramic and brass home accessories. Mic-Mac is open daily from 9am to 2pm and 4 to 9pm.

ACCOMMODATIONS

Ixtapa and Playa Madera have the most expensive hotels, with a couple of choices in the budget to moderate price ranges. Central Zihuatanejo has the most choices in the budget range.

IXTAPA

Very Expensive

✪ Westin Brisas Resort

Bulevar Ixtapa, 40880 Ixtapa, Gro. ☎ **755/3-2121** or 800/228-3000 in the U.S. Fax 755/3-0751. 428 rms, 19 suites. A/C MINIBAR TV TEL. High season, $245 single or double, $275 Royal Beach Club, $475–$1,250 suite. Low season, $165 single or double, $200 Royal Beach Club, $375–$1,000 suite. Free parking.

Sitting above the high-rise hotels of Ixtapa on its own rocky promontory, the Westin is both literally and figuratively a cut above the others. The austere yet luxurious public areas, all in stone and stucco, are bathed in sweeping breezes and announce that this is a special hotel. The spare luxury carries into the rooms with Mexican tile floors, and grand-but-private, half-shaded and plant-decorated patios with hammocks and lounges. All rooms face the hotel's cove and private beach. The six master suites come with private pools. Water is purified in your tap and there's an ice machine on each floor. The 16th floor is reserved as a nonsmoking floor and three rooms on the 18th floor are equipped for disabled travelers.

Dining/Entertainment: From elegant indoor dining to casual open-air restaurants this hotel's five restaurants mean you can stay put and just relax without going out for good food. The airy lobby bar is one of the most popular places to enjoy sunset cocktails while a soothing trio croons romantic songs of Mexico.

Services: Laundry and room service, travel agency, car rental, massage, baby-sitting.

Facilities: Shopping arcade, barber and beauty shop, four swimming pools (one for children), four lighted tennis courts with pro on request, elevator to secluded beach.

Expensive

Krystal

Bulevar Ixtapa s/n, 40880 Ixtapa, Gro. ☎ **755/3-0333** or 800/231-9860 in the U.S. Fax 753/3-0216. 245 rms, 19 suites. A/C MINIBAR TV TEL. High season, $155–$170 single or double, $275–$575 suite. Low season, $125–$155 single or double, $195–$400 suite. Free parking.

Krystal hotels are known in Mexico for the high quality of service and well-maintained rooms. This one is no exception. The multistoried V-shaped building encloses the grounds and pool area. Each spacious, nicely furnished and carpeted room has a balcony with an ocean view, game table, tile bathrooms, and either two double beds or a king-size bed. Master suites have large, furnished triangular-shaped balconies. Ask if the daily buffet breakfast is included in your daily rate. Two children under age 12 can stay free in their parent's room. The eighth floor is nonsmoking, and there's one handicapped-equipped room.

Dining/Entertainment: Among the hotel's five restaurants is the evening-only Bogart's. There's live music nightly in the lobby bar. The Krystal's famous Christine Club, born in Cancún, is reincarnated here with the best disco flash around.

Services: Laundry and room service, travel agency, auto rental, beauty and barber shop, massage.

Facilities: swimming pool, two tennis courts, racquetball court, gym with sauna. Ice machines on floors 2, 5, 8, and 11.

Sheraton Ixtapa

Bulevar Ixtapa, 40880 Ixtapa, Gro. ☎ **755/3-1858** or 755/3-4858, or 800/325-3535 in the U.S. and Canada. Fax 755/3-2438. 322 rms, 12 suites. A/C MINIBAR TV TEL. High season, $175 single or double; $250 junior suite; $300 master suite. Low season, $155–$170 single or double, $250–$350 suite. Free parking.

This grand, resort-style hotel has large, handsomely furnished public areas facing the beach; it's a very inviting place to come for a drink and to people-watch. Rooms are as nice as the public areas. Most have balconies with views of either the ocean or the mountains. Thirty-six rooms on the fifth floor are nonsmoking. Rooms equipped for the disabled are available.

Dining/Entertainment: Four restaurants; nightclub; Wednesday night Mexican fiesta with buffet and live entertainment outdoors.

Services: Room and laundry service, travel agency, concierge, car rental.

Facilities: There's one beachside pool, four tennis courts, a fitness room, ice machine on each floor, beauty and barber shop, boutiques, pharmacy/gift shop.

Villa del Lago

Retorno Alondras 244, (Apdo. Postal 127) 40880 Ixtapa, Gro. ☎ **755/3-1482.** Fax 755/3-1422. 6 rms. A/C TEL. High season, $115–$150 single or double. Low season, $85–$135 single or double. Rates include breakfast. Parking available on street.

Architect Raul Esponda has transformed his private villa into a luxurious, secluded bed-and-breakfast overlooking Ixtapa's golf course. The best room is the trilevel master suite, with a sunken tiled shower, huge bedroom with great views of the golf course, and a large living room and private terrace. Other rooms are smaller but still delightful, decorated with fine folk art and carved furnishings. Breakfast is served on the terrace; get up early enough and you'll probably spot the two resident alligators sunning in the golf course's lake, or a giant gray heron perched in a nearby palm. The lounge chairs by the swimming pool are a perfect spot for reading a novel from the well-stocked library or just watching the golfers cast envious glances your way. The staff of five keeps a watchful eye over the guests, predicting their whims and needs. Reasonable golf, tennis, and meal packages are available. Advance reservations are a good idea, since regular guests sometimes claim the entire villa for weeks at a time.

Dining/Entertainment: Formal dining room for breakfast; lunch and dinner are available on request for both guests and nonguests. TV room with satellite service and a good video library. Family room stocked with games and books. Well-stocked honor bar by the pool.

Services: Transportation to Ixtapa's hotel zone.

Facilities: Swimming pool.

Moderate

Hotel Aristos

Bulevar Ixtapa, 40880 Ixtapa, Gro. ☎ **755/3-0011** or 800/527-4786 in the U.S. Fax 755/3-2031. 250 rms. A/C TV TEL. $60–$80 single or double (including breakfast); $85–$115 single or double (including all three meals). Free parking.

The decor at the bright pink Aristos might be called "Moorish modern," mixing pointed arches with contemporary lines. The standard rooms are in need of renovation and are medium-sized with a sea view (some have balconies) and come with two double beds, marble-trimmed bath, contemporary furniture, and satellite TV with U.S. channels. Check out a few rooms before settling on one; some are in much better condition than others. Parking is in an open lot off Bulevar Ixtapa. The Aristos has an all-inclusive program covering all meals and most activities. This hotel often offers cut-rate deals, and since it's on the same beach as other more expensive hotels, you can enjoy the setting at a fraction of the price. Two restaurants serve buffets only, either included in your all-inclusive package or for a set fee. The one coffee shop has a regular menu. The hotel offers laundry, baby-sitting, and secretarial and business services, and has a swimming pool, travel agency, shops, two tennis courts, and exercise and water-sports equipment.

ZIHUATANEJO

The most economical hotels are in Zihuatanejo rather than in Ixtapa. The term "bungalow" is used loosely in Zihuatanejo, as it is elsewhere in Mexico. A bungalow may be an individual unit with a kitchen and bedroom, or a bedroom only. It also may be hotel-like in a two-story building with multiple units, some of which have kitchens. It may be cozy and nice or rather rustic, and there may or may not be a patio or balcony. Beware of vanishing belongings, however, if your room has a balcony.

Playa Madera and Playa La Ropa, separated from each other only by a craggy shoreline, are both accessible by road. Prices here tend to be higher than those in town, but some people find that the beautiful and tranquil setting is worth the little extra. The town is just 5 to 20 minutes away, depending on whether you walk or take a taxi.

Many long-term guests in Ixtapa and Zihuatanejo search out apartments and condominiums for rent. Information on rentals, as well as hotel reservations and personalized service, are available from Julia Ortíz Bautista at **Job Representatives,** Villas del Pacífico, Edificio C, Dept. 01, 40880 Zihuatanejo, Guerrero. (☎ and fax **755/4-4374**).

In Town

Apartamentos Amueblados Valle

Vicente Guerrero 14, 40880 Zihuatanejo, Gro. ☎ **755/4-2084.** Fax 753/4-3220. 8 apts. FAN. High season, $40 one-bedroom apt, $55 two-bedroom apt. Low season, $30 one-bedroom apt, $45 two-bedroom apt.

You can rent a well-furnished apartment for a little more than the price of a hotel room. The five one-bedroom apartments accommodate up to three people; the three two-bedroom apartments can fit four comfortably. Each apartment is different, but all are clean and airy, with ceiling fans, private balconies, and kitchenettes. Maid service is provided daily. There's a paperback-book exchange in the office. Luís Valle, the owner, can often find cheaper apartments elsewhere for guests who want to stay several months. Reserve well in advance during high season. It's on Guerrero about two blocks in from the waterfront between Ejido and North Bravo.

Casa Aurora

Nicolás Bravo 27, 40880 Zihuatanejo, Gro. ☎ **755/4-3046.** 12 rms. FAN. High season, $9 single; $18 double. Low season, $7 single; $15 double.

Located a few minutes from the beach, this hotel offers small rooms with well-worn furniture, good window screens (unusual in local hotels), and a comfortable second-story porch. All rooms have hot water, two or three lumpy single beds, and louvered windows. The best rooms are no. 12 (a double) and no. 13 (a triple), with windows facing the street. The management also rents apartments on Playa Ropa. From the museum walk inland on Guerrero two blocks to Nicolás Bravo and turn left; the hotel is on your right.

Casa Bravo

Nicolás Bravo 11, 40880 Zihuatanejo, Gro. ☎ **755/4-2548.** 9 rms. FAN. $14 single; $18 double.

A good value for its budget price, this two-story hotel offers clean, plain rooms with mismatched furniture and bare bulbs above the beds. Three second-story rooms at the front of the building have balconies, though they let in a bit of street noise. Guests can lounge in a hammock in the open-ceilinged lobby. You'll find this hotel by walking inland on Guerrero to Bravo and turning right; the hotel is on your left.

Hotel Ávila

Juan Álvarez 8, 40880 Zihuatanejo, Gro. ☎ **755/4-2010.** Fax 755/4-3299. 27 rms. A/C or FAN TV. High season, $35–$45 single or double. Low season, $25–$35 single or double. Parking available on street.

This hotel offers overly expensive rooms conveniently located on the beach—you're paying for location. Eighteen rooms have private balconies facing town, but no ocean view. The rest share a terrace facing the sea. Rooms with ceiling fans are the most inexpensive choice; ocean-view rooms and those with air-conditioning are the highest priced in each category. There's a restaurant bar off the lobby, with tables spreading across the sidewalk and onto the beach. With your back to the water at the basketball court turn right; the Ávila is on your left.

Hotel Imelda

González 11, 40880 Zihuatanejo, Gro. ☎ **755/4-7662.** Fax 755/4-3199. 45 rms. A/C or FAN TV. High season, $20–$30 single; $25–$40 double. Low season discounts. Free parking; enclosed.

Despite its proximity to the market area, this hotel is well maintained and remarkably quiet. Each room has a tile floor and tile bath (no shower curtain), a large closet, louvered windows without screens, and two or three double beds. There's a long lap pool and a cheerful restaurant, Rancho Grande, which offers an inexpensive comida corrida. To get here from the museum, walk inland four blocks and turn left on González; the Imelda is on your right between Cuauhtémoc and Vicente Guerrero.

ⓢ Hotel Susy

Juan Álvarez 3 (at Guerrero), 40880 Zihuatanejo, Gro. ☎ **755/4-2339.** 20 rms. FAN. High season, $25 single or double. Low season, $20 single or double.

Consistently clean, with lots of plants along a shaded walkway set back from the street, this two-story hotel offers small rooms with louvered glass windows with screens. Upper-floor rooms have balconies overlooking the street. Facing away from the water at the basketball court on the Malecón, turn right and walk two blocks; the hotel is on your left at the corner of Guerrero.

✪ Posada Citlali

Vicente Guerrero 3, 40880 Zihuatanejo, Gro. ☎ **755/4-2043.** 17 rms. FAN. $20 single or double.

The small rooms in this pleasant three-story hotel are arranged around a shaded plant-filled courtyard decked out with comfortable rockers and *equipale* (leather-covered) chairs. Bottled water is in help-yourself containers on the patio. Furnishings in each room include an orange chenille bedspread and a large wall mirror with a shelf beneath it. The stairway to the top two floors is narrow and steep. The hotel is near the corner of Álvarez and Guerrero.

Posada Michel

Calle Ejido 14, 40880 Zihuatanejo, Gro. ☎ **755/4-7423.** 17 rms. A/C or FAN. $9 single; $18 double.

Though far from spacious, this small hotel offers immaculately clean rooms for a great price. Pink is the predominant color throughout, from the front doorway down the narrow hallways and on to the rooms. Bathrooms, however, have bright green tile and come without shower curtains or toilet seats. To get here from the waterfront, walk two blocks inland on Guerrero and turn right on Ejido; the hotel is on your right.

Playa Madera

Madera Beach is a 15-minute walk along the street, a 10-minute walk along the beach pathway, or a $2 taxi ride from town. Most of the accommodations are on Calle Eva S. de López Mateos, the road overlooking the beach. If you walk 15 minutes east of town beside the canal, crossing a footbridge and following the road running uphill, you will intersect Mateos. An easier route is along the footpath from the end of Paseo Pescador, by the museum, to Playa Madera. Most hotels are set against the hill and have steep stairways.

Arca de Noa

Calle Eva S. de López Mateos, Playa Madera, 40880 Zihuatanejo, Gro. ☎ **755/4-2272.** 10 rms. FAN. $12 single; $23 double.

An excellent value, the Arca de Noa is a two-story green house set back from a front patio landscaped with flowers and a shaded sitting area. The neat, pleasant rooms have large windows with glass louvers, white walls, and bright-colored bedspreads. Guests can use the kitchen and dining room. Four rooms have sea views. Facing Mateos, take the road to the right; the hotel is midway up the block on your right.

✪ Bungalows Ley

Calle Eva S. de López Mateos s/n, Playa Madera (Apdo. Postal 466), 40880 Zihuatanejo, Gro. ☎ **755/4-4563** or 755/4-4087. 6 rms. A/C or FAN. $25 double with fan; $35 double with A/C; $45 for two-bedroom suite with kitchen and fan for up to four persons, $80 with A/C; $100 for up to six persons.

No two suites are the same at this small complex, one of the nicest on Playa Madera. If you're traveling with a group, you may want to splurge on the most expensive suite (called Club Madero), which comes with a rooftop terrace with tiled hot tub, outdoor bar and grill, and a spectacular view. All the rooms are immaculately clean; the simplest are studios with one bed and a kitchen in the same room. Most rooms have terraces or balconies just above the beach. Clients praise the management. To find the complex, follow Mateos to the right up a slight hill; it's on your left.

⑤ Bungalows Pacíficos

Calle Eva S. de López Mateos, Playa Madera (Apdo. Postal 12), 40880 Zihuatanejo, Gro.☎ and fax **755/4-2112.** 6 rms. FAN. High season, $50 single or double. Low season, $40 single or double.

The three-story building is arranged in tiers down the steep hillside, and the beach is just a 5-minute walk away. Tranquil and comfortable, each room has a bedroom and a narrow alcove with two additional beds facing the doors that open to terraces and sea views. All the rooms have fully equipped (though humble) kitchens with small dining tables and large jugs of purified water, and the rooms open onto large terraces that serve as a living area with a table and chairs, a hammock, flowering plants, and magnificent views. The owner, Anita Hahyner, will gladly answer all your questions in one of four languages, including English, and seems to know everyone in town. Bird-watchers will be delighted here; over 74 species of birds have been spotted and catalogued by guests from their terraces. Facing Mateos, take the road to the right until you reach its terminus overlooking town; the hotel is on the left.

❍ Villas Miramar

Calle Adelita, Playa Madera (Apdo. Postal 211), 40880 Zihuatanejo, Gro. ☎ **755/4-2106** or 755/4-2616. Fax 753/4-2149. 18 suites. A/C FAN TEL. High season, $65 suite for one or two, $85 with ocean view; $100 two-bedroom suite. Low season, $50 suite for one or two, $55 with ocean view. Free parking; enclosed.

Some of these elegant suites are built around a beautiful shady patio that doubles as a restaurant. Those across the street center around a lovely pool and have private balconies and sea views. To find Villas Miramar, follow the road leading south out of town towards Playa La Ropa, then take the first right after the traffic circle, then left on Adelita.

Playa La Ropa

Some travelers consider Playa La Ropa the most beautiful of Zihuatanejo's beaches. It's a 20- to 25-minute walk south of town on the east side of the bay, or a $2 taxi ride.

La Casa Que Canta

Camino Escénico a la Playa La Ropa, 40880 Zihuatanejo, Gro. ☎ **755/4-2722** or 755/4-2782; 800/432-6075 or 800/448-8355 in the U.S. 22 suites. A/C MINIBAR. High season, $250–$400 single or double. Low season, $215–$315 single or double.

La Casa Que Canta (The House that Sings) opened in 1992, and in looks alone it's one of those very special hotels. Meandering down a mountainside overlooking Zihuatanejo Bay, it was designed with striking molded-adobe architecture. Rooms, all with handsome natural-tile floors, are individually decorated in unusual painted Michoacán furniture, antiques, and stretched-leather equipales. Hand-loomed fabrics are used throughout. All units have large, beautifully furnished terraces with bay views. Hammocks under the thatched roof terraces, supported by rough-hewn vigas, are perfectly placed for watching yachts sail in and out of the harbor. The four categories of rooms, all spacious, get larger as you go up the price scale. Beginning with the smallest, there are three terrace suites, four deluxe suites, nine grand suites, and two private pool suites. Rooms meander up and down the hillside, and while no stairs are extensive, there are no elevators. La Casa Que Canta is a member of the Small Luxury Hotels of the World. Technically it's not on Playa La Ropa; it's on the road leading there. The closest stretch of beach (still not yet Playa La Ropa) is down a steep hill. Children under 18 aren't allowed.

Dining/Entertainment: There's a small restaurant/bar on a shaded terrace overlooking the bay.

Services: Laundry and room service.

Facilities: Freshwater pool on the main terrace; saltwater pool on the bottom level.

Hotel Catalina and Hotel Sotavento

Playa La Ropa, 40880 Zihuatanejo, Gro. ☎ **755/4-2032;** 604/652-0456 in Canada. Fax 753/4-2975; 604/652-3571 in Canada. 85 rms, 24 bungalows. $40–$65 standard room; $65–$75 bungalow or terrace room.

Perched high on the hill close to each other and managed together by the same owners, these two attractive hotels were among the first in the area and retain the slow-paced, gracious mood of Zihuatanejo in its early days as a little-known hideaway. While the terrace rooms of the Sotavento rooms are only average in decoration, they are spacious and offer spectacular panoramic views of the bay and Playa La Ropa below. Best of all is the large, shared ocean-view terrace, equipped with hammocks and a chaise lounge for each room—great for sunning and sunset watching. The Catalina has recently remodeled many of its rooms with Mexican tile, wrought iron, and other handcrafted touches; these also have lovely terraces with ocean views and come with two queen-size beds. Between them the two hotels cover eight stories climbing the slope, and two restaurants and bars. Do ask to see at least a couple of rooms first, as they can vary quite a bit in furnishings and price. Also keep in mind the hike down many steps to the beach (depending on the room level) and the lack of air-conditioning, compensated for by the ceiling fans and sea breezes. And there's no swimming pool. To get here, take the highway south of Zihuatanejo about a mile, turn right at the hotels' sign, and follow the road to the hotels.

✪ Villa del Sol

Playa La Ropa (Apdo. Postal Box 84), 40880 Ixtapa/Zihuatanejo, Gro. ☎ **755/4-2239,** 800/223-6510 in the U.S.; 800/422-5500 in Canada. Fax 753/4-2758. 22 standard minisuites, 8 deluxe suites, 6 master suites, 11 condos. A/C. High season, $275–$575 single or double. Low season, $160–$370 single or double. Breakfast and either lunch or dinner, $50 per person, is mandatory in high season. 10% gratuity added to everything.

Few inns in Mexico compare to this one for luxury, attention to quality, service, and tranquillity. This beachfront hotel is one of two in Mexico to meet the tough standards of the French Relais & Châteaux. It's also a member of Small Luxury Hotels of the World. Units lie along the beachfront in a U-shape anchored by immaculately kept grounds and the oceanside restaurant and bar. Each spacious, split-level suite (with either one or two bedrooms) comes with a living room facing a private patio and is tastefully furnished with tile floors, Mexican decorative objects, and a king-size bed draped in white netting. Standard rooms are smaller and don't have TV or telephone. All have fans in addition to air-conditioning, plus hairdryers and luxurious bathrobes in the rooms. Some suites have TV, telephone, minibar, in-room safety-deposit boxes, and a small pool on the patio. Eleven of the 18 condominiums are included in the rental pool. June and September are slow months and last-minute reservations have a better chance then. Children under 14 aren't allowed during high season.

Dining/Entertainment: Open-air restaurant by the beach with classical music and a beachside bar. Friday night Mexican fiesta for $35 at the beachside restaurant.

Nonguests pay $25 each to use the beach and restaurant and $15 of the cost goes toward the purchase of a meal in the hotel's restaurant.

Services: Room service, laundry, beauty shop, travel agency, Tane jewelry store.

Facilities: Two pools, two tennis courts (reserve courts in advance), beauty shop, massage service, paperback lending library.

DINING

IXTAPA

Very Expensive

✪ Villa de la Selva

Paseo de la Roca. ☎ **755/3-0362.** Reservations recommended during high season. Main courses $10–$25. Daily 6–11pm. MEXICAN/CONTINENTAL.

Set on the edge of a cliff overlooking the sea, this elegant restaurant enjoys the most spectacular sea and sunset view in Ixtapa. The elegant candlelit tables are arranged on three terraces; try to come early in hopes of getting one of the best vistas, especially on the lower terrace. The cuisine is delicious and classically rich: Filet Villa de la Selva is red snapper topped with shrimp and hollandaise sauce. The cold avocado soup or hot lobster bisque makes a good beginning; finish with chocolate mousse or bananas Singapore.

Expensive

✪ Beccofino

Marina Ixtapa. ☎ **755/3-1770.** Breakfast $2.75–$3.75; pastas $6–$11; main courses $8–$14. Daily 9:30am–midnight. NORTHERN ITALIAN.

This restaurant is a standout in Mexico. Experienced owner Angelo Rolly Pavia lays before his guests the flavorful northern Italian specialties he grew up knowing and loving. Once seated at the breezy marina location, diners peruse a menu that includes dishes with rice and with short, long, and wide pastas. Ravioli, a house specialty, comes stuffed with the seafood in season. The garlic bread is terrific, and there's an extensive wine list.

Moderate

✪ Golden Cookie Shop

Los Patios Center. ☎ **755/3-0310.** Breakfast $3–$4; sandwiches $3–$5; main courses $3–$6. Mon–Sat 8am–3pm and 6–10pm. PASTRIES/INTERNATIONAL.

Although the name is misleading—there are more than cookies here—Golden Cookie's freshly baked cookies and pastries are worthy of a detour, and the coffee menu is the most extensive in town. The large sandwiches, made with fresh, soft bread, come with a choice of sliced deli meats. Chicken curry is among the other specialty items. To get to the shop, walk to the rear of the shopping center as you face Mac's Prime Rib; walk up the stairs, turn left, and you'll see the restaurant on your right.

✪ Mamma Norma

La Puerta Center, Bulevar Ixtapa. ☎ **755/3-0274.** Breakfast $2.75–$3; main courses $4.50–$8; pizza $5.75–$7. Daily 8am–11pm (deliveries made 3–11pm). ITALIAN/AMERICAN.

At one of the most popular restaurants in Ixtapa, you can choose from 17 kinds of pizza (they deliver too), 8 different pasta dishes (including a spicy puttanesca), and regional Mexican dishes including *cochinita pibil.* You'll also find a generous antipasto, burgers, sandwiches, and ice cream. To get to Mamma Norma from the tourist office, walk to the back of the La Puerta Center and look for the sidewalk tables covered with red cloths.

Toko Tukan Natural

Los Patios Center. ☎ **755/3-0717.** Breakfast $2.75–$3; tacos and sandwiches $3–$4. Daily 8am–11pm. FRUIT/SANDWICHES/VEGETARIAN.

With outdoor tables shaded by umbrellas, this casual restaurant is popular for breakfast and brunch. The fruit plates are amply loaded. Other offerings include fresh-fruit and vegetable drinks, as well as salads, including a noteworthy seafood salad. There's also a good selection of tacos and sandwiches, all of which come with meat. At breakfast, hotcakes come plain or with bananas, nuts, raisins, or apples. The restaurant faces the boulevard beside Aca Joe.

DOWNTOWN ZIHUATANEJO

Zihuatanejo's **central market,** located on Avenida Benito Juárez (about five blocks inland from the waterfront), offers cheap, tasty food. The food is best at breakfast and lunch because the market activity winds down in the afternoon. Be sure to choose what's hot and freshly cooked. The market area is one of the best on this coast for shopping and people watching.

Expensive

El Patio

Cinco de Mayo 3 at Álvarez. ☎ **755/4-3019.** Breakfast $3–$5; Mexican platters $5–$20; seafood $7–$18. Daily 9am–2pm and 3–11pm. MEXICAN/SEAFOOD.

Casually elegant, this patio restaurant is decorated with baskets and at night flickering candles create a romantic atmosphere. Whatever you're a fan of it's likely you'll find it here. There are fajitas and steak, chicken, chiles rellenos, green or red enchiladas, and lobster in garlic sauce. The breakfast menu is typical, but you can also order hamburgers and salads. In the evenings musicians often play Latin American favorites. It's one block inland from Álvarez and next to the church.

Moderate

Casa Elvira

Paseo del Pescador. ☎ **755/4-2061.** Main courses $3.50–$11. Daily noon–10:30pm. MEXICAN/SEAFOOD.

Casa Elvira almost always has a crowd, drawn in by its neat, clean atmosphere and by the wide selection of inexpensive lunches and dinners on its bilingual menu. House specialties are snapper (or whatever fish is in season) and lobster; the restaurant also serves meat dishes and chicken mole. The most expensive seafood platter includes lobster, red snapper, and jumbo butterfly shrimp. Facing the water and the basketball court, turn right; Casa Elvira is on the west end of the waterfront near the town pier.

Garrobos

Álvarez 52. ☎ **755/4-2977.** Main courses $3–$11. Tues–Sun 2–10pm. MEXICAN/SEAFOOD.

This very popular, roomy restaurant offers large meat-and-seafood dishes attractively presented with rice and two vegetables. It also serves the Spanish dish paella and the local specialty, *tiritas de pescado,* little strips of marinated fish (as with ceviche, the fish is "cooked" by the lemon or lime juice). In the evening trios often serenade diners. To reach Garrobos, turn left on Álvarez with your back to the basketball court; the restaurant is on your right beneath the Hotel Raúl Tres Marías Centro.

La Bocana

Álvarez 13. ☎ **755/4-3545.** Breakfast $3–$4.75; main courses $5–$16. Daily 8am–11pm. MEXICAN/SEAFOOD.

One of Zihuatanejo's finest seafood restaurants, La Bocana is known for its huge *plato de mariscos*—a seafood platter that feeds two to four people. It comes heaped with lobster, crayfish, shrimp, fish filet, rice, and salad. Mariachis and marimba bands come and go on Sunday. It's on the main street near the town plaza.

✪ Restaurant Paul's

Cinco de Mayo s/n. ☎ **755/4-2188.** Main courses $7–$12. Daily 6–10pm. INTERNATIONAL/ SEAFOOD.

It's hard to find a seat after 7pm at this small open-air restaurant, where the Swiss chef has attained a fanatical following. It must be the only place in town that serves fresh artichokes as an appetizer, and the ubiquitous fish filet is covered with a smooth, delicately flavored shrimp and dill sauce. The pasta comes topped with a pile of shrimp and fish in a light cream sauce, and the pork chops and beef medallions are thick and juicy. To get to Paul's from the main pier, turn right on Álvarez and walk one block, then turn left onto Cinco de Mayo; Paul's is on your right before the church.

Inexpensive

Café La Marina

Paseo del Pescador 9. ☎ **755/4-2373.** Pizzas $3.75; sandwiches $1.50–$3; Wed-night spaghetti $3.50. Mon–Sat 11am–9pm. PIZZA/SANDWICHES.

This popular beachfront hangout has only a handful of tables on its front porch and its service is lackadaisical. Yet it dishes out pizza, with toppings that range from pineapple to ham and seafood. Large tortas (sandwiches) come with bean sprouts and avocado. The Wednesday-night spaghetti with pesto or bolognese sauce is said to be the best in town. While you wait, browse through the many shelves stacked with English-language paperbacks for sale. Facing away from the water at the basketball court, turn left and walk down Paseo del Pescador; the cafe is on your right by the Casa Marina shops.

Casa Puntarenas

Calle Noria, Colonia Lázaro Cárdenas. No phone. Soup $1.35; main courses $2.25–$5. 6:30– 9pm. MEXICAN/SEAFOOD.

A modest spot with a tin roof and nine wooden tables, Puntarenas is one of the best spots in town for fried whole fish served with toasted *bolillos,* sliced tomatoes, onions, and avocado. The chiles rellenos are mild and stuffed with plenty of cheese; the meat dishes are less flavorful. To get to Puntarenas from the pier, turn left on Álvarez and cross the footbridge on your left. Turn right after you cross the bridge; the restaurant is on your left.

ⓢ Nueva Zelanda

Cuauhtémoc 23 at Ejido. ☎ **755/4-2340.** Tortas $2–$3.50; enchiladas $2–$4; fruit-and-milk licuados $1.50; cappuccinos $1.65. Daily 8am–10pm. MEXICAN.

One of the most popular places in town, this clean open-air snack shop welcomes diners with rich cappuccinos sprinkled with cinnamon and pancakes with real maple syrup. But the mainstays of the menu are tortas and enchiladas. For only 5¢ more, you can order a cappuccino to go (say *"para llevar"*) and get twice as much coffee.

You'll find Nueva Zelanda by walking three blocks inland from the waterfront on Cuauhtémoc; the restaurant is on your right. There's a second location (☎ **755/ 3-0838**) in Ixtapa in the back section of the Los Patios shopping center.

Ruben's

Calle Adelita s/n. ☎ **755/4-4617.** Burgers $2.25–$3.25; vegetables $1.50; ice cream $1. Daily 6pm–11pm. BURGERS/VEGETABLES.

The choices are easy here—you can order either a big sloppy burger made from top sirloin beef grilled over mesquite, or a foil-wrapped packet of baked potatoes, chayote, zucchini, or sweet corn. Homemade ice cream plus beer and soda fills out the menu, which is posted on the wall by the kitchen. Guests snag a waitress and rattle off their orders, grab their own drinks from the cooler, and tally their own tabs. Rolls of paper towels hang over the tables on the open porch and shaded terrace. Ruben's is a popular fixture in the Playa Madera neighborhood—though the customers come from all over town. To get here from Mateos, turn right on Adelita; Ruben's is on your right.

⑤ La Sirena Gorda

Paseo del Pescador. ☎ **755/4-2687.** Breakfast $2–$3; main courses $3–$5. Thurs–Tues 7am–10pm. MEXICAN.

For the best inexpensive breakfast in town, head to La Sirena Gorda for a variety of eggs and omelets, or hotcakes with bacon, as well as fruit with granola and yogurt. For lunch or dinner try the house specialty, seafood tacos with fish prepared to taste like *machaca* or *carnitas* or covered with mole. There's always a short list of daily specials, such as blackened red snapper, steak, or fish kebabs. Patrons enjoy the casual sidewalk-cafe atmosphere. To get here from the basketball court, face the water and walk to the right; La Sirena Gorda is on your right just before the town pier.

PLAYA MADERA & PLAYA LA ROPA

Kon-Tiki

Camino a Playa La Ropa. ☎ **755/4-2471.** Pizza $7–$18. Daily 1pm–midnight; happy hour 6–7pm. PIZZA.

In the air-conditioned dining room on a cliff overlooking the bay, enjoy 13 types of pizzas in three different sizes. The vegetarian pizza is topped with beans, peanuts, onion, mushroom, bell pepper, garlic, pineapple, and avocado. There's also a big-screen sports-video bar, open the same hours.

La Perla

Playa La Ropa. ☎ **755/4-2700.** Breakfast $2.50–$5; main courses $6–$11. Daily 10am–10pm; breakfast served 10am–noon. SEAFOOD.

There are many palapa-style restaurants on Playa La Ropa, but La Perla is one of the best. Cloth-covered tables under the trees and thatched roof make for pleasant dining. Plus the long swath of pale sand stretching out in either direction and an array of wooden chairs under palapas combine with good food to make La Perla a favorite with visitors. The "filet of fish La Perla" is cooked deliciously, wrapped in foil with tomatoes, onions, and cheese. Around sunset, visitors gather in the bar to watch the news on the TV, which shows American channels. It's near the southern end of La Ropa Beach. Take the right fork in the road; there's a sign in the parking lot.

Rossy

Playa La Ropa. No phone. Breakfast $2.50–$4; tacos $2–$3; seafood $3.50–$11; beer $1.50; margarita $2.50. Daily 9am–10pm. SEAFOOD/SANDWICHES/TACOS.

Another locally favorite beachside restaurant, this one too is casual with orange and yellow cloth-covered tables and peach and orange chairs and lounges near the water. The menu emphasizes seafood with a short beef and taco section. Seafood includes ceviche, breaded lobster, and river crawfish during the rainy season. It's at the far end of La Ropa Beach. Take the left fork in the road and follow it to the end.

Two Bakeries

El Buen Gusto

Guerrero 4. ☎ **755/4-3231.** All items 25¢–$2.25. Mon–Sat 7:30am–10pm. BAKED GOODS.

Small but packed with goodies, this pastry shop offers what's usually found in a Mexican bakery—then goes beyond expectations by offering banana bread, French bread, doughnuts, and cakes. To get here from the museum, walk half a block up Guerrero; the bakery is on your left.

Panadería Francesa

Gonzalez 15, between Cuauhtémoc and Guerrero. ☎ **755/4-4520.** Bread and pastries 25¢–$1.80. Daily 7am–9pm. BAKED GOODS.

Here you can buy sweet pastries to accompany your take-out cappuccino to go from nearby Nueva Zelanda (see above). You can also grab a long baguette or loaf of whole-wheat bread for picnic supplies. To get here from Nueva Zelanda, turn left on Gonzalez; the shop is on your right.

IXTAPA & ZIHUATANEJO AFTER DARK

With an exception or two, Zihuatanejo nightlife dies down around 11pm or midnight. For a good selection of clubs, discos, hotel fiestas, special events, and fun watering holes with live music and dancing, head for Ixtapa. But keep in mind that the shuttle bus stops at 11pm, and a taxi ride back to Zihuatanejo after midnight costs 50% more than the regular price. During off-season (after Easter or before Christmas) hours vary: Some places are open only on weekends, while others are closed all season.

The Club & Music Scene

Many discos and dance clubs stay open until the last customers leave, so closing hours vary. Most discos have a ladies' night at least once a week when admission and drinks are free for women. Call to check the days.

The Bay Club and Samba Café

Camino a Playa La Ropa, Zihuatanejo. ☎ **755/4-4844.** No cover.

It's fun to dance under the stars on the beautifully lit patio surrounded by tropical plants. The restaurant/bar is perched on a hillside with a splendid view of the town lights and bay. Live music ranges from jazz and tropical to soft rock. The mesquite-grilled dinners are expensive, but come after dinner to enjoy the music with an appetizer or dessert. Drinks cost between $1.75 and $3.50, and snacks range from $3 to $7. A full dinner goes for $9 and up. The club is open daily during high season from 9:30pm to midnight; happy hour is 5 to 7pm. Closed in the off-season.

Carlos 'n' Charlie's

Bulevar Ixtapa (just north of the Best Western Posada Real), Ixtapa. ☎ **755/3-0085.** Cover (including drink tokens) after 9pm for dancing $2.50.

Decorated with all sorts of nostalgia, bric-a-brac, silly sayings, and photos from the Mexican Revolution, this restaurant/nightclub offers party ambiance and good food. The eclectic menu humorously includes iguana in season (Alka-Seltzer and aspirin are on the house). Out back by the beach is an open-air section (part of it shaded) with a raised wooden platform called the "pier" for "pier-dancing" at night, thus mixing the sound of the surf with recorded rock and roll. The restaurant is open daily from noon to midnight; pier dancing is nightly from 9pm to 3am.

Christine

In the Hotel Krystal, Bulevar Ixtapa, Ixtapa. ☎ **755/3-0456.** Cover $2.50.

This flashy streetside disco is famous for its midnight light show, which features classical music played on a megasound system. A semicircle of tables in tiers overlooks the dance floor. No tennis shoes, sandals, shorts, or jeans are allowed, and reservations are advised during high season. Drinks cost $1.50 to $5. It's open daily during high season from 10:30pm to the wee hours; the light show is at midnight. (Off-season hours vary.)

Euforia Disco

Bulevar Ixtapa, Ixtapa. ☎ **755/3-1190.** Cover $4.50.

You can't miss the Euforia Disco, next to the Lighthouse Restaurant and in front of the Best Western Posada Real at the turnoff to Carlos 'n' Charlie's. Levels of tables rise on one side of the circular dance floor, behind which is a volcano that actually erupts. Go early to see the sound-and-light show. No shorts are allowed. Drinks cost between $1.75 and $4. Ask about seasonal admission discounts. It's open daily during high season and on holidays from 10pm to the wee hours, and is closed in the off-season.

Señor Frog's

Bulevar Ixtapa in the La Puerta Center, Ixtapa. ☎ **755/3-0272.** Cover (including drink tokens) after 9pm for dancing $3–$5.

A companion restaurant to Carlos 'n' Charlie's, Señor Frog's has several dining sections and a warehouselike bar with raised dance floors. Rock and roll blares from large speakers, and even those stopping by for dinner sometimes dance by their tables between courses. The restaurant is open daily from 6pm to midnight; the bar is open until 3am.

HOTEL FIESTAS & THEME NIGHTS

Many hotels hold Mexican fiestas and other special events that usually include dinner, drinks, live music, and entertainment for a fixed price ($30–$40). The **Sheraton Ixtapa** (☎ 755/3-1858) is famous for its Wednesday-night fiesta; good Mexican fiestas are also held by the **Krystal Hotel** (☎ 755/3-0333) and **Dorado Pacífico** (☎ 755/3-2025) in Ixtapa and the **Villa del Sol** (☎ 755/4-2239) on Playa La Ropa in Zihuatanejo. The Sheraton Ixtapa is the only one that offers these in the off-season. The **Westin Brisas Ixtapa** (☎ 755/3-2121) and the **Sheraton Ixtapa** also put on theme nights featuring the cuisine and music of different countries. Call to make reservations (travel agencies also sell the tickets) and be sure you understand what the fixed price covers (drinks, tax, and tip are not always included).

A SIDE TRIP TO SLEEPY TRONCONES

The tiny fishing settlement of Troncones, 20 miles northwest of Ixtapa, has become a favorite escape for visitors to Ixtapa and Zihuatanejo. The main thing to do is stroll the long, empty beaches, swim in the sea (if the surf is not high), and feast on seafood at one of the fishermen's-shack restaurants or at El Burro Borracho (see below). But there are other things to do here: Horse rentals can be arranged; hotel owners can provide information on hiking in the jungle or to nearby caves; you can take part in the small village's fiestas.

There are no direct telephone lines yet to Troncones, which is inhabited by all of 250 people. The phones listed below are cellular and the fax lines are in Ixtapa or Zihuatanejo. Unfortunately, no public buses serve this area; to get here, you'll have to join a tour or hire a taxi in Ixtapa/Zihuatanejo. For about $20, a driver will take you and return at the hour you request to bring you back to town.

If you have your own car, follow the highway northwest through Ixtapa, past the Marina Ixtapa, and continue past the Ciudad Altamirano turnoff. Mark your odometer at this turnoff—14 kilometers (8.7 miles) ahead is the sign pointing left to El Burro Borracho. When you reach it, turn and continue 3.5 kilometers (2.2 miles) until you reach the ocean. Turn left. El Burro Borracho is the last restaurant on the right. From that location you can get directions to the rest of the inns.

WHERE TO STAY

All of the lodgings mentioned below may offer discounts on rentals of as much as 50% in low season.

El Burro Borracho

Los Troncones, Guerrero, 6 miles north of Ixtapa on Hwy. 200. ☎ **755/7-0777.** Fax 755/3-2417. 3 bungalows. 5 RV spaces. High season, $45 single; $55 double. Low season $25 single or double; RV space $10–$15. Rates include continental breakfast.

Anita Lapointe, the owner of El Burro Borracho, offers three rustic stone bungalows all with private bathroom, king-size bed, and a hammock on the porch. In addition, guests can use the fully equipped kitchen, library, and satellite TV. Boogie boards and kayaks are available for rent. Five full-hookup RV spaces and a place to camp are available as well. Local artisans from Troncones provide El Burro Borracho with hand-embroidered dresses and blouses, lace, and other locally made art. The beachfront restaurant is the one recommended for the area.

Casa Canela

Los Troncones, Guerrero, 6 miles north of Ixtapa on Hwy. 200. ☎ **755/7-0777.** Fax 755/4-3296. Two-bedroom house (three baths). High season, $90 per day for the house; $535 per week. Rates include continental breakfast.

Opposite El Burro Borracho, Anita Lapointe also offers this complete house, with two bedrooms, three bathrooms, a kitchen, porch, garden, and satellite TV. The house will sleep up to six people. It isn't on the beach, but the beach is just across the road.

Casa de la Tortuga B&B

Los Troncones, Guerrero, 6 miles north of Ixtapa on Hwy. 200. ☎ **755-7-0732.** Fax 755/3-2417. (Reservations: write Apdo. Postal 37, 40880 Zihuatanejo, Gro.) 6 rms. High season, $50–$100 single or double. Rates include full breakfast.

Dewey and Karolyn MacMillan, a young American couple, recently renovated their isolated paradise on the beach at Troncones; they've used Mexican tiles and created a garden setting. Casa Tortuga is a six-bedroom home with four bathrooms, a dining room, kitchen, laundry, pool, TV and VCR, and a book and video library. Individual rooms are available or you could rent the whole place for your vacation; it will sleep up to 12 people. A palapa-covered bar is just steps from the beach and ocean.

Casa Ki

Los Troncones, Guerrero, 6 miles north of Ixtapa on Hwy. 200. No phone. Fax 755/3-2417. 3 bungalows. $45 single; $55 double. Rates include continental breakfast.

Ed and Ellen Weston offer these three separate bungalows in a garden setting right on the beach. Each one is furnished with a king-size bed, private bathroom, and porch with a hammock to while away some relaxing hours.

La Puesta del Sol

Los Troncones, Guerrero, 6 miles north of Ixtapa on Hwy. 200. No phone. Fax 755/3-2417. 2 rms (both with bath). $55–$65 single; $60–$70 double. Rates include continental breakfast.

Next to El Burro Borracho is this small inn, run by Malury Wells. Its two large separate units are on the beach. One has a kitchenette and commands the higher rates.

In either room, you have a choice of a king-size or single bed. Guests use the El Burro Borracho restaurant.

WHERE TO EAT

Several palapa-topped restaurants are near Troncones and are worth a try—just make a casual inspection for cleanliness. Or you can try this place:

El Burro Borracho

Troncones Beach. ☎ **755/3-0089.** Fax 755/3-2417. Main courses $2–$9. Daily 8am–9pm. AMERICAN/SEAFOOD.

Mike Bensal's casual beachfront restaurant is not your ordinary greasy-spoon beach shack. Here are a few winners from the menu, which features a lot of seafood and grilled dishes: shrimp tacos, filet mignon with mashed potatoes and mushroom gravy, the "ultimate" hamburger, barbecued pork ribs, and grilled chicken breast with tamarindo chipotle sauce. You can kick back with a margarita, iced cappuccino, a glass of wine, or cold beer.

If you're here on a day-trip from Ixtapa/Zihuatanejo, you can spend the day here if you like, using the beach and this restaurant as headquarters, and have your taxi return here to pick you up.

2 Acapulco

262 miles S of Mexico City, 170 miles SW of Taxco, 612 miles SE of Guadalajara, 158 miles SE of Ixtapa/Zihuatanejo, 470 miles NW of Huatulco

To the world, Acapulco has a perennially romantic reputation and a jet-set image. Acapulco first grabbed the world's attention in the 1950s when it was the stomping ground of Hollywood celebrities. And though by now it could be considered old-hat among Mexico's resorts, it is still growing and attracting celebrities. A plethora of new villas and condominiums has appeared seemingly overnight on the mountain slopes. The latest development is the enormous Acapulco Diamante project running along the coast from Puerto Marqués almost to the airport. It includes the new Sheraton, Camino Real, and Vidafel resort hotels, and even more hotels are on the drawing board.

Acapulco's nightlife never dims; the vibrant variety of this city's discos and clubs is hard to top in Mexico. And to anyone who knows it, the view of Acapulco Bay, flanked by mountains and beaches, is breathtaking day or night.

Acapulco, however, is a real city of about 1 million now, rather than simply a resort. It has its share of grit along with glitz. There are slums as well as villas, and some of the hotels could use a face-lift. The city continues to work hard to maintain the glamour that originally put it on the map. A program called "ACA-Limpia" ("Clean Acapulco") has cleaned up the bay, where whales have been sighted recently for the first time in years, and has spruced up the Costera. And the itinerant vendors that once hawked their wares to tourists on the beaches and sidewalks have been moved to newly created market areas, such as the Diana traffic circle on the Costera.

ESSENTIALS

GETTING THERE & DEPARTING

BY PLANE   See Chapter 2, "Planning a Trip to Southern Pacific Mexico," for information on flying from the United States or Canada to Acapulco. Local numbers for major airlines that have nonstop or direct service to Acapulco are: **Aeroméxico** (☎ 74/85-1600 for reservations; 74/66-9104 at the airport); **American** (☎ 74/84-1244 or 74/84-1179 for reservations; 74/84-0372 at the airport); **Continental**

(☎ **74/66-9063** or 74/66-9064 at the airport); **Mexicana** (☎ **74/84-6943** or 74/84-6890; 74/84-1815 at the airport); and **Taesa** (☎ **74/66-9067** or 74/86-4576 for reservations; 74/81-1214 at the airport).

Within Mexico, Aeroméxico flies from Guadalajara, Mexico City, Toluca, and Tijuana; Mexicana flies from Mexico City; and Taesa flies from Laredo, Mexico City, and Guadalajara. Regional carriers include **AeroLibertad,** flying from Ixtapa/Zihuatanejo and Oaxaca, and **AeroMorelos,** flying from Cuernavaca and Puebla. Check with a travel agent about charter flights.

Transportes Terrestres (☎ **74/83-6500**) has colectivo service to and from the airport. Call the day before your departure for a reservation. The one-way trip costs $7 per person. The service picks you up 1¹⁄₂ hours (for flights within Mexico) to two hours (international flights) before your departure time. **Taxis** cost about $20.

BY BUS   To/From Mexico City: From the Ejido/Central Camionera station in Acapulco, **Estrella de Oro** and **Estrella Blanca** have almost hourly service for the 5- to 7-hour trip to Mexico City. Return frequency is about the same. **Turistar** (the nicest line, with video movies and complimentary snacks and soft drinks) offers almost hourly service from Acapulco to Mexico City. In Acapulco service begins at 8am with the last bus at 6:35pm. **Futura** and **Turistar Plus** are the super deluxe lines of Turistar, with fewer seats and lots of room to spread out; but their service to Mexico City is limited. There's little difference in quality between express and deluxe service, but get a *directo/sin escalas* (direct, nonstop) if you want to arrive without a lot of stops in between; using *economico* service from this station means your first born will grow up and have children before you arrive at your destination. Travel time depends on the number of stops and whether travel is by the toll road (faster—5 hours) or the old road (slower—6 to 7 hours or more). Most buses from Acapulco will arrive at Mexico City's **Terminal Central de Autobuses del Sur** (also known as Tasqueña) but some go to the **Norte** station. The terminal destination (either Tasqueño or Norte) is usually clearly marked on the wall schedules, but verify it anyway.

From its separate station in Acapulco, **Estrella de Oro** has frequent direct buses to Mexico City. From the same station **Oro Plus** has service to Mexico City daily at 7:45, 10, and 11am; 10:15pm; and 1am. All passengers at this station must check luggage that is over 1 foot long. The baggage-check counter is to the right of ticket sales.

To Ixtapa & Zihuatanejo: From the Ejido/Central Camionera station in Acapulco **Turistar** has two buses daily. **Estrella Blanca** has several daily direct buses, and **Turistar** has Plus service daily at 6:30am and 5pm, while **Futura** service runs seven times daily. From its own station **Estrella de Oro** runs several daily buses to Ixtapa/Zihuatanejo.

To Other Points in Mexico: From Acapulco's Ejido/Central Camionera station the following buses serve several routes: **Turistar** buses go from Ejido/Central Camionera to Chilpancingo (five times daily) and Cuernavaca (twice daily); **Estrella Blanca** has service to Chilpancingo every few minutes, Cuernavaca (four times daily), and Iguala frequently; **Elite** has limited departures heading for Manzanillo and Puerto Vallarta; **Lineas Unidos del Sur** offers second class service to the small towns on the Costa Chica south of Acapulco. From its separate station **Estrella de Oro** offers three daily buses to Taxco (at 7 and 9am and 4:30pm).

BY CAR   From Mexico City, you can take Highway 95 south or the curvy toll-free highway (six hours). You can also take Highway 95D, the toll highway (3¹⁄₂–4 hours), which costs around $80 one way. The free road from Taxco is in good condition,

Acapulco Bay Area

To Pie de la Cuesta
Ixtapa - Zihuatanejo

Guerrero

Av. Constituyentes

Mendoza

Av. Cuauhtémoc

Parque
Papagayo

Hotel Pa
Radiss

Vasco Nuñez

Río Camarón

La Quebrada

Plaza
Las Glorias/
El Mirador

Market

Escudero Serdán

6

Playa Hornos

Playa
Hornit

5 Zócalo

Commercial Wharfs

Playa
Langosta

Downtown Acapulco
(See Inset)

Costera M. Alemán

Bahía de Acapulco

La Pinzona

Playa Larga

Av. de la Aguada

Gran Vía Tropical

3

Av. A. López Mateos

2

Peninsula de las Playas

4

Playa Caletilla

Playa Caleta

Playa Roqueta

Isla de la Roqueta

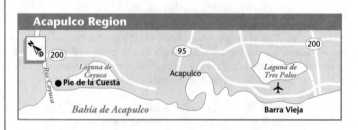

Acapulco Region

200

95

200

*Laguna de
Coyuca*

Acapulco

*Laguna de
Tres Palos*

Río Coyuca

Pie de la Cuesta

Barra Vieja

Bahía de Acapulco

Centro Internacional de
  Convivencia Infantil (CICI) **8**
Cliff divers **1**
Convention Center **7**
Fort San Diego/Museo
  Histórico de Acapulco **6**

Jai Alai Fronton/Stadium **3**
Mágico Mundo Marino **4**
Plaza de Toros **2**
Zócalo/Plaza Alvarez **5**

2-0010

84

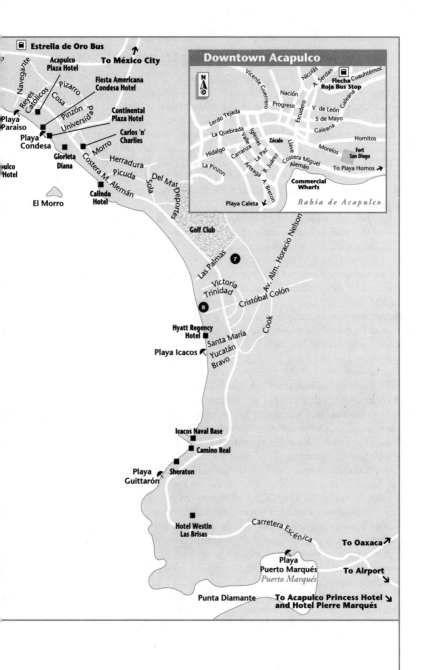

Estrella de Oro Bus

Acapulco
Plaza Hotel

To México City

Fiesta Americana
Condesa Hotel

Navegante
Reyes
Católicos
Pizarro
Cosa
Pinzón
Universidad

Continental
Plaza Hotel

Carlos 'n'
Charlies

Playa
Paraiso

Playa
Condesa

Glorieta
Diana

Morro

Herradura

ulco
Hotel

Picuda

Costera M. Alemán

Sola

Del Mar
Deportes

El Morro

Calinda
Hotel

Downtown Acapulco

N

Vicente Guerrero

Nicolás

A. Serdán

Flecha
Roja Bus Stop

Cuauhtémoc

Nación

A. de León

Galeana

Progreso

Escudero

5 de Mayo

Lerdo Tejada

Galeana

La Quebrada

Valle

Iglesias

Zócalo

Morelos

Hornitos

Hidalgo

Carranza

La Paz

Llave

La Pinzón

Arteaga

B. Juárez

A. Breton

Costera Miguel
Alemán

Fort
San Diego

To Playa Hornos

Commercial
Wharfs

Playa Caleta

Bahía de Acapulco

Golf Club

Las Palmas

7

Victoria

Trinidad

8

Cristóbal Colón

Av. Alm. Horacio Nelson

Cook

Hyatt Regency
Hotel

Santa María

Playa Icacos

Yucatán

Bravo

Icacos Naval Base

Camino Real

Playa
Guittarrón

Sheraton

Hotel Westin
Las Brisas

Carretera Escénica

To Oaxaca

Playa
Puerto Marqués

Puerto Marqués

To Airport

Punta Diamante

To Acapulco Princess Hotel
and Hotel Pierre Marqués

85

The Spice Bazaar: Acapulco's Colonial Past

It's hard to see past all the highrise hotels, sun-browned bodies, and boisterous nightclubs to Acapulco's preresort days, but for centuries one of the Spanish Empire's most important trade hubs in the New World was located here.

Acapulco's post-Conquest history really begins in 1573, when a Spanish galleon arrived from Manila, loaded with treasures from China: porcelain, ivory, silk, inlaid furniture, spices, gold jewelry, pearls, precious stones, bricks of silver and gold, and much more. This newly discovered trade route linked three continents (Asia, America, and Europe), and for the next 250 years, merchants in both Manila and Acapulco eagerly awaited the annual arrival of the magnificent sailing ships.

Few people lived in the insect-infested Acapulco of the 16th century, yet the arrival of the galleons became the occasion of grand fairs that would attract as many as 10,000 people. Sometimes merchants would spend months on the beaches waiting for the moment when the galleons' white sails appeared on the horizon. And when the big day arrived, one can only imagine what the beaches of Acapulco Bay must have looked like: hundreds of temporary camps dotting the shore, makeshift sunshades billowing over valuable foreign cargo spread out on the sand, and thousands of eager merchants making deals and hauling off their take. In payment for the cargo, ships set forth from Acapulco to the Philippines loaded with silver, as well as *cochinil* (a natural dye), *cacao* (chocolate), and wool, all prized trade items.

Both coming and going, pirates dogged the galleons' watery trails, and almost 4 dozen ships were lost either by shipwreck or pirate attack during the 250 years of trade. To defend against attacks, Acapulco's Fuerte de San Diego was designed in 1617, by a Dutch engineer, but was not completed until 1783.

Acapulco was but a way station for the treasures of the Far East. Much of this exotic merchandise was carried inland by mule over the Sierra Madre, ending its passage through Mexico at Veracruz on the Gulf Coast, where it was sent on to the Spanish Crown. Goods were also shipped toward Mexico's colonial centers—Mexico City, Guadalajara, Jalapa, Puebla, Oaxaca, and Morelia, to name a few. Other goods were repacked into the holds of ships bound for Spain's outposts in Peru.

Until the opening in 1928 of an auto highway connecting Acapulco and Mexico City, the *arriero* (mule driver) was the only means of transport across the rugged Mother Range. Genuine folk heroes, their arduous journeys were made doubly dangerous by the presence of bandits. Vicente Guerrero, Mexico's second president and the man for whom Acapulco's home state is named, was an *arriero*. His knowledge of the rugged terrain inland from Acapulco stood him well in Mexico's fight for independence.

Though it was one of the most important ports in the world, and the only one authorized by Spain in the Americas, it wasn't until 1799 that the king of Spain officially named it Acapulco and recognized it as a city. Only 11 years later Mexico began its fight for independence from Spain. The turmoil of Mexico's independence war and changes in world trade diminished the influence of both Mexico and Spain and the famed Manila galleons stopped coming in 1815. Today, the Fort of San Diego houses the Museo Histórico de Acapulco (Acapulco Historical Museum), devoted to Acapulco's history including its centuries of trade with Asia and Europe through Acapulco.

A fascinating account of Mexico's 250 years of trade with Asia appears in a 1990 issue of *National Geographic* magazine (see *Reader's Guide to Periodical Literature*).

so it's worth taking to save around $40 in tolls from there through Chilpancingo to Acapulco. From points north or south along the coast, the only choice is Highway 200.

ORIENTATION

ARRIVING BY PLANE The **airport** is 14 miles southeast of town near Puerto Marqués, over the hills east of the bay. **Transportes Terrestre** has desks at the front of the airport where you can buy tickets for minivan colectivo transportation into town ($7 per person); you can also go by taxi ($20).

ARRIVING BY BUS **Estrella Blanca** terminal at Ejido 47 is north of downtown and farthest from the hotels I have recommended below; however, it has the most complete service of any Acapulco bus station. The station has a hotel-reservation service. The **Estrella de Oro** bus station is a distance from downtown at Cuauhtémoc 1490 and Massieu. Local buses pass the terminal going both directions on Cuauhtémoc. Just before you exit you'll see a taxi ticket booth where rates are set for every hotel.

INFORMATION The **State of Guerrero Tourism Office** operates the **Procuraduria del Turista** on street level in front of the Convention Center (☎ 74/84-4583 or 74/84-7050, ext. 165 or 175). It offers maps and information about the city and state and is open daily from 9am to 9pm.

CITY LAYOUT Acapulco stretches for more than 4 miles around the huge bay, so walking to see it all is impractical. The main boulevard, **Costera Miguel Alemán** (the Costera), follows the outline of the bay from downtown on the west side, where "Old Acapulco" began, to the Hyatt Regency Hotel on the east side. It continues by another name (**Carretera Escenica**) all the way to the airport. Most hotels are either on the Costera and the beach or a block or two away; as you go east from downtown they become increasingly luxurious. **Avenida Cuauhtémoc** is the major artery inland and runs roughly parallel to the Costera.

Street names and numbers in this city can be confusing and hard to find—many streets are not well marked or change names unexpectedly. Fortunately, you're seldom far from the Costera, so it's hard to get really lost. Street numbers on the Costera seem to have nothing to do with their location, so don't conclude that similar numbers will necessarily be close together.

GETTING AROUND **By Bus** Even though the city has such a confusing street system, it's amazingly easy and inexpensive to use city buses. Two kinds of buses run along the Costera: pastel color-coded buses and regular "school buses." The main difference is the price. The new air-conditioned tourist buses (**Aca Tur Bus**) are 65¢; the old buses are 30¢. Covered bus stops are located all along the Costera, with handy maps on the walls showing bus routes to major sights and hotels.

The best place near the zócalo to catch a bus is beside Sanborn's, two blocks east. **CALETA DIRECTO** or **BASE–CALETA** buses will take you to the Hornos, Caleta, and Caletilla beaches along the Costera. Some buses return along the same route; others go around the peninsula and return to the Costera. To get to the restaurants and nightspots in the upscale hotel district on the north and east sides of the bay, catch a **BASE–CINE RÍO–CALETA** bus beside Sanborn's. It runs inland along Cuauhtémoc to the Estrella de Oro bus terminal, then heads back to the Costera and beach at the Ritz Hotel and continues east along the Costera to Icacos Beach near the Hyatt Regency Hotel. **ZÓCALO DIRECTO** and **CALETA DIRECTO** buses follow the same route in the opposite direction.

For expeditions to more distant destinations, there are buses to Puerto Marqués to the east (the bus is marked PUERTO MARQUÉS–BASE) and Pie de la Cuesta to the west (the bus is marked ZÓCALO–PIE DE LA CUESTA). Be sure to verify the time and place of the last bus back if you hop one of these!

For a cheap way to get to the discos and restaurants east of town near the Las Brisas Hotel, take a BASE bus as far as the Hyatt Regency. Then take a LAS BRISAS bus the rest of the way. City buses discontinue service at 10pm.

By Taxi   Taxis charge $2 to $8 for a ride within the city and more if you go far-ther out. For approximate prices, ask at your hotel or scan one of the taxi tariff lists found in the lobbies of most major hotels. Hotel taxis often charge three times the rate of a taxi hailed on the street. Always establish the price with the driver before starting out. Report any trouble or overcharges to the Procuraduria del Turista—the tourist assistance office on the Costera next to the Convention Center (☎ 74/84-4416).

FAST FACTS: ACAPULCO

American Express   The main office is at Costera Alemán 709, east of the Diana traffic circle (☎ 74/84-1095 for travel services, 74/84-5200 for financial services, 74/84-5550 for customer service, 74/84-6060 for tours); another branch is at the Hyatt Regency on Costera Alemán near the naval base (☎ 74/84-2888).

Area Code   The telephone area code is 74.

Climate   June through October is the rainy season; June, September, and October are the wettest months, while July and August are relatively dry.

Consular Agents   The United States has an agent at the Hotel Club del Sol on Costera Alemán at R. Católicos (☎ 74/85-6600), across from the Hotel Acapulco Plaza; it's open Monday through Friday from 10am to 2pm. The agent of Canada is also at the Hotel Club del Sol (☎ 74/85-6621), open Monday through Friday from 9am to 1pm. The agent of the United Kingdom is at the Las Brisas Hotel on Carretera Escénica near the airport (☎ 74/84-6605); it's open Monday through Fri-day from 9am to 6pm.

Currency Exchange   Banks along the Costera are open Monday through Friday from 9am to 1 or 1:30pm (though hours for exchanging money may be shorter) and generally have the best rates. Casas de cambio (currency-exchange booths) along the street may have better exchange rates than hotels.

Parking   It is illegal to park on the Costera at any time.

Post Office   The central post office (*correo*) is on the Costera near the zócalo and Sanborn's. Other branches are located in the Estrella de Oro bus station on Cuauhtémoc, inland from the Acapulco Ritz Hotel, and on the Costera near Caleta Beach.

Safety   Pay careful attention to warning flags posted on Acapulco beaches! Riptides claim a few lives every year. Red or black flags mean stay out of the water, yellow flags signify caution, and white or green flags mean it's safe to swim. Don't swim on any beach that fronts an open sea. But don't let down your guard on the bays either. It's difficult to imagine how powerful an undertow can be.

As always, tourists are vulnerable to thieves. This is especially true when you're shopping in a market; lying on the beach; wearing jewelry; or carrying a camera, purse, or bulging wallet. Tourists out for a morning walk on the beach should be es-pecially alert. Pay attention to joggers coming from both directions—one knocks you down, then they rob you. To remove temptation from would-be thieves, purchase a waterproof plastic tube on a string to wear around your neck at the beach—it's big enough for a few bills and your room key. Street vendors and hotel variety shops sell them.

Telephone Numbers   As mentioned above, the area code for Acapulco is 74, a recent change from the old code, which was 748. Be aware that now all Acapulco numbers begin with "8," but many people have not made the transition and still give their numbers without the "8" or still print the area code as 748.

Tourist Police   If you see policemen in uniforms of white and light blue, they're from a special corps of English-speaking police who assist tourists.

FUN ON & OFF THE BEACH

Great beaches and water sports abound in Acapulco. It's also pleasant to take a walk early in the day (before it gets too hot) around the **zócalo,** called Plaza Álvarez. Visit the **cathedral**—the bulbous blue onion domes make it look more like a Russian Orthodox church, and it was actually designed as a movie theater! From the church, turn east along the side street going off at a right angle (Calle Carranza, which doesn't have a marker), where there's an arcade with newsstands and shops.

A fabulous view of Acapulco awaits you from the top of the hill behind the cathedral. Take a taxi up the hill from the main plaza, following the signs leading to **La Mirador.**

City tours, day-trips to Taxco, cruises, and other excursions and activities are offered through local travel agencies. Taxco is about a 3-hour drive inland from Acapulco.

THE BEACHES

Here's the rundown, from west to east around the bay. **Playa la Angosta** is a small, sheltered, and often-deserted cove just around the bend from **La Quebrada** (where the cliff divers perform).

South of downtown on the Peninsula de las Playas lie **Caleta Beach** and **Caletilla Beach.** They are separated by a small outcropping of land containing the new aquarium and water park, Mágico Mundo Marino. Here you'll find thatch-roofed restaurants, water-sports equipment for rent, and the brightly painted boats that ferry passengers to Roqueta Island. You can rent beach chairs and umbrellas for $5 per day. Mexican families favor these beaches because they're close to several inexpensive hotels. In the late afternoon, fishermen pull their colorful boats up on the sand and sell their catch and sometimes oysters on the half shell.

The pleasure boats dock at **Playa Larga,** also south of the zócalo. Charter fishing trips sail from here. In the old days, these downtown beaches—Larga, Caleta, and Caletilla—were what Acapulco was all about. Nowadays the beaches and the resort development stretch the entire 4-mile length of the bay's shore.

Going east from the zócalo, the major beaches are **Hornos** (near Papagayo Park), **Hornitos, Condesa,** and **Icacos,** followed by the naval base (La Base) and **Punta del Guitarrón.** After Punta del Guitarrón, the road climbs to the legendary hotel Las Brisas, where many of the 300 *casitas* (bungalow-type rooms) have their own swimming pools (there are 250 pools in all). Past Las Brisas, the road continues to **Puerto Marqués** and **Punta Diamante,** about 12 miles from the zócalo. The fabulous Acapulco Princess and Pierre Marqués hotels dominate the landscape.

The bay of Puerto Marqués is an attractive area for **swimming.** The water is calm, the bay sheltered, and waterskiing available. Past the bay lies **Revolcadero Beach** and a fascinating jungle lagoon.

Warning: Each year in Acapulco at least one or two unwary swimmers drown because of deadly riptides and undertow (see "Safety" in "Fast Facts," above). Swim

---

Death-Defying Divers

High divers perform at La Quebrada each day at 12:45, 7:30, 8:30, 9:30, and 10:30pm for $4 admission. From a spotlit ledge on the cliffs in view of the lobby bar and restaurant terraces of the Hotel Plaza Las Glorias/El Mirador, each solitary diver plunges into the roaring surf 130 feet below after praying at a small shrine nearby. To the applause of the crowd that has gathered, he then climbs up the rocks and accepts congratulations and gifts of money from onlookers. The best show is at 10:30pm, when they dive with torches.

You can watch from the hotel's terraces for a cover charge in the form of an obligatory drink for $9. However, you might try arriving at the lobby bar 30 minutes before a performance and ordering less expensive drinks; they don't always collect the cover charge from people who are already there. You could also get around the cover by having dinner at the hotel's La Perla restaurant. The buffet is $20 to $25. Reservations (☎ 74/83-1155) are recommended during the high season.

---

only in Acapulco Bay or Puerto Marqués Bay—but be careful of the undertow no matter where you go!

Other beaches are difficult to reach without a car. **La Pie de la Cuesta** is eight miles west of town (buses leave town every 5 or 10 min.). You can't swim here, but it's a great spot for watching big waves and the sunset, especially over coco locos (refreshments made with a fresh coconut with the top whacked off) at one of the rustic beachfront restaurants hung with hammocks. If boys try to collect money from you for sitting under the thatched palapas on the public beach, you don't have to pay them.

If you are driving, continue west along the peninsula, passing Coyuca Lagoon on your right, until you have almost reached the small air base at the tip. Along the way, you'll be invited to park near different sections of beach by various private entrepreneurs, mostly small boys.

BAY CRUISES & ROQUETA ISLAND

The deck of a boat is a wonderful place from which to view the whole bay, and Acapulco has a variety of them to choose from—yachts, huge catamarans and trimarans, single- and double-decker—you name it. Cruises are offered morning, afternoon, and evening. Some offer buffets, open bars, and live music; others have snacks, drinks, and taped music. (The music, by the way, may be loud enough to preclude talking.) Prices range from around $20 to $60. The operators of these cruises come and go, and their phone numbers change so frequently from year to year that it's pointless to list them here; to find out what cruises are currently operated, contact any Acapulco travel agency or hotel tour desk. They usually have a scrapbook with pictures and brochures so you can get a good idea about what a cruise entails before booking it.

Boats from Caletilla Beach to **Roqueta Island**—a place to snorkel, sunbathe, hike to a lighthouse, visit a small zoo, or eat lunch—leave every half hour from 10am until the last one returns at 5pm. The cost is $5 round-trip or $7 on a glass-bottom boat (use the same ticket to return on any launch). You may disagree, but I don't think the glass-bottom boat ride is worth the bucks; you circle the bay looking down at a few fish, then a diver swims down to a statue of a Madonna. Purchase tickets directly from any boat that's loading or from the **information booth** on Caletilla Beach

(☎ **74/82-2389**). The booth also rents inner tubes, small boats, canoes, paddleboats, and beach chairs; it can also arrange waterskiing and scuba diving.

WATER SPORTS & BOAT RENTALS

An hour of **waterskiing** can cost as little as $30 or as much as $60. Caletilla Beach, Puerto Marqués Bay, and Coyuca Lagoon have waterskiing facilities.

Scuba diving costs $40 for $1^1/_2$ hours of instruction if you book directly with the instructor on Caleta Beach. It costs $45 to $55 if you make arrangements through a hotel or travel agency. Dive trips start around $50 per person for one dive.

Boat rentals are the least expensive on Caletilla Beach, where an information booth rents inner tubes, small boats, canoes, paddleboats, and beach chairs; it can also arrange waterskiing and scuba diving (see "Bay Cruises & Roqueta Island," above).

For **deep-sea fishing** excursions, go to the pale-pink building of the boat cooperative opposite the zócalo. Charter fishing trips from here run from $100 to $150 for seven hours, arranged through the **boat cooperative** (☎ **74/82-1099**). Booked through a travel agent or hotel, fishing trips start around $150 to $200 for four people. The fishing license, food, and drink are extra.

Parasailing, though not without risks (like landing on a palm tree or a building), can be a fantastic thrill. The pleasure of floating high over the bay hanging from a parachute towed by a motorboat is yours for $35. Most of the parachute rides operate on Condesa Beach.

GOLF, TENNIS, RIDING & BULLFIGHTS

A round of 18 holes of **golf** at the **Acapulco Princess Hotel** (☎ **74/84-3100**) costs $107 for nonguests and $70 for guests. At the **Club de Golf Acapulco,** off the Costera next to the Convention Center (☎ **74/84-0781** or 74/84-0782), you can play nine holes for $35 or 18 holes for $46.

Tennis at one of the tennis clubs open to the public costs around $11 per hour. Try the **Club de Golf Acapulco** (☎ **74/84-4824** or 74/84-0782), open daily from 7am to 7pm. Singles cost $11 per hour; doubles, $16.

Horseback-riding tours on the beach are available through the **Lienzo Charro "México Real,"** near the Acapulco Princess Hotel (☎ **74/85-0331**). The 2-hour rides depart at 9:30 and 11:30am and 3:30pm daily and cost $40, including two beers or soft drinks.

Traditionally termed the Fiesta Brava, the **bullfights** are held during Acapulco's winter season at a ring up the hill from Caletilla Beach. Tickets purchased through travel agencies cost around $40 and usually include transportation to and from your hotel. The festivities begin each Sunday in winter at 5:30pm.

MUSEUMS & WATER PARKS

The original **Fuerte de San Diego,** Costera Alemán, east of the zócalo, was built in 1616 to protect the town from pirate attacks. At that time, the port was wealthy from its trade with the Philippine Islands, which like Mexico were part of Spain's enormous empire. The fort you see was rebuilt after extensive damage by an earthquake in 1776. Today the structure houses the **Museo Histórico de Acapulco** (Acapulco Historical Museum), filled with exhibits that tell the fascinating story of Acapulco, beginning with its role as a port for conquest of the Americas and going through the conversion of the natives to Catholicism and the city's trade with the Orient. The first room has changing shows. Recently, it displayed artifacts from the Aztec Templo Mayor excavation in Mexico City. Other rooms chronicle Acapulco's pre-Hispanic past and the coming of the conquistadores, complete with Spanish armor. There are also displays about the Spanish imperial conquest of the South Seas, for which Acapulco was a base, and a 6-foot-tall model of a *Manila galeón,* the famous ships that sailed back laden with treasures from China. Artifacts from the China trade, including fine chests, vases, textiles, and furniture, are also on exhibit.

To reach the fort, follow Costera Alemán past Old Acapulco and the zócalo; the fort is on a hill on the right. You can also reach the fort by a road through a military zone; coming from the main plaza, look for the road on the left (landward) side of the Costera. If you're in good shape, you can climb a cascade of stairs opposite the cargo docks. The museum is open Tuesday through Sunday from 10:30am to 4:40pm, but the best time to go is in the morning, since the "air-conditioning" is minimal. The $2.50 admission is waved on Sunday.

The **Centro Internacional de Convivencia Infantil (Cici),** Costera Alemán, at Colón (☎ 74/84-1970) is a sea-life and water park east of the Convention Center. It offers a variety of swimming pools with waves, water slides, and water toboggans. The park is open daily from 10am to 6pm. Dolphin shows at noon, 2:30, and 5pm are in English and Spanish. Bird shows are at 11:15am, 1:15, and 3:45pm. Amenities include a cafeteria and rest rooms. Admission is $5 for adults and $3 for children. Children under 2 are free.

SHOPPING

Acapulco is not the best place to buy Mexican crafts, but there are a few interesting shops. The best places are at the **Mercado Parazal** (often called the **Mercado de Artesanías**) on Calle Velásquez de León near Cinco de Mayo in the downtown zócalo area (when you see Sanborn's, turn right, walk behind it for several blocks, and ask for directions). Stall after covered stall of curios from all over the country are here, including silver, embroidered cotton clothing, rugs, pottery, and papier-mâché. Artists paint ceramics with village folk scenes while waiting for patrons. It's a pleasant place to spend a morning or afternoon.

Shopkeepers are vigilant and not too pushy, but they'll test your bargaining mettle. The starting price will be astronomical, and getting the price down may take more time than you have. But as always, acting uninterested often brings down prices in a hurry. Before buying silver here, examine it carefully and be sure it has ".925" stamped on the back (this signifies that the silver is 92.5% pure). The market is open daily from 9am to 8pm.

For a familiar, brightly lit department store with fixed prices, try **Artesanías Finas de Acapulco** (☎ 74/84-8039), called AFA-ACA for short. To find it, go east on the Costera until you see the Hotel Romano Days Inn on the seaward side and Baby-O disco on the landward side. Take Avenida Horacio Nelson, the street between Baby-O and the Hotel El Tropicana. On the right, half a block up, is AFA-ACA, a huge air-conditioned store that's popular with tour groups. The merchandise includes clothes, marble-top furniture, saddles, luggage, jewelry, pottery, papier-mâché, and more. The store is open Monday through Saturday from 9am to 7:30pm and Sunday from 9am to 2pm. **Sanborn's** is another good department store.

The **Costera Alemán** is crowded with boutiques selling resort wear. These stores have an abundance of attractive summer clothing at prices lower than those you generally find in the United States. If they have a sale, that's the time to stock up on some incredible bargains. Pay close attention to the quality of zippers; sometimes Mexican zippers are not up to the task. One of the nicest air-conditioned shopping centers on the Costera is **Plaza Bahía,** Costera Alemán 125 (☎ 74/86-2452), which has two stories of shops and small fast-food restaurants, including a tempting pastry shop—

Café Paris. The center is located just west of the Fiesta Americana Acapulco Plaza Hotel. In front of the hotel there is a fine-silver shop called **Fini.**

ACCOMMODATIONS

The descriptions below begin with the very expensive resorts south of town (nearest the airport) and continue along the famous main avenue, Costera Miguel Alemán, to those less expensive hotels north of town in what is considered the zócalo, downtown, or "Old Acapulco" part of the city. Rather than pay the rates quoted here at the "very expensive" and "expensive" hotels, inquire first about promotional rates or check airlines to see what airfare and hotel packages are available. During Christmas and Easter weeks, some hotels double their normal rates. **Fiesta Americana** premiers a special hotel and tour package (you book your hotel and tours at the same time) that can be booked alone or with airfare included. **Camino Real** created a "Little Rascals Club" especially for entertaining children. Acapulco bus stations also have both partial and impartial reservation services. The impartial one is operated by the Acapulco Hotel Association. The clerk will call a member hotel of your choice or try to find one to suit your requirements. If they make the reservation, you pay them for 1 night in advance (they'll give you a voucher for the hotel). Other hotels (the partial reservation desks) may have a booth promoting only their property.

Private, very secluded villas are available for rent all over the hills south of town; renting one of these luxurious and palatial homes makes an unforgettable Acapulco vacation alternative. See Chapter 3, Section 9 for U.S. companies handling Acapulco villa rentals.

SOUTH OF TOWN

The steep forested hillsides south of town between the naval base and Puerto Marqués hold some of Acapulco's most exclusive hotels, restaurants, and villas for which Acapulco is justly famous. The **Hotel Camino Real** is on Playa Guitarrón, the **Sheraton** is on a secluded cove, the super exclusive **Acapulco Princess** faces the open ocean, and next to it is the enormous **Vidafel** resort.

Very Expensive

Acapulco Princess

El Revolcadero Beach, 39868 Acapulco, Gro. ☎ **74/84-3100** or 800/223-1818 in the U.S. Fax 74/84-7185. 916 rms, 92 suites, 11 penthouses. A/C MINIBAR TV TEL. High season (including breakfast and dinner), $300–$600 single or double. Free parking.

The first luxury hotel most people see on arriving in Acapulco is the 480-acre Acapulco Princess on El Revolcadero Beach just off the road to the airport. Set apart from the Manhattan of skyscraper hotels downtown, the Princess complex, framed by the fabulously groomed and palm-dotted golf course, reminds one of a great Aztec ceremonial center. Its pyramidlike buildings dominate the flat surrounding land.

Within the spacious and gracious complex of buildings at the Acapulco Princess is a self-contained tropical-paradise world: a system of waterfalls, fountains, and pools set amid tropical trees, flowers, and shrubs, with swans, peacocks, and flamingos. Though the beach is long, inviting, and beautifully kept, there is no bay and therefore swimming in the open here is unsafe; look but don't go in. The dramatic lobby is enormous, and other public spaces are bold and striking in the best Mexican fashion. Guest rooms at the Acapulco Princess are big, bright, and luxurious, with marble floors and balconies. Room rates vary from selection of standard, superior, and deluxe rooms, and two types of suites, with the highest prices for the one- and two-bedroom penthouses.

During high season, prices include two meals. During low season, children within a certain age group may share a room with two adults at no extra charge. Ask about special packages which may include unlimited golf and daytime tennis, free use of the fitness center, and other perks, and, during high season, perhaps a 7-night stay for the price of five nights.

Next door is the older, more sedate **Hotel Pierre Marqués,** open during high season only and offering Princess amenities and privileges at a fraction of Princess prices.

Dining/Entertainment: Seven restaurants in all (some subject to seasonal closings); in general all are excellent and you may find no reason to go elsewhere to eat. Fine dining; sheltered outdoor dining. Bars include Laguna and La Cascada, where mariachis often entertain; La Palma and La Palapa by the beach; and Grotto, the swim-up bar. Tiffany's is the trendy disco that gets going late and stays open until the wee hours of the morning. Garden theme parties, with regional music and dancing, are often offered.

Services: Laundry and room service, travel agency, baby-sitter, cribs, wheelchairs.

Facilities: Five free-form swimming pools, a saltwater lagoon with water slide, two 18-hole golf courses, and nine outdoor tennis courts (all lit for night play) and two indoor courts with stadium seating. Fishing and other water sports can be arranged with the hotel's travel agency. There's also a barber and beauty shop with massage available, a fitness center with aerobic classes, boutiques, a flower shop, and an ice machine on each floor.

Camino Real Diamante

Carretera Escénica km 14, Calle Bajacatitia 18, Pichilinque, Puerto Marqués, 39887 Acapulco, Gro. ☎ and fax **74/81-2010** or 800/7-CAMINO in the U.S. and Canada. 156 rms. A/C MINIBAR TV TEL. High season, $180–$250. Ask about low season and midweek discounts and "The Little Rascals Club" for children.

One of Acapulco's finest, this hotel opened in 1993 in a secluded location on 81 acres as part of the enormous Acapulco Diamante project. From the Carretera Escénica, you wind down, down, down a handsome brick road to the hotel's location beside and overlooking Puerto Marqués Bay. Reception is gracious in the expansive lobby, which offers a sitting area and an enormous terrace facing the water. Elevators whisk you to all but the outside terrace levels. The spacious rooms, each with a small sitting area, have cool marble floors, and are furnished in an elegantly austere way. Televisions and minibars are sequestered within lightly hued wooden armoires. Each room has a ceiling fan in addition to air-conditioning and a safety-deposit box in the closet.

It's secluded here in this relaxing, completely self-contained resort. And it's an ideal choice for accommodations if you already know Acapulco and don't need to explore much, since a taxi to town costs $7 or more one way.

Dining/Entertainment: Outdoor seafood grill overlooking the bay. Cabo Diamante features both Mexican and international food. The open-air lobby bar facing the bay is the place to be for evening cocktails.

Services: Room and laundry service, travel agency, car rental.

Facilities: Trilevel pool, tennis courts, beauty and barber shops, and shopping arcade. The health club offers aerobics, massage, and complete workout equipment.

Westin Las Brisas

Apdo. Postal 281, Carretera Escénica, 39868 Las Brisas, Acapulco, Gro. ☎ **74/84-1580** or 800/ 228-3000 in the U.S. Fax 74/84-2269. 300 units. A/C MINIBAR TV TEL. High season (including continental breakfast), $235 single or double, $272 Royal Beach Club, $481–$1,250 suite.

Low season, $162 single or double, $200 Royal Beach Club, $375–$1,138 suite. $15 per day service charge extra (in lieu of all tips).

Some consider this the ultimate hostelry in Acapulco. Perched in tiers on a hillside overlooking the bay, it presents a pink stucco facade that is a traditional trademark in Acapulco. The pink theme is carried on to the 175 pink Jeeps rented exclusively to Las Brisas guests. The hotel is a community unto itself: The elegantly simple, marble-floored rooms are like separate little villas built into a terraced hillside, and each has a private (or semiprivate) swimming pool with a panoramic bay view. Spacious Regency Club rooms are at the top of the property and all have private pools and fabulous commanding views of the bay. Altogether, there are 300 casitas and 250 swimming pools. Although its location on the airport road southeast of the bay means that Las Brisas is a long way from the center of town, guests tend to find this an advantage rather than a drawback. Outsiders aren't permitted on the property without an invitation.

Prices for this luxury (wait till you see the lights of all Acapulco twinkling across the bay) depend on the number of bedrooms you want, whether you want a room with a private or shared pool, and whether you choose to be a Regency Club guest.

Dining/Entertainment: Complimentary breakfast of fruit, rolls, and coffee served to each room daily. Bella Vista is the reservation-only (and now open to the public) panoramic-view restaurant, open 7 to 11pm daily. El Mexicano Restaurant on a starlit terrace is open Saturday to Thursday evenings. La Concha Beach Club offers seafood daily from 12:30 to 4:30pm. The Deli Shop is open from 11am to 7pm daily.

Services: Travel agency and gas station, express checkout with advance notice, 24-hour shuttle transportation around the resort, laundry and room service, beauty and barber shops.

Facilities: Private or shared pools with each room with fresh floating flowers daily; private La Concha Beach Club at the bottom of the hill has both fresh and saltwater pools—the hotel provides transportation; five tennis courts; pink Jeeps rent for $85 a day and include tax, gas, mileage, and insurance.

Expensive

Acapulco Sheraton Resort

Costera Guitarrón 110, 39300 Acapulco, Gro. ☎ **74/84-3737** or 800/325-3535 in the U.S. Fax 74/84-3760. 226 rms, 8 suites. A/C MINIBAR TV TEL. High season, $145 double. Parking $5 daily. Ask about "Sure Saver" and weekend rates.

Opened in 1992, this is one of the newest resort hotels north of town. Secluded and tranquil, and completely invisible from the scenic highway, it's nestled in a landscaped ravine with a waterfall and wonderful bay view. The 17 multistoried units descend to a small beach beside the pool. Each building unit has an elevator, making it possible to come and go from the lobby to the rooms without climbing stairs—though you may need a trail of rice to remember your route. Rooms have travertine tile floors and rattan furniture and come with a private or shared balcony, purified tap water, and in-room safety-deposit boxes. Some have a separate living room and kitchenette. The 32 Sheraton Club rooms have extra amenities. All rooms have remote-control TV, alarm clocks, and tub/shower combinations. It's located between La Base and Las Brisas, off the Carretera Escénica at Playa Guitarrón at the eastern end of the bay. A small sign marks the turnoff.

Dining/Entertainment: Besides a restaurant with kosher service, there's La Bahía Restaurant, with a magnificent semicircular bay view, elegantly set tables, and international cuisine. The Lobby Bar offers live piano music nightly and a bay view. The famous Jorongo Bar of the Sheraton María Cristina in Mexico City is re-created here with its cantina atmosphere, live trio music, and regional food specialties. Restaurants and bars are seasonal and all may not be open during low season.

Services: Laundry and room service, travel agency, car rental; scheduled shuttle service to and from town may be offered.

Facilities: Beach, two swimming pools, two handicapped-equipped rooms, 20 nonsmoking guest rooms, boutiques, beauty shops, and small gym with sauna, steam room, and massage. The hotel has a tennis membership at the Club Brittanica and provides guests with free transportation.

CONVENTION CENTER & ICACOS BEACH AREA

These hotels are all on the far eastern side of the bay, near the Convention Center (*Centro Acapulco*) and CICI (*Centro Internacional de Convivencia Infantil*), Acapulco's fabulous water amusement park for children.

Expensive

Hotel Elcano

Costera Alemán 75, 39690 Acapulco, Gro. ☎ **74/84-1950** or 800/222-7692 in the U.S. Fax 74/84-2230. 144 rms. A/C TV TEL. $165 studio and standard room; $180 junior suite. Ask about promotional discounts.

If you knew the old El Cano, you'll see that this new one is nothing like it. Completely gutted during 2 years of renovation, it reopened without showing even a hint of its former frumpy self. The lobby is a sea of Caribbean blue and white and the rooms are themed around trendy navy-and-white tile. All have tub/shower combinations and ceiling fans in addition to the central air-conditioning; all except studio rooms have balconies. The very large junior suites, all located on corners, have two queen-size beds and huge closets. Standard rooms are a little smaller than suites. Studios are quite small, with king-size beds and small sinks outside the bathroom area. In the studios a small portion of the TV armoire serves as a closet. The studios don't have balconies, but full sliding doors open to let in the breezes. All rooms have purified tap water and in-room safety-deposit boxes.

Dining/Entertainment: The informal and excellent Bambuco restaurant (see "Dining" below) is by the pool and beach and is open from 9am to 11pm daily. The more formal Victoria is on an outdoor terrace overlooking the pool and beach and is open from 6 to 11pm daily.

Services: Room and laundry service, travel agency.

Facilities: One beachside pool, workout room, gift shop, boutiques, travel agency, beauty shop, massages, video-game room, an ice machine on each floor.

Hyatt Regency

Costera Miguel Alemán 666, 39869 Acapulco, Gro. ☎ **74/69-1234** or 800/233-1234 in the U.S. and Canada. Fax 74/84-3087. 645 rms. A/C TV TEL. High season, $243 single or double, $525–$2,680 suite. Low season, $128 single or double, $370–$1,630 suite.

The multistoried Hyatt has regained its glamour after several years of remodeling and a multimillion dollar face-lift. The sleek lobby offers a welcoming sitting/bar area that's become a popular place for drinks and conversation. Rooms on the first six floors are furnished a little less lavishly than those on upper floors—no minibars for example—but are still worthy of the Hyatt stamp. Those on floors 7 to 22, including the Regency Club rooms, offer stylish furnishings using a rich green to accent bright colors inspired by the ocean. All rooms are large, with balconies overlooking the pool and ocean, and come with in-room security boxes and purified tap water. Robes, hairdryers, and remote control TVs are standard in deluxe rooms and the

Regency Club. Regency Club guests have complimentary continental breakfast and afternoon canapés, separate check-in and checkout, and a paperback exchange library.

Dining/Entertainment: Four restaurants serve all three meals, including one by the beach and pool featuring pasta and pizza. Another poolside restaurant converts to full kosher food from December through April.

Services: Laundry, room service, concierge, travel agency, car rental, direct-dial telephone, gift shops and boutiques. Synagogue services are held on the premises from December through April.

Facilities: A large, shaded free-form pool.

Moderate

Hotel La Palapa

Playa Icacos, Fracc. Costa Azul, Fragata Yucatán 210, 39850 Acapulco, Gro. ☎ **74/84-5363** or 91/800-10-9777 in Mexico. Fax 74/84-8399. 333 rms. A/C TEL. High season, $75 single or double (including breakfast). Low season, $55 single or double. Two children stay free in parents' room. Free parking.

You can't fail to see this hotel's 30 stories towering over the beach between the naval base and the Convention Center. While not in the luxury category, with white Formica furniture, every room has an ocean view and balcony. Some rooms are smaller than others but all are suites, with living area separate from the bedroom, many have small bars and a dining table, and all have in-room safety-deposit boxes. The palm-lined beachside pool is the hotel's relaxing focal point. Mariscos is the poolside restaurant, open 7:30am to 11pm daily. La Nouvell is off the lobby and open for all three meals daily. El Muelle Pizzaria, with seafood specialties, is open daily in high season only from 1 to 11pm. There's a travel agency in the lobby, and the hotel offers laundry and room service.

CONDESA BEACH & DIANA CIRCLE AREA

The row of gigantic hotels along the northern shore of Acapulco Bay has been photographed over and over for travel brochures and posters, and at dusk as the lights twinkle on, these giants certainly do offer a romantic vista.

Expensive

Fiesta Americana Condesa Acapulco

Costera Miguel Alemán 1220, 39300 Acapulco, Gro. ☎ **74/84-2355** or 800/223-2332 in the U.S. Fax 74/84-1828. 475 rms, 13 suites. A/C MINIBAR TV TEL. High season, $150–$175 single or double. Low season, $125–$140 single or double. Ask about "Fiesta Break" packages that combine hotel, sightseeing, and air.

Once called the Condesa del Mar, the Fiesta Americana Condesa Acapulco is among Acapulco's long-standing favorite deluxe hotels. The 18-story hotel towers above Condesa Beach, just east up the hill from the Glorieta Diana. The attractive and very comfortable rooms are furnished in soft pastels. Each has a private terrace with an ocean view. The more expensive rooms have the best bay views and all rooms have purified tap water.

Dining/Entertainment: Coffee shop, poolside restaurant, and lobby bar with live entertainment most nights.

Services: Laundry and room service, travel agency.

Facilities: Dramatic adults-only swimming pool perched atop a hill with the land dropping off toward the bay, affording swimmers the best view of Acapulco from any pool in the city. Smaller pool for children. Two handicapped-equipped rooms, beauty shop, boutiques, and pharmacy.

Moderate

Calinda Acapulco Quality Inn

Costera Miguel Alemán 1260, 39300 Acapulco, Gro. ☎ **74/84-0410** or 800/228-5151 in the U.S. Fax 74/84-4676. 358 rms. A/C TV TEL. Year-round $115 double. Numerous discount rates apply to senior citizens, government and military employees, corporations, and travel clubs such as AAA.

You can't miss this tall cylindrical tower rising at the eastern edge of Condesa Beach. The design allows each room to have a view, usually of the bay. The guest rooms, though not strikingly furnished, are large and comfortable and most come with two double beds. Remodeling in recent years has given it a modern face-lift. A package price will reduce the rates listed above, which otherwise are too high for the quality of accommodations. Three restaurants from snacks by the pool to indoor informal dining cover most guests' needs. For cocktails, the Lobby Bar party gets going around 6pm and stops at 1am; there's a happy hour from 4 to 9pm when drinks are two for the price of one, and live music between 9pm and 1am. Laundry and room service and a travel agency round out the routine services. Plus there's one swimming pool, several lobby boutiques, a pharmacy, beauty shop, ice machine on the third floor, two handicapped-equipped rooms, and four nonsmoking floors.

✪ Hotel Acapulco Tortuga

Costera Miguel Alemán 132, 39300 Acapulco, Gro. ☎ **74/84-8889** or 800/832-7491 in the U.S. Fax 74/84-7385. 250 rms. A/C TV TEL. High season, $65–$80 single or double. Low season, $55–$65 single or double.

The Acapulco Tortuga is a modern eight-story hotel on the landward side of the Costera Alemán near Condesa Beach, almost across the street from the Fiesta Americana Condesa hotel and Beto's Safari Restaurant. You enter the hotel to find a cavernous atrium lobby, in the midst of which are the restaurants Los Portales and La Fonda. Despite its modern construction, the decor in the atrium is theatrical Spanish colonial, with lots of greenery. The reception desk is at the left-rear side of the cavernous atrium. The rooms have wall-to-wall carpeting, color TVs with cable, and radios, though upkeep could be better. At the very back of the hotel is a nice little swimming pool with a shady palapa (thatched shelter). By the way, the toll-free number (which you dial in the U.S.) rings in Mexico and those who answer may not speak English if you call before 9am, in midafternoon, or in the late evening.

✪ Hotel Sands

Costera Alemán 178, 39690 Acapulco, Gro. ☎ **74/84-2260.** Fax 74/84-1053. 93 rms. A/C TV TEL. $55 single or double all year except Christmas, Easter, and other major Mexican holidays.

Nestled on the landward side opposite the giant resort hotels and away from the din of Costera traffic is this unpretentious and comfortable hostelry. From the street, you enter the hotel lobby through a stand of umbrella palms and a pretty garden restaurant. The rooms are light and airy in the style of a good modern motel, with fairly dressy furniture and wall-to-wall carpeting. The Sand's has four swimming pools (one of them for children), a squash court, as well as volleyball and Ping-Pong areas. The price here is more than reasonable, the accommodations are satisfactory, and the location opposite the Acapulco Plaza Hotel is excellent.

PAPAGAYO PARK TO DIANA CIRCLE

Hotel del Valle

Espinoza 150, 39300 Acapulco, Gro. ☎ **74/85-8336** or 74/85-8388. 18 rms. A/C or FAN. High season, $20 single or double with fan; $23 single or double with A/C. Lower rates available in low season.

This little hotel has a small pool in front, and the beach is only a block away. There are a variety of rooms. Those with air-conditioning have telephones, and those with fans have two twin beds. Six rooms have tiny kitchens and rent for $8 more. To find the hotel, use the Hotel Plaza Las Glorias on the Costera as a landmark. Walk opposite it half a block inland, and you'll see the hotel on the right facing Papagayo Park.

Hotel Howard Johnson Maralisa

Calle Alemánia s/n, 39670 Acapulco, Gro. ☎ **74/85-6677** or 800/446-4656 in the U.S. Fax 74/85-9228. 90 rms. A/C TV TEL. High season, $85–$150 single or double.

Of the smaller hotels in the row of giants, this, the former Hotel Maralisa, is one of the most congenial. It's got all the things the huge hotels have without the tremendous size: a fine palm-shaded swimming pool, plus a smaller pool, a nice stretch of beach, La Mar bar between the beach and the swimming pool, and a dining room overlooking the bay. Lower-priced rooms have two twin beds and higher-priced ones have two double beds and balconies. Whichever accommodation you choose, you'll have a comfortable, modern, air-conditioned room with sliding glass doors (in most cases) opening onto a balcony or back interior walkway—the latter are the least expensive rooms. Besides standard rooms there are three handicapped-equipped rooms, a travel agency, and pharmacy/gift shop. It's just off the Costera at Alemánia; turn when you see the Baskin-Robbins and follow the side street going toward the beach.

Plaza Las Glorias Paraío

Costera Miguel Alemán 163, 39300 Acapulco, Gro. ☎ **74/85-5050** or 800/342-AMIGO in the U.S. Fax 74/85-5543. 422 rms. A/C MINIBAR TV TEL. High season, $130–$150 single or double.

Formerly the Paraío Radisson, it stands right at the eastern end of Papagayo Park on Hornos Beach. Though it's among the resort's older hotels, it has been well maintained. The lofty lobby is an expanse of gleaming black marble leading to large windows overlooking the beach, dotted with little palapas. The hotel's attractive sundeck next to the beach is set with comfy lounge chairs. The guest rooms are spacious, with nice tiled bathrooms, marble vanities, and little balconies. More expensive rooms are those with a sea view. Land-view rooms can be a bit noisy because of the busy traffic along the Costera.

Dining/Entertainment: Two informal restaurants, a rooftop restaurant with fabulous view of the bay, and a poolside bar.

Services: Laundry and room service, travel agency, car rental.

Facilities: Oceanside pool, ice machine on each floor, one handicapped-equipped guest room; floors 2 and 17 are nonsmoking.

DOWNTOWN—ON LA QUEBRADA

Numerous budget-quality hotels dot the streets fanning out from the zócalo (Acapulco's official and original downtown) and they are among the best buys in Acapulco if you aren't looking for luxury. Be sure to check your room first to see that it has the basic comforts you expect.

Expensive

Plaza Las Glorias/El Mirador

Quebrada 74, 39300 Acapulco, Gro. ☎ **74/83-1221** or 800/342-AMIGO in the U.S. Fax 74/82-4564. 100 rms. A/C TV TEL. High season, $115 single or double. Parking available on street.

One of the landmarks of "Old Acapulco," the former El Mirador Hotel overlooks the famous cove where the cliff divers perform. Renovated with lush tropical landscaping and lots of handsome Mexican tile, this romantic hotel offers attractively furnished rooms with double or queen-size beds, minifridge and wet bar, and large bathrooms with marble counters. Most have a separate living room area and all are accented with handsome Saltillo tile and other Mexican decorative touches. Ask for a room with a balcony (there are 42) and ocean view (95 rooms).

To get there, follow the Costera past the Club de Esquies (on the left), the Pemex station (on the right). Turn right at the Hotel Avenida and follow the street right around the mountain. You'll see the Quebrada and the hotel across the small, deep cove on the left.

Dining/Entertainment: The evening buffet ($20–$25) offers great views of the cliff-diving show; the coffee shop features mediocre food and slow service. The large, comfortable, and breezy lobby bar is a favorite spot to watch day fade into night on the beautiful cove and bay.

Services: Room service for breakfast and lunch, laundry service, travel agency.

Facilities: Three pools, protected cove with good snorkeling, saltwater pool accessed by mountainside elevator.

Inexpensive
Hotel Angelita

Quebrada 37, 39300 Acapulco, Gro. ☎ **74/83-5734.** 10 rms. FAN. $8 single; $12 double.

This three-story white stucco hotel on Quebrada a few blocks west of the zócalo advertises *limpieza absoluta* (absolute cleanliness), and that's what you'll find in this bright place. Simply furnished white rooms have blue-tile baths, and the airy central hallway is lined with plants. The two largest rooms have balconies.

⑤ Hotel Asturias

Quebrada 45, 39300 Acapulco, Gro. ☎ **74/83-6548.** 15 rms. FAN. $9 single; $14 double.

This little, charming budget hotel gets high marks for cleanliness and friendly management. There's also a nice pool which is just big enough to cool off. Rooms are clean and airy, with tile floors and small tile baths (no toilet seats). Louvered glass windows in each room face the open common walkways of the hotel's interior, letting in light and air—as well as mosquitoes. To find the hotel from the zócalo, walk up Quebrada three blocks; the hotel is on the left opposite the Secretaría de Finanzas. You will notice it by its blue columns flanking a wide stucco arch over the front porch.

DOWNTOWN—THE ZÓCALO/LA PAZ AREA
⑤ Hotel California

La Paz 12, 39300 Acapulco, Gro. ☎ **74/82-2893.** 24 rms. A/C or FAN. High season, $10 single; $20 double. Year-round, $22 rm with A/C.

The rooms at the Hotel California are arranged around a paved open patio. All have fans (two are air-conditioned) and are decorated with nice white drapes and Formica furniture. The hotel is a block southwest of the zócalo; two blocks east on the Costera are convenient bus stops.

Hotel Isabel

La Paz 16 Centro, 39300 Acapulco, Gro. ☎ **74/83-9816.** 36 rms. FAN. $6 single; $10 double.

A short walk from the zócalo, the Isabel offers four stories of plain, clean rooms with marble-tiled floors and tile baths with pull-string showers. Windows have built-in louvers; they have no glass or screens and are not closable. Rooms in the front have small balconies overlooking bustling La Paz. Those in the back have windows on the interior. It stands out a bit from other buildings since it's the only four-story building in the area and has a dark-blue base with white on top.

Hotel María Antonieta

Azueta 17, 39300 Acapulco, Gro. ☎ **74/82-5024.** 30 rms. A/C or fan. $7–$10 single; $10–$20 double.

This well-kept two-story hotel offers rooms off an airy central corridor festooned with plants. Each clean white room comes with two double beds, white spreads and curtains, and louvered glass windows, but only 15 have hot water. Upstairs rooms have larger windows and are brighter. Higher-priced rooms have air-conditioning. The hotel, located at the corner of La Paz, three blocks southwest of the zócalo, has a communal kitchen and dining area.

✪ Hotel Misión

Felipe Valle 112, 39300 Acapulco, Gro. ☎ **74/82-3643.** 27 rms. FAN. $14 single; $27 double.

Enter this hotel's plant-filled brick courtyard, shaded by an enormous mango tree, and you'll step back to an earlier Acapulco. This tranquil 19th-century hotel lies two blocks inland from the Costera and the zócalo. The original L-shaped building is at least 100 years old. The rooms have colonial touches such as colorful tile and wrought iron and come simply furnished with one or two beds. Breakfast and lunch are served on the patio. On Thursdays, beginning at 2pm, the specialty is an elaborate pozole spread cooked out on the patio; bowls of the regional favorite cost around $3. Soft drinks and beer are usually available all day.

ON PLAYA LA ANGOSTA

If you stand on the zócalo and face the water, to your right the Costera leads to hotels on the hilly peninsula that curves back into the bay. Their location gives some of these hotels great views of the city and bay; luxury hotels were built here in the 1950s. On the back side of the peninsula is Playa la Angosta. To get there, take any bus along the Costera, which runs along the base of the peninsula, and get off at the Hotel Avenida. Walk a block to Playa la Angosta; the hotels are on the left facing the bay.

⑨ Hotel Villa Romana

Av. López Mateos 185, Fracc. Las Playas, 39300 Acapulco, Gro. ☎ **74/82-3995.** 9 rms. A/C. High season, $27 single; $30 double. Low season, $20 single; $25 double.

With terraces facing the sparkling Playa la Angosta, this is one of the most comfortable inns in the area, ideal for a long stay. Some rooms are tiled and others carpeted, and all have small kitchens with refrigerators. There is a small plant-filled terrace on the second floor with tables and chairs, and a fourth-floor pool with a splendid view of the bay.

NEAR PLAYAS CALETA & CALETILLA

The layout of streets on the peninsula that separates the two beaches is confusing, and the disorganized street names and numbers are enough to drive one loco. A street will be named Avenida López Mateos, but so will the street meeting it at a 90° angle. Some streets have two names, while others have none; many buildings have two street numbers.

The following hotels are easy to find. Simply take a CALETA bus to Mágico Mundo Marino, a popular local tourist attraction, and you'll be within walking distance (one to four blocks) of any of the hotels.

Hotel Belmar

Gran Vía Tropical and Av. de las Cumbres, 39360 Acapulco, Gro. ☎ **74/82-1525** or 74/82-1526. 80 rms. A/C or FAN MINIBAR. Year-round $20 double.

Two pools and shady patios fill the grassy lawn in front of this hotel. Built in the 1950s, it features large, breezy rooms, enormous balconies, and relaxing views; 70 rooms are air-conditioned. It's an ideal place to spread out and unwind. There's a comfortable restaurant/bar open for breakfast and lunch. Dust from an adjacent un-paved street, however, can be a problem here. To get here, stand at the crossroads and put your back to the Hotel Meiga (a very large and visible all-inclusive hotel), and you'll see the Belmar sign up the hill. Take the street to your left up and up and up the hill about 1¹/₂ blocks.

Hotel Lindavista

Playa Caleta s/n (Apdo. Postal 3), 39300 Acapulco, Gro. ☎ **74/82-5414.** Fax 74/82-2783. 43 rms. A/C or FAN. $42 single or double with fan; $50 single or double with A/C. Rates include breakfast. Ask for a discount. Free parking.

The old-fashioned Lindavista snuggles into the hillside above Caleta Beach. Older American and Mexican couples are drawn to the well-kept rooms, beautiful views, and slow pace of the area here. Most of the rooms have air-conditioning, and those that don't have fans. There is a small pool and a terrace restaurant/bar. Cozy as the Lindavista is, the quoted prices are way too high—negotiate a discount or ask about their packages for a stay of several nights. Coming from Caleta Beach, you'll find the hotel up the hill to the left of the Hotel Caleta.

Motel La Jolla

Costera Alemán and Av. López Mateos, 39300 Acapulco, Gro. ☎ **74/82-1525** or 74/83-8098. Fax 74/82-1526. 80 rms. A/C TEL. High season, $45 single, $55 double; low season, $35 single, $45 double.

This L-shaped two-story motel, with bright and modern rooms, surrounds a very pleasant swimming pool handsomely shaded by coconut palms. Although there is no view of the sea whatsoever, you are within a block of the bay and of Caleta and Caletilla beaches here. It's almost always full on weekends. You'll know you've reached the hotel when you see the flying-saucer–shaped restaurant.

DINING

Dining out in Acapulco can be one of the best experiences you'll ever have in Mexico—whether you're clad in a bathing suit and munching a hamburger on the beach, or seated at a candlelit table with the glittering bay spread out before you.

The price of a meal in a deluxe establishment in Acapulco may not be much higher than what you'd pay for something of inferior quality at a mass market restaurant. The proliferation of U.S. franchise restaurants (McDonald's, Subway, Shakey's Pizza, Baskin-Robbins, Tony Roma's, etc.), has increased competition in Acapulco and more expensive places have reduced prices in response; the quality of their food is much better, offering more value for the money than supposedly budget restaurants.

The restaurants I've taste-tested below reflect a mixture of both value and good food. And if it's a romantic place you're looking for, you won't have to look far, since Acapulco fairly brims over with such inviting places.

SOUTH OF TOWN: LAS BRISAS AREA

Very Expensive

Restaurant Miramar

Plaza La Vista, Carretera Escénica. ☎ **74/84-7874.** Reservations required. Main courses $17–$25; desserts $4–$9. Daily 6:30pm–midnight. ITALIAN/FRENCH/MEXICAN.

The Miramar is about as formal as an Acapulco restaurant gets, and with the view of the bay and outstanding food, the dining experience is something not soon forgotten. Waiters wearing black suits and ties are quietly solicitous as you make your selection and ponder the view between courses. The menu, as refined as the service, offers familiar continental classics such as duck in orange sauce, coq au vin, and tournedos Rossini, all exquisitely presented. But save room for a dessert, all as memorable as the main courses. Dress up a bit for dining here, but as lightly as possible, since bay breezes are few and the fans aren't quite adequate. When the tab for your wonderful meal comes, check it carefully; I don't know if they get busy and make mistakes or what exactly happens, but sometimes unordered items appear on the bill, or the total is more than the sum of the prices. The Miramar is in the La Vista complex near the Hotel La Brisas.

Spicey

Carretera Escénica. ☎ **74/81-1380** or 74/81-0470. Reservations recommended on weekends. Main courses $11–$30. Mon–Fri 1:30–5pm; daily 7–11:30pm. INTERNATIONAL.

For original food with a flair, you can't beat this trendy new restaurant in the Las Brisas area, next to Kookaburas. Diners (in cool attire that's on the dressy side of casual) can enjoy the air-conditioning indoors or the completely open rooftop terrace, with its sweeping view of the bay. To begin, try the shrimp Spicey, in a fresh coconut batter with an orange marmalade and mustard sauce. Among the main courses, the grilled veal chop in pineapple and papaya chutney is a good choice, as is the beef tenderloin—prepared with the flavors of Thailand, or Santa Fe–style, or blackened a la Louisiana. The chiles rellenos in mango sauce win raves.

Expensive

✪ Madeiras

Carretera Escénica 33. ☎ **74/84-4378.** Reservations required. Fixed-price dinner $28. Daily 7–11pm (two seatings: 7–8:30pm and 9–11pm). MEXICAN/CONTINENTAL.

Enjoy an elegant meal and a fabulous view of glittering Acapulco Bay at night at Madeiras, east of town on the scenic highway before the Las Brisas Hotel. The several small dining areas have ceiling fans and are open to the evening breezes. If you arrive before your table is ready, have a drink in the comfortable lounge. Selections might include roast quail stuffed with tropical fruits; or fish cooked in orange sauce. There are such old favorites as filet mignon, beef Stroganoff, and frogs' legs in garlic and white wine. Wines are reasonably priced if you stick to the Mexican labels.

THE CONVENTION CENTER/NAVAL BASE AREA

Moderate

✪ Bambuco's

Hotel Elcano, Costera Alemán 75. ☎ **74/84-1950.** Breakfast $2.50–$5.50; main courses $6–$14; daily specials $14. Daily 7am–11pm. INTERNATIONAL/SEAFOOD.

You can't beat this hotel restaurant for dining in stylish surroundings by the palm-filled beach—ocean sounds lull you into an afternoon of lingering over dessert or more margaritas. Appetizers include fried calamari that's plenty for three people. Daily specials might include lamb with apples and salad, and the house specialty of charbroiled fish with a selection of sauces is always available. Of course there are sandwiches too. At breakfast it's hard to avoid the waffles stuffed with fruit and nuts, or hotcakes with apples in a vanilla sauce. It's on the beach side of the Costera, almost opposite but slightly north of the Convention Center.

✪ Su Casa/La Margarita

Av. Anahuac 110. ☎ **74/84-4350** or 74/84-1261. Reservations recommended. Main courses $8–$18. Daily 6pm–midnight. INTERNATIONAL.

Relaxed elegance and terrific food at moderate prices are what you get at Su Casa (Your House), one of the most delightful restaurants for dining on some of the best food in the city. Owners Shelly and Angel Herrera created this pleasantly breezy open-air restaurant on the patio of their hillside home overlooking the entire city. Both are experts in the kitchen, and both are on hand nightly to greet guests to their patio. The menu changes often, so each time you go there's something new to try—ask about off-the-menu specials. But some things are standard, such as the unusual chile con carne, which is served both as a main dish and as an appetizer. Shrimp a la patrona in garlic; grilled fish, steak, and chicken; and flaming filet al Madrazo, a delightful brochette marinated in tropical juices, are also served daily. Most entrees come with refreshing garnishes of cooked banana or pineapple, and often a baked potato or rice. The margaritas are big and delicious. Su Casa is the hot pink building on the hillside above the Convention Center.

THE COSTERA: ICACOS BEACH TO PAPAGAYO PARK
Very Expensive
✪ Suntory

Costera Alemán at Maury. ☎ **74/84-8088** or 74/84-8766. Reservations recommended. Suntory course $12; Midori course $20; Imperial course $40; sushi plates $11–$25; a la carte meals $8–$35. Daily 2pm–midnight. JAPANESE.

For a refreshingly cool and serene respite from Acapulco's heat, sand, and zooming Costera, try this touch of Japan in Mexico. Though prices are expensive, the food is outstanding. The extensive menu includes the Suntory course, a teppanyaki with a choice of U.S. rib eye, chicken, or fish, all with vegetables, crisp salad, a small bowl of soup, and a heaping main platter (bring a big appetite), most of which is cooked at your table. The more expensive Midori course includes much of the Suntory course plus an appetizer, pickled vegetables, and dessert. The extensive Imperial course, for which you'll need a huge appetite, incorporates those items already mentioned but with shrimp salad, lobster soup, and a teppanyaki that includes lobster, and fresh fruit. The à la carte menu includes grilled and fried main courses, tempuras, and sushi. The delicious sushi platters come with between 16 and 22 beautifully prepared and presented pieces, and include a glass of wine and misoshiro soup; either platter is enough for two or three people to share. Drinks to try besides the traditional hot or cold sake include the jarra Suntory, a mixture of white wine with mango and peach flavorings, and Midori, a melon-based liqueur. There's also a full list of imported and domestic wines and liquors. Highly recommended.

Expensive
✪ Dino's

Costera Alemán .s/n. ☎ **74/84-0037.** Reservations recommended. Main courses $10–$20. Daily 4pm–midnight. (May be closed in low season.) NORTHERN ITALIAN.

A popular dining spot for years, Dino's continues with its combination of good food and service at respectable prices. Plus from its second story dining room there's a modest bay view between high-rise hotels. The restaurant is famous for its fettuccine Alfredo and waiters prepare it with fanfare, often tableside. Other main courses include broiled seafood and steak, all of which come with a baked potato, vegetables, and Dino's special fresh-baked bread. It's on the landward side of the Costera beside the Hotel Tortuga.

El Olvido

Diana Circle, Centro Marbello. ☎ **74/81-0203** or 74/81-0256. Main course $15–$45. Daily 7pm–2am. NOUVELLE MEXICAN.

Once past the front door of this handsome terrace restaurant, you'll almost forget that it's tucked back in a shopping mall—you have all the glittering bay-view ambiance of the posh Las Brisas restaurants, without the taxi ride. The menu is one of the most sophisticated in the city. It's expensive, but each dish is delightful not only in looks but in taste. Start with one of the 12 house specialty drinks such as Olvido: a tequila, rum, contreau, tomato and lime juice mixture. Soups include a delicious cold melon soup and thick black-bean soup with sausage. Among the innovative entrees is quail with honey and pasilla chiles; the thick sea bass comes on a mild sauce of cilantro and avacado. For dessert try the chocolate fondue or the guanabana mousse in a rich zapote negro sauce.

El Olvido is in the shopping center fronted by Aca-Joe clothing store on the Diana Circle. Walk into the passage to the left of Aca-Joe and bear left; it's at the far back.

Moderate

El Cabrito

Costera Alemán 1480. ☎ **74/84-7711.** Breakfast $3–$5; main courses $4–$8. Daily 8am–1am. NORTHERN MEXICAN.

With its arched adobe decor, waitresses in embroidered dresses, and location in the heart of the Costera, this restaurant is aimed at the tourist trade. But its authentic and well-prepared specialties attract Mexicans in the know—a stamp of approval I find comforting. Among its specialties are *cabrito al pastor* (roasted goat), charro beans, northern-style steaks, and burritos de machaca. Regional specialties from other areas include Jalisco-style birria and Oaxaca-style mole. Dine inside or outside on the patio facing the Costera. It's on the ocean side of the Costera opposite the Hard Rock Cafe, and south of the Convention Center.

Italianissimo

Diana Circle, Costera Alemán. ☎ **74/84-0052.** Main courses $5–$11. Daily noon–midnight. ITALIAN.

This restaurant's new location, beside/behind the Aca-Joe clothing store at the Diana traffic circle, is easy to miss if you don't know it's there. This branch has air-conditioning and cool gray-marble floors in an Italian-style decor. The restaurant makes dishes with pizzazz—try the scampi Stroganoff with vodka sauce. The pastas are homemade. For appetizers, try the Caesar salad or heavenly mussels in white-wine sauce. Dessert includes Irish coffee and chocolate cake.

✪ Restaurant Cocula

Costera Alemán 10. ☎ **74/84-5079.** Breakfast $3–$5; main courses $3–$9. Daily 7am–1am; happy hour 6pm until closing. MEXICAN.

You can dine on the patio out front or on one of the two levels of terraces. Appetizers include guacamole, black-bean soup, and watercress salad. Grilled meats are the specialty, and you can choose from among red snapper, shrimp, broiled chicken, quail, spiced pork sausage, ribs, shish kebab, and mixed grill. The restaurant is on the inland side of the east end of the Costera, across from Acapulco 2000.

Sanborn's

Costera at Condesa Beach near the El Presidente Hotel. ☎ **74/84-4465.** Breakfast $3.50–$5; main courses $3.50–$10. Daily 7:30am–11pm. AMERICAN/MEXICAN.

The best of the American-style restaurants, Sanborn's offers a cool dining area. Reminiscent of upscale dining rooms of the 1950s, it features American colonial decor, brass light fixtures, and well-padded booths. It's especially good for breakfast, though it also has good enchiladas, club sandwiches, burgers, sincronizadas (ham and cheese melted between corn tortillas), pastas, and fancier fare such as fish and steaks. Beer, wine, and cocktails are served. For an inexpensive snack, buy pastries to go at the store's bakery. Upstairs are clean bathrooms. You'll find this branch two blocks east of the zócalo on the Costera.

Another Sanborn's is in Old Acapulco near the zócalo at Costera Alemán and Escudero, and yet another is on Costera Miguel Alemán in the new shopping complex Oceano 2000, just north of the Hyatt Regency.

Inexpensive

Antojitos Mayab

Alemán 151. No phone. Main courses $2–$5; comida corrida $3. Daily noon–midnight (comida corrida served noon–5pm). YUCATECAN.

A cool, clean little eatery, this place has carved its own niche among Acapulco's quick-food places, offering a few specialties from the Yucatán area. Nowhere else in town will you find tacos filled with *cochinta pibil* or *escabiche,* in addition to the usual fillings of chicken or shrimp. *Antojitos* include turkey *panuchos* (a small flat corn-cake topped with turkey, onions, beans, and cheese), empanadas, and tostadas. Yucatecan tamales are served after 5pm. You'll find this restaurant opposite the new blue La Gran Plaza shopping center, next to McDonald's and half a block from the Ritz Hotel.

100% Natural

Costera Alemán at Yucatán. ☎ 74/84-4462. Breakfast $2–$3.50; main courses $3–$6; fruit and vegetable drinks $1.75–$2.50; sandwiches $2.50–$4. Daily 7am–11pm. MEXICAN/ VEGETARIAN.

You'll see branches of 100% Natural in just about every area of Acapulco, some with green awnings and others with yellow. Those with green signs are actually rival chains of those with yellow signs, but their menus are quite similar. They both feature soups, salads, sandwiches, fruit, yogurt, shakes, and pasta dishes that please vegetarians and carnivores alike. Although each restaurant is part of a franchise, they're individually owned, so the hours vary; some stay open 24 hours. This branch is on the east end of the Costera between the Romano Days Inn and the Magic Disco.

Restaurant Fersato's

Costera Alemán 44. ☎ 74/84-3949. Breakfast $2.50–$4; main courses $3–$8. Daily 7am–midnight; happy hour 7–10pm. MEXICAN.

The big dining room at Fersato's, beneath the tile roof and stone arches, is decorated with colorfully clad tables. There's an extensive menu of authentic Mexican food, plus seafood, chicken, and steak. Try the mole, the black beans, or the mixiotes with chicken or lamb wrapped in maguey leaves. The restaurant is on the inland side of the Costera across from the State of Guerrero Cultural Center, CICI, and the Acapulco Dolphins Hotel.

La Tortuga

Lomas del Mar 5. ☎ 74/84-6985. Main courses $3.50–$7. Daily 10am–1am. MEXICAN.

This small, congenial outdoor restaurant with cloth-covered tables occupies two greenery-filled terraces shaded by enormous mango trees. The extensive menu offers a good sampling of food from several Mexican regions, such as Oaxaca tamales, chicken mixiotes, and tortilla soup. Specialties include shrimp-filled crêpes and the Tortuga combination, which has grilled meat, tostadas, enchiladas, stuffed peppers, guacamole, beans, and chips. You can also select from one of the 13 kinds of tortas.

To find this place, walk half a block inland from the Costera at the corner of Lomas del Mar and across from the Hotel Torre de Acapulco, which is next door to the better-known El Presidente.

DOWNTOWN: THE ZÓCALO AREA

The old downtown area of Acapulco is packed with simple, inexpensive eateries serving up tasty food. It's easy to pay more elsewhere in Acapulco and not get such consistently good food as what you'll find at the restaurants in this part of town. To explore this area, start right at the zócalo and stroll west along Juárez. After about three blocks you'll come to Azueta, lined with small seafood cafes and streetside stands.

Moderate

✪ Mariscos Pipo

Almirante Breton 3. ☎ **74/83-8801** or 74/82-2237. Main courses $3–$11. Daily 11am–8pm. SEAFOOD.

Diners can look at photographs of Old Acapulco on the walls while sitting in the airy dining room of this place, decorated with hanging nets, fish, glass buoys, and shell lanterns. The English-language menu lists a wide array of seafood, including ceviche, lobster, octopus, crayfish, and baby-shark quesadillas. This local favorite is five blocks west of the zócalo on Breton, just off the Costera, behind the large curved building boasting in sky-high green letters EDIFÍCIO STIBADORES. Another branch, open daily from 1 to 9pm, is at Costera M. Alemán and Canadá (☎ **74/84-0165**).

Inexpensive

✪ Cafe Los Amigos

Av. de la Paz 10 at Ignacio Ramirez. Breakfast $2.50; sandwiches $1.50–$3; fresh fruit drinks $1.25; daily specials $3–$4. MEXICAN/INTERNATIONAL.

With umbrella-covered tables set out on one of the coolest and shadiest sections of the zócalo, this little restaurant gets my vote for the best breakfast in town. Breakfast specials include a great fresh fruit salad with mango, pineapple, and cantaloupe and free coffee refills. Other specials include fish fingers, empanadas, breaded chicken, and burgers and fries. Fruit drinks, including fresh mango juice, come in schooners. To find the restaurant, enter the zócalo from the Costera and walk toward the kiosk. On the left, about midway into the zócalo, you'll see a wide, shady passageway that leads onto Avenida de la Paz and the umbrella-covered tables under the huge shady tree.

✪ El Amigo Miguel

Juárez 31, at Azueta. ☎ **74/83-6981**. Main courses $3–$6. Daily 10:30am–9:30pm. MEXICAN/SEAFOOD.

Locals all know that El Amigo Miguel is a standout among downtown seafood restaurants—you can easily pay more but not eat any better elsewhere. Fresh seafood is king here and the large open-air dining room, three blocks west of the zócalo, is usually brimming with seafood lovers. Try the delicous *camarones borracho* (drunken shrimp) in a delicious sauce made with beer, applesauce, ketchup, mustard, and bits of fresh bacon—yet it tastes nothing like the ingredients. The filete Miguel is a red snapper filet stuffed with seafood and covered in a wonderful poblano pepper sauce. To accommodate the crowds, El Amigo II is open directly across the street.

La Granja del Pingue

Juárez 10. ☎ **74/83-5339**. Breakfast $2.50; main courses $2–$4; lunch special $3.50. Daily 7am–10pm. ECLECTIC/PASTRIES/ICE CREAM.

This restaurant is housed in one of the few remaining original Acapulco buildings. The eclectic menu includes burgers and fries, Tex-Mex chili, and a lunch special usually in the American home-cooking genre. It also claims to have the best coffee in town, with free refills. The dining area, an attractive shaded patio hung with piñatas, is prime gathering ground for foreigners in town and a great place to exchange paperbacks. This place is two blocks west of the zócalo.

San Carlos
Juárez 5. ☎ **74/82-6459.** Breakfast special $2; main courses $2.50–$4; comida corrida $2. Daily 7:30am–11pm (comida corrida served 1–6pm.) MEXICAN.

Western-style food such as charbroiled chicken and fish is served at chuck-wagon prices on the front patio of this place or in its open, fan-cooled dining room. Colorful tablecloths brighten this cheery cafe a few steps west of the zócalo. On Sunday one of the many specialties is chicken mole. There are at least 11 main-course choices for the comida corrida.

CALETA/CALETILLA BEACH AREA

The area around Caleta and Caletilla beaches used to be rather down-at-the-heels, but not long ago the municipal authorities pumped lots of money into public facilities here. Now the beaches have nice shady palapas, clean sand, and fine palm trees. Three buildings have been built to house *vestidores* and *regarderas* (changing rooms, showers, and lockers) and restaurants.

Little dining places line the outer periphery of the buildings. To find a good meal, wander along the rows of restaurants, looking for busy spots where people are eating (*not* just sipping drinks). Study menus, which will either be displayed or handed to you on request. Although the restaurants may tend to look all the same, you'll be surprised at the differences in price. *Filet de pescado* (fish filet) might be $4 at one place and twice as much at another; beer can cost anywhere from $1 to $2. Some places offer inexpensive fixed-price meals for around $2 to $3.

DINING WITH A VIEW

Among the pleasures of vacationing in Acapulco is dining with a fabulous view of the city spread out before you. Good places for this include **Madeiras** and **Restaurant Miramar,** both in the Las Brisas area; **Bambuco** at the Hotel Elcano; **Su Casa** on a hill above the Convention Center; **La Bahía Restaurant** at the Sheraton Hotel; and the **Bella Vista Restaurant** (now open to the public) at the Hotel Las Brisas.

ACAPULCO AFTER DARK
SPECIAL ATTRACTIONS

The **"Gran Noche Mexicana"** given by the **Acapulco Ballet Folklórico** is held in the plaza of the Convention Center every Tuesday, Thursday, and Saturday night at 8pm. With dinner and open bar the show costs $45; general admission (including three drinks) is $20. Call for reservations (☎ **74/84-7050**) or consult a local travel agency.

Another excellent **Mexican fiesta/folkloric dance show,** which includes *voladores* (flying pole dancers) from Papantla, is held at Marbella Plaza near the Continental Plaza Hotel on the Costera on Monday, Wednesday, and Friday at 7pm. The $35 fee covers the show, buffet, open bar, taxes, and gratuities. Make reservations through a travel agency.

Many major hotels also host Mexican fiestas and other theme nights that include dinner and entertainment. Consult a travel agency for information.

NIGHTCLUBS & DISCOS

Acapulco is more famous for its nightclubs than for its beaches. The problem is that the clubs open and close with shocking regularity, making it very difficult to give specific recommendations that will remain accurate. Some general tips will help. Every club seems to have a cover charge of around $20 in high season, $10 in low season, and drinks can cost anywhere from $2.50 to $7.

Many periodically waive their cover charge or offer some other promotion to attract customers. Another trend is to have a high cover charge with an open bar. For more information, call the disco or look for promotional material around hotel reception areas, at travel desks or concierge booths, and in local publications. A sign announcing the coming of **Planet Hollywood** was plastered on a wall next to the Hard Rock Cafe, so look for yet another lively place to be open when you are there.

In addition, the high-rise hotels have their own bars and sometimes discos. Informal lobby or poolside cocktail bars often offer live entertainment to enjoy for the price of drinks.

Note: When the managers of local discos say no shorts, they mean no shorts for men; they welcome women in them.

Acapulco also has its own spectacular cultural and Convention Center, the **Centro Acapulco,** on the eastern reaches of the bay between Condesa and Icacos beaches. Within the modern center are several forms of entertainment, including a mariachi bar, a piano bar, a disco, a movie theater, a live theater, a cafe, a nightclub, several restaurants, and outdoor performance areas.

Afro Antillanos
Costera Alemán at Cuando la Cosa 32. ☎ **74/84-7235.** Cover $15–$20.

Live tropical salsa music is the specialty of the house at this relatively new disco not far from the Continental Plaza Hotel. Shorts are a no-no. It's open nightly from 9:30pm to 4am; open bar closes at 3am.

Baby-O
Costera Alemán. ☎ **74/84-7474.** Cover $15–$20.

Baby-O's can be very selective about who they let in when it's crowded. Your chances of getting in here increase greatly if you're young, pretty, and female. Your next best shot is to be older, affluent looking, and male. Across from the Romano Days Inn, this intimate disco has a small dance floor surrounded by several tiers of tables and sculpted, cavelike walls. It even has a hot tub and breakfast area. Drinks run $4 to $5.

Carlos 'n' Charlie's
Costera Alemán 999. ☎ **74/84-1285** or 74/84-0039. Nightly 6:30pm–midnight.

For fun, high-decibel music (you can't talk above it) plus good food, you can't go wrong with this branch of the Carlos Anderson chain. It's always packed, an indication that people like what they get for the price they pay. Come early and get a seat on the terrace overlooking the Costera. It's east of the Diana traffic circle and across the street from the El Presidente Hotel and the Fiesta Americana Condesa.

Extravaganzza
Carretera Escénica. ☎ **74/84-7154** or 74/84-7164. Cover $15–$20.

If you have something trendy and dressy to wear, you might venture into this snazzy neo-deco chrome-and-neon extravaganza, perched on the side of the mountain between Los Rancheros Restaurant and La Vista Shopping Center. You can't miss the neon lights. The plush, dimly lit interior dazzles patrons with a sunken dance floor and panoramic view of Acapulco Bay. The door attendants wear tuxedos, so don't expect to get in wearing shorts, jeans, T-shirts, sneakers, or sandals. It opens nightly at 10:30pm; fireworks blast off at 3am. Call to find out if reservations are needed. National (as opposed to imported) drinks run $5 to $6.

Fantasy

Carretera Escénica. ☎ **74/84-6727** or 74/84-6764. Cover $15–$20.

This club has a fantastic bay view and sometimes waives the cover charge as a promotion. Periodically during the evening it puts on a good show with green lasers, which it also shoots out across the bay. The dress code does not permit shorts, jeans, T-shirts, or sandals. Reservations are recommended. Located in the La Vista Shopping Center, it's open nightly 10:30pm to 4am. Drinks go for $6.

Hard Rock Cafe

Costera Alemán 37. ☎ **74/84-0077.** Cover for live music. Daily noon–2am; live music Wed–Mon 11:30pm–1:30am.

If you like your music loud and your food trendy, dip into this cool and interestingly decorated place. The decor is a combination of nostalgia and museum, all with a modern twist. Elvis memorabilia greets you in the entry area, and among the other numerous framed or encased mementos is the Beatles' gold record for "Can't Buy Me Love." Naturally there's a bandstand for the live music and a small dance floor. It's on the seaward side towards the southern end of the Costera, south of the Convention Center and opposite El Cabrito.

News

Costera Alemán. ☎ **74/84-5902.** Cover (including open bar) $15–20.

The booths and love seats ringing the vast dance floor can seat 1,200, so this disco can double as a concert hall. But while high-tech in style, News is laid-back and user-friendly. It doesn't even have a dress code! Across the street from the Hyatt Regency, it opens at 10:30pm nightly.

3 Puerto Escondido

230 miles SE of Acapulco, 150 miles NW of Salina Cruz, 50 miles NW of Puerto Angel

Puerto Escondido (*pwer*-toe es-con-*dee*-do) translates to "Hidden Port"; although this town of 50,000 has been "discovered," touristic development here hasn't yet transformed it. Anyone who wandered into Acapulco half a century ago might have found a similar scene and a similar ambiance. So catch Puerto Escondido before it's gone forever. The lush palm-lined beach off the town center is one of the most beautiful in the country, with colorful boats pulled up on the sand—it makes for the kind of scene long since gone from more developed resorts.

When looking out on the Bahía Principal and its beach, you'll see to your left the eastern end of the bay, consisting of a small beach, Playa Marinero, followed by rocks jutting into the sea. Beyond this is Playa Zicatela, which attracts surfers like a magnet. By way of contrast, the western side of the bay, to your right, is about a mile long with low green hills (and a lighthouse) descending to meet a long stretch of fine sand. The coastline is slowly being developed. Where there was once nothing, Zicatela Beach now has restaurants, bungalows, surf shops, and hotels, although the construction there is well back from the shoreline. Westward, the beaches are not quite as accessible by land, but hotels are overcoming this by constructing beach clubs reached by steep private roads and jeep shuttles.

Laziness is a state of mind here—sipping a cool bottle of something refreshing, feeling the sea breeze, watching the pelicans soar and wheel and then come down to race across the surface of the water. Duck into a fan-cooled restaurant by day or return in the cool evening and find informal groups discussing the day's events.

ESSENTIALS
GETTING THERE & DEPARTING

BY PLANE **AeroMorelos** has several daily flights between Oaxaca and Puerto Escondido flying a 40-passenger turboprop. **Aerovega** also serves the route to and from Oaxaca with one, and sometimes two daily morning flights using a five-passenger AeroCommander. Tickets for both these lines are handled by Turismo Rodimar (see below). **Mexicana** (☎ 958/2-0098) flies from Mexico City to Puerto Escondido five days per week.

If space on flights to Puerto Escondido is booked solid, you have the option of flying Aeroméxico into the Huatulco airport six days per week. This is an especially viable option if your destination is Puerto Angel, which lies between Puerto Escondido and Huatulco but is closer to the Huatulco airport. There is frequent bus service between the three destinations.

Aerotransportes Terrestres sells colectivo transportation tickets for travel to the airport through **Turismo Rodimar** near the east end of the pedestrians-only zone (☎ **958/2-0734** or ☎/fax 958/2-0737). The price is $2.25 one way and includes pickup at your hotel.

BY BUS Buses are frequent between Acapulco, Oaxaca, and south along the coast to and from Huatulco and Pochutla, the transit hub for Puerto Angel. Puerto Escondido's several bus stations are all within a three-block area. For **Gacela** and **Estrella Blanca,** the station is just north of the coastal highway where Perez Gasga crosses it. First-class buses go from here to Pochutla and Huatulco hourly, and almost hourly to Acapulco and Zihuatanejo. Five daily direct buses with assigned seats go to Acapulco, one to Zihuatanejo and two to Mexico City. The most comfortable bus to Mexico City (12 hours) is the deluxe Futuro de Lujo bus leaving at 7 and 10pm.

A block north at Hidalgo and Primera Poniente is **Transportes Oaxaca Istmo.** The office is in a small restaurant. Several buses daily leave for Pochutla (1 hour), Salina Cruz (5 hours), or Oaxaca (10 hours via Salina Cruz). **Autotransportes Turisticas** has twice daily first-class service to Oaxaca, via Pochutla (7 hours). The terminal for **Lineas Unidas, Estrella del Valle,** and **Oaxaca Pacífico** is two blocks farther down on Hidalgo, just past 3rd Oriente. All buses go to Oaxaca via Pochutla; four are *ordinario* and three are *directo* buses, leaving at 8:15am, and 10:15 and 10:45pm.

Cristóbal Colón buses, Primera Norte 207, serve Salina Cruz, Tuxtla Gutiérrez, and San Cristóbal de las Casas. They also have two first-class buses to Oaxaca at 4 and 9pm, via Salina Cruz, where you can enjoy an air-conditioned waiting room.

BY CAR From Oaxaca, Highway 175 via Pochutla is the least bumpy road. The 150-mile trip takes 5 to 6 hours. Highway 200 from Acapulco is also a good road. Don't attempt to come from Oaxaca via Zimatlán—about 100 miles of it is unpaved and in poor condition.

From Salina Cruz to Puerto Escondido is a 4-hour drive, past the Bahías de Huatulco and the turnoff for Puerto Angel. The road is paved but can be rutty in the rainy season.

ORIENTATION

ARRIVING The airport is about $2\frac{1}{2}$ miles from the center of town near Playa Bacocho. Prices for the Aerotransportes Terrestres minibus to hotels are posted: $3.25

per person. Arriving by bus, you will be deposited at one of the terminals described above. Minibuses from Pochutla or Huatulco will let you off anywhere en route, including the spot where Perez Gasga leads down to the pedestrians-only zone.

INFORMATION   The **State Tourist Office, SEDETUR** (☎ **958/2-0175**), is about a half mile from the airport, at the corner of Carretera Costera and Bulevar Benito Juárez. It's open Monday through Friday from 9am to 2pm and 5 to 8pm and Saturday from 10am to 1pm. A kiosk at the airport is open for incoming flights, and another, near the west end of the paved tourist zone is open Monday through Saturday from 9am to 2pm and 5 to 8pm.

CITY LAYOUT   Puerto Escondido is oriented roughly east-to-west, with the long Zicatela Beach turning sharply southeast. Residential areas lying behind (east of) Zicatela Beach tend to have unpaved streets, while the older town (with paved streets) lies north of the Carretera Costera (Hwy. 200). The town streets were recently numbered, with Avenida Oaxaca the dividing line between east (*oriente*) and west (*poniente*), and Avenida Hidalgo the divider between north (*norte*) and south (*sur*). Formerly they were named after historic dates and famous people. But the streets are not marked, so finding your way involves a bit of guesswork and asking directions.

South of this is the tourist zone, through which Avenida Perez Gasga makes a loop. Part of this loop is a paved pedestrian-only zone (or PZ) along which are found many hotels, shops, restaurants, travel agencies, and other services. Actually, in the morning, taxis, delivery trucks, and private vehicles are allowed. But at noon it becomes a closed zone, and chains are fastened at each end. However, motorbikes and bicycles get in, so don't become complacent.

Avenida Perez Gasga angles down from the highway at the east end, and on the west, where the PZ terminates, it climbs in a wide northward curve to cross the highway, after which it becomes Avenida Oaxaca.

The **beaches,** Playa Principal in the center of town and Marinero and Zicatela, southeast of the town center, are interconnected and it's easy to walk from one to the other, crossing behind the separating rocks. Puerto Angelito, Carrizalillo, and Bacocho beaches are west of town and can be reached by road or boat. Surfers find Zicatela Beach's big curling waves are the best for board surfing. Playa Bacocho hosts most of the expensive hotels.

GETTING AROUND   Almost everything is within walking distance of the pedestrian-only zone. Taxis cost no more than $1.50 to $4.50 to beaches or anywhere in town. Mountain bikes ($9/day or $2.25/hour) and Honda motor bikes ($33.50/day or $7.75/hour) can be rented at Mango Club, Av. Perez Gasga 605-E, on your right just as you enter the PZ on the east. For intrepid walkers, it is now possible to walk beside the sea from the Playa Principal to the tiny beach of Puerto Angelito. However, I recommend the hike only for the hardy because it's rather arduous and the sun beats down unrelentingly. Carry water and wear a hat!

FAST FACTS: PUERTO ESCONDIDO

Area Code   The telephone area code is 958.

Currency Exchange   Near the middle of the PZ is a money-exchange office, Puerto Bahias, open Monday through Saturday from 9am to 2pm and 5 to 8pm.

Safety   Crime in Puerto Escondido is on the rise, and beach muggings are common even in broad daylight. Don't carry money or other valuables while walking on the beach, don't leave your belongings unattended on the beach, and be sure to deposit other valuables in a hotel safe. Positively do not take a midnight stroll down the deserted beach—even one in daylight is chancy. Above all respect the power of the waves and undertow. Drownings occur all too frequently.

Seasons   Seasons vary from business to business. Most, however, consider high season to be mid-December through January, then again before, during, and after Easter week. A third high season occurs in July and August, during school and business vacations.

Telephone   There are numerous businesses offering long-distance telephone service, and several offer credit card convenience. One is several doors west of the Hotel Las Palmas (near the center of the PZ) and is open daily from 9am to 10pm. Another is at the west end of the PZ (beach side) and is open daily from 7:30am to 10pm.

FUN AT THE BEACH
BEACHES

Playa Principal and Playa Marinero, both adjacent to the town center and on a deep bay, are the best swimming beaches. Zicatela beach adjoins Playa Marinero and extends southeasterly for several miles. The surfing part of Zicatela, with large curling waves, is about 1¹/₂ miles from the town center.

Barter with one of the fishermen on the main beach for a ride to **Puerto Angelito** and other small coves just west of town, where the swimming is safe and the pace decidedly calmer than in town. Both places have palapas and hammock rentals for $1 per day. Both also boast clear blue water excellent for snorkeling and can provide equipment. After you've worked up an appetite, enjoy fresh fish, tamales, and other Mexican dishes cooked right at the beach by local entrepreneurs. **Playa Bacocho** is on a shallow cove farther to the northwest and is best reached by taxi or boat rather than walking.

Warning: Swimming at a beach that fronts on open sea is a risk to your life. The waves (and undertow) are unpredictable—you're floating peacefully in shoulder-deep water when suddenly the water sinks to knee level and before you can blink it's crashing over your head. Don't follow the surfers' examples; they have surfboards to cling to, and they know waves and tides. Despite big warning signs, there are several drownings every year. Swim at the beach in town or at other sheltered beaches in bays and coves.

SURFING

Zicatela Beach, 1¹/₂ miles southeast of Puerto Escondido's town center, is a world-class surf spot. A **surfing competition** in August, and **Fiesta Puerto Escondido,** held for at least 10 days each November, feature Puerto Escondido's well-known surfing waves. The tourism office can supply exact dates and details. It's also prime territory for muggers—so don't take much money or any valuables with you to this beach.

SEEING NESTING RIDLEY TURTLES

The beaches around Puerto Escondido and Puerto Angel are nesting grounds for the endangered ridley turtle. Tourists can sometimes see the turtles laying eggs or observe the hatchlings trekking to the sea.

Escobilla beach near Puerto Escondido and another near Barra de la Cruz beach near Puerto Angel seem to be favored among other nesting grounds for ridley turtles. Furthermore, in 1991 the Mexican government established the **Centro Mexicano la Tortuga,** known locally as the Turtle Museum, for the study and life-enhancement of the turtle. Present are examples of all species of marine turtles living in Mexico, plus six species of freshwater turtles and two species of land turtles. The center is located on Mazunte Beach, near the town of the same name. Hours are 9am–5pm daily, and entry is $2.25. Buses go to Mazunte from Puerto Angel (50¢) about every half hour, and a taxi will take you there for $3.50 to $4.50. You can fit this in with a trip to Zipolite Beach, the next one closer to Puerto Angel.

Ecotours & Other Unusual Explorations

The **Turismo Rodimar Travel Agency,** on the landward side just inside the PZ (☎ **958/2-0734** or 958/2-0737; open daily 7:30am–10pm), is an excellent source of information and can arrange all types of tours and travel. Manager Gaudencio Díaz speaks English. He can arrange individualized tours or formal ones such as **Michael Malone's Hidden Voyages Ecotours.** Malone, a Canadian ornithologist, takes you on a dawn or sunset trip to **Manialtepec Lagoon,** a bird-filled mangrove lagoon about 12 miles northwest of Puerto Escondido. The cost is $25 to $30 and includes a stop on a secluded beach for a swim. Probably the best all-day tour is to **Chacahua Lagoon National Park** about 42 miles west at a cost of $30. These are true ecotours—small groups touching the environment lightly. You visit a beautiful sandy spit of beach, and the lagoon with incredible birdlife and flowers, including black orchids. Locals can provide fresh barbecued fish on the beach. If you know Spanish, and get information from the tourism office, it's possible to stay overnight under a small palapa, but bring plenty of insect repellent. If no agency-led tour is available, ask at the tourism office for the names of a couple of locals who also lead these trips.

An interesting and slightly out-of-the-ordinary endeavor is **Jorge Perez's Aventura Submarina,** located "on the strip" (Zicatela Beach, Calle del Morro s/n, in the Acuario building near the Cafecito; ☎ **958/2-1026**). Jorge, who speaks fluent English and is a certified scuba-dive instructor, guides individuals or small groups of qualified divers along the Coco trench, just offshore. He also arranges surface activities such as deep-sea fishing, surfing, trips to lesser-known yet nearby swimming beaches, and dirt-bike tours into the mountains. If you want to write ahead, contact him at Apdo. Postal 159, 71980 Puerto Escondido, Oaxaca.

Fishermen keep their colorful *pangas* (small boats) on the beach beside the PZ. A **fisherman's tour** around the coastline in his boat will cost about $35, but a ride to Zicatela or Puerto Angelito Beaches will cost only $3. Most hotels offer or will gladly arrange tours to meet your needs.

SHOPPING

The PZ sports a row of tourist shops selling straw hats, postcards, and Puerto Escondido T-shirts, plus a few stores featuring Guatemalan and Oaxacan clothing as well as art and souvenirs from various parts of the country. Interspersed among the hotels, restaurants, and shops are pharmacies and minimarkets selling basic necessities.

ACCOMMODATIONS

Note: Even the more expensive hotels have their share of mosquitos, so come armed with a small container of your favorite insect repellent.

MODERATE

✪ Hotel Santa Fe

Calle del Morro (Apdo. Postal 96), 71980 Puerto Escondido, Oax. ☎ **958/2-0170.** Fax 958/2-0260. 51 rms, 8 bungalows. A/C TEL. High season, $65 single; $75 double; $85 bungalow. Low season, $49 single; $56 double. Free parking.

This very good hotel is about half a mile southeast of the town center off Highway 200. It is located just where Marinero and Zicatela Beaches join, and overlooks a rock outcropping that's a prime sunset-watching spot. The hacienda-style buildings have tiled stairs and archways laden with blooming bougainvillea. The ample rooms have large tile baths, colonial furnishings, handwoven fabrics, Guerrero pottery lamps, and both air-conditioning and ceiling fans. There's a small pool in the central patio. Some rooms don't have telephones, but who are you going to call anyway? Bungalows are next to the hotel, and each comes equipped with a living room, a kitchen, and a bedroom with two double beds. Park in front of the hotel entrance.

Hotel Suites Villasol

Loma Bonita s/n, Fracc. Bacocho, 71980 Puerto Escondido, Oax. ☎ **958/2-0061.** Fax 958/ 2-0451. 72 rms, 24 junior suites, 12 suites. A/C TV TEL. High season, $65 single or double. Low season, $45 single or double.

Only 5 minutes from the airport and about the same from Puerto Escondido's tourist zone, this four-story hotel offers a great deal for the money. It's built around a large courtyard with a swimming pool and palapa bar/snack bar, restaurant, and bakery at ground level. All rooms open onto this courtyard. The nice-size standard rooms have one double and one single bed and moderate-size bathrooms. Although the hotel is away from the bluff on the top of the hill, a shuttle service whisks you either to town or to the beach club (on Bacocho Beach) where another restaurant and bar tends to your after-swim needs.

INEXPENSIVE

⑤ Castillo de los Reyes

Av. Perez Gasga s/n, 71980 Puerto Escondido, Oax. ☎ **958/2-0442.** 16 rms. FAN. High season, $11.50 single; $13 double. Low season, $10 single; $11.50 double.

Don Fernando, the proprietor at Castillo de los Reyes, has a gift for making his guests feel at home. Guests converse around tables on a shady patio near the office. Your white-walled room may have a special touch—perhaps a gourd mask or carved coconut hanging over the bed. There's hot water, and the rooms are shaded from the sun by aging palms. It's on your left as you go up the hill on Perez Gasga after leaving the pedestrian-only zone (you can also enter Perez Gasga off Hwy. 200).

✪ Hotel Flor de María

Playa Marinero, 71980 Puerto Escondido, Oax. ☎ and fax **958/2-0536.** 24 rms. FAN. $30 single; $35 double.

This is a real find. Canadians María and Lino Francato built their cheery three-story hotel facing the ocean, which you can see from the rooftop and common walkways linking rooms in the upper stories. Built around a garden courtyard, each room is colorfully decorated with beautiful trompe l'oeil still-lifes and landscapes painted by Lino, some of which are headboards. All rooms have windows facing the outdoors, double beds with orthopedic mattresses, and small safes. On the roof you'll find great views, a small pool, shaded hammock terrace, and an open-air bar (open 5–9pm) with evening happy-hour specials and a TV that receives American channels. This is a great place to be for sunset. The first floor restaurant is highly recommended (see María's Restaurant in "Dining," below). Ask about off-season discounts for long-term guests. The hotel is a third of a mile from the PZ and 200 feet up a sandy road from Marinero Beach on an unnamed street at the eastern end of the beach.

Hotel Las Palmas

Av. Perez Gasga s/n, 71980 Puerto Escondido, Oax. ☎ **958/2-0230** or 958/2-0303. 38 rms. FAN. High season, $20 single; $25 double. Low season, $15 single; $20 double.

This traditional favorite has an overgrown courtyard surrounded by a three-story U-shaped building in the center of the tourist zone facing the ocean and the beach.

Each nicely furnished room has a double and a twin bed covered with tasteful foot-loomed bedspreads and matching drapes. The windows and glass doors offer two choices: You either shut all the curtains for privacy (no natural light) or leave them open and have natural light but no privacy. The louvered windows are screenless. The best rooms are on the second and third floors, facing the sea. While the food isn't particularly outstanding, the hotel's beachfront restaurant location is a comfortable place to dawdle away the hours watching the beach scene. Beside the restaurant is a comfy shaded bar with lounge chairs where guests become engrossed in thick novels.

Hotel Loren
Av. Gasga 507, 71980 Puerto Escondido, Oax. ☎ **958/2-0057.** Fax 958/2-0591. 23 rms. FAN. High season, $25 single or double. Low season, $20 single or double. Free parking; enclosed.

This four-story hotel is tucked in a shady bend of Avenida Perez Gasga past the west end of the pedestrian-only zone (it can also be reached off Hwy. 200), around the corner from both the Hotel Nayar and the Hotel Paraío Escondido. It faces an open interior patio with an inviting pool. The best views are from small private balconies on the upper levels (no elevators). Rooms are immaculate but sparsely furnished, each with two double beds, a chair, and a table.

Hotel Nayar
Av. Gasga 407, 71980 Puerto Escondido, Oax. ☎ **958/2-0113** or 958/2-0319. Fax 958/2-0547. 41 rms. FAN TV. High season, $15 single; $19 double. Low season, $11 single; $15 double. Free parking.

Enter the Nayar via a cobbled drive shaded by enormous palms. There's parking for several cars along the entryway. On the left is a nice-size pool. This is an old-fashioned, rambling two-story hotel with clean but dated rooms, each with either one or two double beds or two twin beds. All have balconies, but only upper-story rooms have views. Fifteen rooms have air-conditioning ($5.50 extra). It's past the PZ, up the hill where Avenida Perez Gasga turns north.

Hotel Rincón del Pacífico
Av. Perez Gasga 900, 71980 Puerto Escondido, Oax. ☎ **958/2-0056.** Fax 958/2-0101. 28 rms, 5 suites. FAN. Year-round $25 double; $35–$40 suite.

This two-story, U-shaped hotel surrounds a patch of sand shaded by a few tremendous palms. It's opposite Bancomer, close to the center of the PZ and to the Hotel Las Palmas, facing the Pacific. In fact, the rooms are similar to those at Las Palmas, with a glass wall and doors, although the decor is from the 1960s. All except two rooms have a double and one twin bed. The suites have a living room, a minibar, air-conditioning, a TV, and a small patio overlooking the beach. The beach-level restaurant, Danny's Terrace, is open daily from 7am to 10pm, with two drinks for the price of one. Happy hour from 4 to 6pm.

Hotel San Juan
Felipe Merklin 503, 71980 Puerto Escondido, Oax. ☎ **958/2-0336** or 958/2-0518. Fax 958/2-0612. 26 rms. FAN. High season, $14.50 single; $18 double. Low season, $11.25 single; $14.50 double. Free parking; limited.

The San Juan is a good budget choice in the area, located at the top of the hill, just off Avenida Perez Gasga and near the Hotel Crucero. It's easy to get to as you come into town on the bus or by car, but the return trip on foot up the hill after a hot day at the beach is rough. A new restaurant (open only during the high season) has been added to the pretty patio on the right as you enter. The sparkling clean and bright but spare rooms have painted concrete floors. Each has either two double beds and one twin bed or a double and a twin bed, small closets, and windows with screens. Second- and third-floor rooms have fantastic views from the balcony walkway. *Note:* The hotel will not quote rates or make reservations by phone.

DINING
MODERATE

✪ Art & Harry's Bar and Grill
Av. Morro s/n. No phone. Seafood $2.25–$6.75; steaks $8–$11. Daily 10am–10pm. SEAFOOD/STEAKS.

Located about three-fourths of a mile southeast of the Hotel Santa Fe on the road fronting Zicatela Beach, this is the robust watering hole where the sun seems to go down in a more spectacular fashion if you are eating one of their monster shrimp cocktails, or savoring fork-tender pieces of budget- and diet-busting grilled beef. A few hours spent here in the late afternoon and early evening watching the surfers and tourists, the sun as it sinks, and the resident cat (no dogs allowed) will give you a sense of Puerto Escondido.

Nautilus
Av. Perez Gasga. No phone. Breakfast $1.75–$2.75; main courses $3.50–$9; comida corrida $5. Daily 8am–midnight. INTERNATIONAL/SEAFOOD.

Here at the west end of the pedestrian-only zone, you may hear exhilarating mariachi music, Billie Holiday, or Patsy Cline coming from the tape player. From the second-story dining room there's a fabulous bay view for watching fishermen and brown pelicans. Breakfast selections include German and continental dishes. Usually there are several tourist specials featuring soup through dessert in various price ranges. For splurge specialties, try huachinango or vegetarian dishes Hindu-style with fruit, wine, and curry. Pastas are more moderately priced, as well as chicken and a small selection of vegetarian dishes.

✪ Restaurant Santa Fe
In the Hotel Santa Fe, Calle del Morro s/n. ☎ **958/2-0170.** Breakfast $2–$4; main courses $4–$9. Daily 7am–10:30pm. INTERNATIONAL.

The atmosphere here is cool and breezy, with great views of the sunset and the waves on Zicatela Beach. The seafood dishes are a little expensive, but the vegetarian and pasta dishes are reasonably priced and creative, adapting traditional Mexican and Italian dishes. One of my favorites is the house specialty, chiles rellenos: mild green peppers stuffed with cheese, raisins, and nuts, baked in a mild red-chile sauce, and served with brown rice, beans, and salad. My other favorite is the tostada special—big crispy tortillas heaped high with beans, lettuce, cheese, avocado, and salsa. The restaurant is across the street from the beach about half a mile southeast of the town center.

Spaghetti House
Playa Principal. ☎ **958/2-0005.** Main courses $5–$7.25; pasta $3.25–$5; pizza $4.25–$11.25. Daily noon–11pm. ITALIAN.

This restaurant faces the beach and is open to great sea breezes and the sound of pounding rolling surf. Pasta runs the gamut from basic spaghetti napoletana to cannelloni and seafood fettuccine. Seven salads and seven varieties of pizza, plus an extensive bar list, ought to please most anyone. It is a couple of doors toward the beach at the eastern entry to the PZ.

INEXPENSIVE

Bananas

Av. Perez Gasga s/n. ☎ **958/2-0005.** Breakfast $1.75–$2.25; sandwiches $1.75–$3; breakfast buffet $2.75. Daily 7:30am–12:30am. MEXICAN.

You'll see this bamboo-and-thatch–roofed two-story restaurant/bar at the eastern entrance to the PZ. Breakfast includes fresh yogurt, crepes, and fresh-fruit drinks. A range of light appetizers includes quesadillas with potato or squash flowers, tacos, and stuffed tortillas. Happy hour is every night from 6 to 8pm, with live music in high season.

✪ Carmen's La Patisserie

Playa Marinero. ☎ **958/2-0005.** Pastries 50¢–$1.25; sandwiches $1.50–$2. Daily 7am–7pm. FRENCH PASTRY/SANDWICHES/COFFEE.

Dan and Carmen are the proprietors of this tiny-but-excellent cafe/bakery which has a steady and loyal clientele. Carmen's baked goods are positively unforgettable. By 8am on one weekday there was only one mango creme roll left, and other items were disappearing fast. The coffee, perhaps the best in town, has a flavor and fullness which keeps you asking for refills. Taped international music provides a soothing background, and a paperback exchange creates another reason to linger. Fruit, granola, and sandwiches (croissant or whole wheat) round out the menu. Dan and Carmen also provide space for an English-speaking AA group here.

La Patisserie is across the street from the Hotel Flor de María. A second shop, El Cafecito (open 6am) is on Zicatela Beach, near Bruno's Surf Shop. Surfers and observers gather here to critique each other.

✪ María's Restaurant

In the Hotel Flor de María, Playa Marinero. ☎ **958/2-0536.** Breakfast $2.25; main courses $3.50–$5.50. Daily, breakfast 8–11am; lunch noon–3pm; dinner 6–10pm. INTERNATIONAL.

Probably the best restaurant in Puerto Escondido, meals are served in the first-floor open-air dining room of this hotel near the beach. The menu changes daily and includes specials such as María Francato's homemade pasta dishes, the ingredients based on what's fresh that day. María's is a third of a mile from the PZ and 200 feet up a sandy road from Marinero Beach on an unnamed street at the eastern end of the beach.

Restaurant Alicia

Av. Perez Gasga. ☎ **958/2-0690.** Breakfast $1.50–$3.50; main courses $1.75–$4.50. Daily 8am–11pm. MEXICAN.

Here in the middle of the pedestrian-only zone, a few doors from the Hotel Las Palmas, is Puerto Escondido's honorary United Nations. Visitors from all over wait in line to enjoy the inexpensive meals and good service here. Decor is simple; half a dozen cloth-covered tables look onto Perez Gasga's passing scene. The menu is posted on a large board facing the street and features fish, chicken, and beef dishes as well as tacos and enchiladas served with small salads. Drink specialties are licuados and fruit milk shakes.

Taquería Fiord

Av. Perez Gasga. No phone. Tacos, quesadillas, and sandwiches $1.25–$3.50. High season, daily 7am–midnight. Low season, daily 3–11pm. MEXICAN.

Take a seat on a backless chair at one of the uncovered wooden tables here and try the food. Chances are you'll forget what the place looks like once you've tried an inexpensive taco de pollo on a whole-wheat tortilla with its generous portion of chicken, sliced onion, fresh cilantro, lime, and salsa. The restaurant is at the east end of the PZ, on the landward side.

PUERTO ESCONDIDO AFTER DARK

Sunset watching is a ritual you won't tire of since there are many good lookout points. Watch the surfers at Zicatela from the **Los Tres Osos restaurant** or mingle with them at **Art and Harry's Bar and Grill,** both about a quarter of the way down the beach near the end of current development. For another great sunset view, go to the **Hotel Santa Fe** at the junction of Zicatela and Marinero beaches or the rooftop bar of **Hotel Flor de María.** Dedicated sun worshipers might want to spring for a cab (about $1.75) or walk half an hour or so west to the **Hotel Posada Real,** overlooking Playa Bacocho. The hotel's cliff-top lawn is a perfect sunset-watching perch. Or you might climb down the cliff side (or take the hotel's shuttle bus) to the pool-and-restaurant complex on the beach below. The food isn't great, but the restaurant is an amazing sight, with an artificial tropical lagoon in the middle and leopard-skin swings at the bar.

There are several choices for after-dark entertainment in Puerto Escondido. **El Tubo** is an open-air beachside disco just west of Restaurant Alicia on the PZ. **Son y la Rumba** features live Latin music and dancing, across and up the hill from Las Palmas. **Cocos,** near the east end of the PZ, and **Tío Mac,** also near the east end, feature live music during high season and have happy hours from 6 to 8pm. Both the **Posada Real and Villa Sol,** on Bacocho Beach, have Beach Clubs where one can dance the night away. Most nightspots are open until 3am or until the customers leave.

4 Puerto Angel: Laid-Back Sun & Sand

Fifty miles southeast of Puerto Escondido and 30 miles northwest of the Bays of Huatulco is the tiny fishing port of Puerto Angel (*pwer*-toe on-*hel*). Once known only to a handful of vacationers who came here regularly (mostly from Mexico City and Oaxaca), today Puerto Angel, with its unpaved streets and budget hotels, is very popular with the international backpacking set and those looking for an inexpensive and restful vacation. A small, beautiful bay and several inlets provide peaceful swimming and good snorkeling, and the village's out-of-the-way position assures a sleepy, tranquil atmosphere. The population of Puerto Angel is listed as 15,000, but the figure is misleading because it includes the surrounding farming area. On any given day you'll see very few people in the village, and many of them are tourists. Fishermen leave very early in the morning and return with their catch by late afternoon. Taxis make up most of the traffic, although the bus from Pochutla passes every half hour or so.

ESSENTIALS
GETTING THERE & DEPARTING

There are no direct **buses** from Puerto Escondido or Huatulco to Puerto Angel; however, numerous buses leave Puerto Escondido and Huatulco for **Pochutla,** 7 miles north of Puerto Angel, where you can transfer for the short ride to the village. If you arrive at Pochutla from either Huatulco or Puerto Escondido, you may be dropped at one of several bus stations that line the main street; if so, walk one or two blocks toward the large sign reading POSADA DON JOSÉ. The buses to Puerto Angel are in the lot just before the sign. Ask for the "amarillos" buses (to Puerto Angel). That's what the locals call them—they're yellow—although the name of the line is Estrella del Valle. Estrella del Valle buses originating in Huatulco (about every hour, $1.50) drop passengers at their station in Pochutla. Buses depart from Pochutla for Puerto Angel every 20 or 30 minutes and cost 50¢. Pochutla has many taxis, and they will be glad to take you to Puerto Angel or Zipolite Beach for $3.50 to $4.50, or to the Huatulco airport ($18) or Puerto Escondido ($23).

The bus will let you off in Puerto Angel near the small market in the central part of town. The town center is only about four blocks long, oriented more or less east-to-west. There are few signs in the village giving directions, and off the main street much of Puerto Angel is a narrow sand-and-dirt path. The navy base is toward the far (west) end of town, just before the creek-crossing toward Playa Panteón (Cemetery Beach).

If you're traveling **by car,** take coastal Highway 175 to Puerto Angel.

ORIENTATION

Puerto Angel now has several **public telephones.** Primary of these is a TelMex office, just past the turnoff to La Buena Vista, and across from the Casa de Huespedes Anahi. It's open daily from 7am to 10pm. Their numbers are 958/4-3055 and 958/4-3063, and they will accept messages to be picked up (Spanish only). Another public long distance phone is available at the small restaurant next to Gambusino's Travel Agency and near the entrance to the Hotel Soraya. The office is open daily from 7pm to 10pm.

If you want to stash your luggage while you look for lodgings, Gambusino's Travel Agency offers **luggage storage** for $1.25 during their office hours (Mon–Sat 10:30am–2pm and 4–6pm). It's about half a block up the street opposite the pier.

The closest **bank** is Bancomer in Pochutla, which will change money Monday through Friday from 9 to 10:30am; however, it's not uncommon for it to run out of cash. It may be hard to change foreign currency with locals in Puerto Angel. Your best bet is simply to come with enough pesos for your stay.

The **post office** (*correo*), open Monday through Friday from 9am to 3:30pm, is on the curve as you enter town.

BEACHES, WATER SPORTS & BOAT TRIPS

The golden sands of Puerto Angel and the peaceful village life are the attractions here, so in the "where to soak" category let's begin with **Playa Principal** in the central village. You can't miss it, as the beach lies between the pier (from which the bulk of the local fishing fleet works) and the Mexican navy base. On one end near the pier, fishermen pull their colorful boats on the beach and unload their catch in the late morning while trucks wait to haul it off to processing plants in Veracruz. The rest of the beach is for enjoyment, and except on Mexican holidays, it's relatively deserted. It's important to note that Pacific coast currents deposit trash on Puerto Angel beaches. The townsfolk do a fairly good job of keeping it picked up, but those currents are constant.

Playa Panteón is the main **swimming** and **snorkeling** beach. It's about a 15-minute walk from the town center, straight through town on the main street that skirts the beach. Just before you reach Playa Panteón you pass the panteón (cemetery), on the right, for which the beach is named.

The 3.7 miles of paved road to the village of **Playa Zipolite** (See-*poh*-lee-teh) is walkable, albeit only for the hardy in the midday sun. Taxis charge around $4.50 for a single passenger (taxis are expensive here), or you can catch a taxi colectivo on the main street in the town center and share the cost. If you walk, the heat can sap the last bit of your energy, so at least wear a hat and, better still, carry drinking water.

Zipolite is a beach without protection from the open sea. Consequently, swimming can be very dangerous—*people die swimming here.* The dangerous currents attract rather than deter surfers, however; along the beach you'll find many surfers ensconced in hammocks under numerous palapas. Beyond a large rock outcropping at the far end of the beach is an area where nude bathing has been tolerated for several years. One caveat: Police could roust au naturel bathers at any time, as they are technically breaking the law. Even more serious is the possibility of drug busts. Mexican jails are more unpleasant than those in the United States. Remember, in Mexico you are under Mexican law. *Don't risk it!*

Hotels in Playa Zipolite are basic and rustic—most are made with crude walls and palapa roofs. Prices run from $10 to $35 a night with the highest prices being charged on Mexican holidays. Thefts from hotel rooms are not uncommon, and hotel operators sometimes band together to run off tourists who keep hanging around even though it's well known that they've run out of money.

Besides these beaches, there are others reachable primarily by boat. One of the pleasures of a lengthy stay in Puerto Angel is discovering these hidden beaches; taking a lunch and drinks and spending the day. Local boatmen can give details and quote rates for this service, or ask at your hotel.

In Playa Panteón some of the palapa restaurants and a few of the hotels rent **snorkeling** and **scuba** gear and can arrange **boat trips,** but it all tends to be quite expensive. Above all, be cautious about the gear—particularly scuba gear. Often the chaps who rent from the beach have rusted and worn equipment, and are hardly interested in either your capability or safety. One reliable boatman, **Mateo López,** at the Posada Cañon Devata (See "Where to Stay," below), will take you fishing or snorkeling. He emphasizes that aside from being a lifelong fisherman, he is also fully insured.

ACCOMMODATIONS

Two areas in Puerto Angel have accommodations: **Playa Principal** in the tiny town and **Playa Panteón,** the pretty beach area beyond the village center. The bus will let you out at either place—but in Playa Panteón you'll be stuck with your luggage while you look for lodging. A taxi to Playa Panteón from town is around $1.75.

Between Playa Panteón and town are numerous bungalow and guest-house setups with budget accommodations.

Most hotels now receive mail in Puerto Angel, although some still maintain a P.O. Box in Pochutla. During the high season—December, January, around Easter, and July and August—rates can go up and you should reserve well in advance.

✪ La Buena Vista

Apdo. Postal 48, 70902 Puerto Angel, Oax. ☎ and fax **958/4-3104.** 18 rms. FAN. $24 single; $29 double.

To find La Buena Vista, follow the road through town and shortly you'll see a sign on the right pointing to the hotel. It's on a hillside, so to get to the lobby/patio you follow the sign, taking a left at Casa de Huespedes Alex, after which you climb a formidable flight of stairs. This will take you to the lobby, where you'll discover why this hotel's name means "good view," with the bay and village in the distance. The rooms, each with a natural tile floor, one or two double beds, and well-screened windows, are tastefully furnished with Mexican accents. On the upper floor is a wonderful little reasonably priced restaurant with bay views. It's open for breakfast from 7:30 to 11am and for dinner from 6 to 10pm.

Capy's

Apdo. Postal 44, 70902 Puerto Angel, Oax. ☎ **958/4-3002**. 14 rms. FAN. Year-round, $6–$8 single; $10–$12 double.

You'll see Capy's sign hanging over the street; it's on the right, before the cemetery and Playa Panteón. Go up a flight of stairs to the second-story restaurant and someone can show you one of the very clean rooms. It's a good budget choice, with simple furnishings and well-screened windows. Room 6 has a great patio out front with a splendid bay view.

The pleasant, covered open-air restaurant is open daily from 7am to 10pm. Breakfast is served between 7am and noon; lunch and dinner are served from 1 to 10pm.

⊖ Hotel La Cabaña de Puerto Angel

Apdo. Postal 22, 70902 Pochutla, Oax. ☎ **958/4-0026**. 23 rms. FAN. Year-round, $16.50 single or double.

Covered in vines and plants, with lots of shade, this hacienda-style hotel is efficient and accommodating, with a friendly, helpful staff; owner Diego Oropeza is truly gracious. The clean, sunny rooms have louvered windows and screens, ceiling fans, and double beds. The rooftop patio is a nice place to sunbathe peacefully, and a hot pot of free coffee awaits guests every morning at 7am in the lobby. The hotel is on Playa Panteón on the landward side of the road, just steps from the beach and several restaurants.

✪ Posada Cañon Devata

Calle Cañon del Vata (Apdo. Postal 10), 70902 Puerto Angel, Oax. ☎ and fax **958/4-3048**. 10 rms, 4 bungalows (13 with bath). $14–$25 single; $17–$29 double; $38 bungalow or El Cielo room for two. Closed May–June.

One of the most inviting places in Puerto Angel is a 3-minute walk almost straight up from Playa Panteón. Americans Suzanne and Mateo López run this ecologically sound, homey, cool, green and wooded oasis in a narrow canyon. All water is recycled for the benefit of the resident plants and critters. Rooms are agreeably rustic-chic, with fans, beds covered in Guatemalan tie-died cloth, and Mateo's paintings hanging from the walls (the paintings can be bought). The patio restaurant serves delicious food featuring home-baked bread and the posada's own organically grown vegetables. Don't miss climbing to the appropriately named El Cielo to see the bay bathed in the light of the setting sun, and to enjoy the happy hour from 5pm until dark. Mateo also offers fishing and snorkeling trips (see "Beaches, Water Sports & Boat Trips," above).

To find it, walk just past the Hotel Cabaña del Puerto Angel to where the road more or less ends; turn right and go down the sandy path to an area with a few parked cars. Walk across the tiny bridge on your right and follow the stairs on the left until you reach the restaurant, where someone is around to rent rooms and serve food.

Posada Rincón Sabroso

Playa Principal, 70902 Puerto Angel, Oax. No phone. 8 rms. FAN. $9 single; $15 double. Low-season discounts available.

A sign on the street marks the entrance and a flight of stairs takes you up to the Posada. Rooms have nice tile floors, plaster walls, and screened windows. Hammocks hang between posts on the tile patio walkway which is also furnished with tables and chairs outside each room. Recent sprucing up, plus its attractive prices, make this one of the best budget choices for in-town stays. The posada is on the right as you enter town, opposite the main pier and by the Hotel Soraya.

DINING

In addition to the restaurants below and those mentioned under hotels above, there are four or five palapa-topped restaurants on the main beach in town as well as on Playa Panteón. Hawkers from these various establishments implore you to try their restaurants, but they're all similar in price, menu, and service. Breakfasts generally cost $2.25 to $4.50, and meat or seafood plates run $3.50 to $11. Watch out for over-billing in these restaurants.

✪ Restaurant Cañon Devata

At Posada Cañon Devata, Calle Cañon Devata. ☎ **958/4-3048.** Breakfast $1.75–$4.50; sandwiches $3.50; dinner $6–$7. Daily 7:30am–4pm and 7–8:30pm. Closed May–June. VEGETARIAN.

It's always a few degrees cooler under the thatched palapa in the middle of the canyon area. Fresh flowers centered on the thick wooden tables set the mood. Guests partake of some of the healthiest cooking around, mainly vegetarian dishes with occasional fish specialties. The restaurant is in the hotel by the same name, on the right, past the Hotel Cabaña de Puerto Angel.

✪ Villa Florencia

Bulevar Virgilio Uribe. ☎ **958/4-3044.** Breakfast $1.50–$2.25; pasta dishes $3.50–$5; pizzas $4–$6. Daily 7am–10pm. ITALIAN.

One of the best restaurants in town is Lulu and Walter Pelliconi's delightful slice of Italy. Their generous servings are prepared in a spotlessly clean kitchen that contains a purifier for all water used on the premises. Pasta products are imported from Italy, and the chefs use only extra virgin olive oil. The restaurant is located near the pier and the bus drop-off in the central village.

5 Bahías de Huatulco

40 miles SE of Puerto Angel, 425 miles SE of Acapulco

"The next Cancún!" trumpets the tourist literature—but it's going to be a while before this statement is true. Oaxaca's coastline is one of the last undeveloped stretches of pure white sands and isolated coves in Mexico, and it's a joy to see. Birds and tropical blossoms abound. The sea is crystal clear and bathwater warm, the air blessedly free of gasoline fumes.

The FONATUR development of the Bahías de Huatulco, a government megaresort on the nine pristine bays of Huatulco, is an ambitious project that will sprawl across 124,000 acres of land, most still undeveloped. The small communities of locals have been transplanted away from the coast into Crucecita, and corporate giants are vying for the rights to huge parcels of prime, pristine bayfront jungle.

It's unlikely that the developers' ambitious original projections of a million visitors annually by the year 2000 will be realized. Huatulco's growth pace has (for some) been painfully slow and measured. Perhaps this leisurely development will help spare Huatulco from thoughtless overdevelopment and from the ruination of the unspoiled beauty of its setting. Right now, the area is distinctly divided into three sections—Santa Cruz, Crucecita, and Tangolunda (see "City Layout," below).

ESSENTIALS

GETTING THERE & DEPARTING

BY PLANE   Three times daily **Mexicana** (☎ **958/7-0243;** 958/1-0208 at the airport), connects Huatulco with Cancún, Guadalajara, and Los Angeles by way of

Mexico City. **Aeroméxico** (☎ **958/1-0336,** 958/1-0329, or toll free 91-800/9-0999), offers service from Mexico City once daily Monday through Saturday. **AeroVega** arrives daily from Oaxaca. **AeroMorelos** (through Servicios Turísticos del Sur, ☎ **958/1-0055**) has direct flights from Oaxaca five days per week, and via Puerto Escondido three days per week. **Continental** ☎ 958/1-9028) flies from Houston several times a week. **Club Med charter flights** originate at the Dallas/Fort Worth Airport.

　Transportes Terrestres minibuses to the hotels from Huatulco's international airport, about 13 miles northwest of the Bahías de Huatulco, cost $4.50 per person. It's $8–$10 by taxi to Santa Cruz/Tangolunda.

BY BUS　Reaching Huatulco by bus has become easier. There are three bus stations in Crucecita, but none in Santa Cruz or Tangolunda, so a bus trip to any destination begins and ends in Crucecita. The stations in Crucecita are all within a few blocks of one another. The **Gacela and Estrella Blanca** station (☎ **958/7-0103**) is at the corner of Gardenia and Palma Real. Here you'll find ten daily buses traveling semidirect to Acapulco, as well as one direct service to Mexico City. Others go hourly to Puerto Escondido and to Pochutla. Gacela and **Oaxaca Pacífico** have several buses daily to Puerto Escondido.

　The **Cristóbal Colón** station (☎ **958/7-0261**) is at the corner of Gardenia and Ocotillo, four blocks from the Plaza Principal. Most of these buses go east to Salina Cruz, Tehuantepec, and Juchitán, and then either across the isthmus to Acayucan, or on to Tuxtla Gutiérrez and San Cristóbal de las Casas. But there are also several to Oaxaca (via Salina Cruz), Puerto Escondido (9 trips), and Pochutla. There's also service to Huatulco from Acapulco. If you come from tiny Puerto Angel you must change buses in Pochutla. The fare is 50¢ for the 30-minute ride to Pochutla and $1.50 for the hour-long ride into Huatulco. Any bus going to Huatulco will drop you off at Crucecita. To avoid confusion, read the "City Layout" section, below.

　To get to the **Estrella del Valle** station (☎ **958/7-0193**), start from the corner of Guanacostle and Gardenia. Go eight blocks on Gardenia (passing the Colón station) to Palo Verde, then left one block to Jasmin, then right half a block to the station (it is between Sabali and Carrizal). From here, three buses leave for Oaxaca daily.

　The stations in Crucecita are all within a few blocks of one another.

BY CAR　The coastal Highway 200 leads to Huatulco (via Pochutla) from the west and is generally in good condition. Allow at least eight hours for the trip from Oaxaca City on mountainous Highway 175.

ORIENTATION

ARRIVING　The airport is 13 miles from town, and the trip costs $4.50 by Transporte Terrestre to Santa Cruz or Crucecita and $8–$10 to Tangolunda. If you arrive by bus you'll be dropped off in Crucecita.

INFORMATION　The closest thing to a **tourist office** the area has is a quasi–tourism office located in Crucecita on Guamúchil, near the corner of Bugambilia, just off the Plaza Principal. It is run by the tourist publication *Huatulco Espacio 2000* (☎ 958/7-0027), though they speak little English and are seldom there. Best to go to Sunrise Tours (Plaza Gardenia #2-B, across Calle Flamboyan from the Plaza Principal). Here Lic. Miguel Gonzaléz will provide you with maps of Puerto Angel and Puerto Escondido and advice on everything in the area. They're open Monday through Saturday from 9am to 10:30pm and Sunday 4 to 10:30pm.

The **State Tourism Office** (*Oficina del Turismo*) once again is said to be open in the shopping center area of Tangolunda Bay. It's always offered erratic service and uncertain hours, so don't count on it. Supposedly it's open Monday through Saturday from 9am to 3pm and 6 to 8pm.

CITY LAYOUT   Just naming where you want to go in Huatulco can be confusing. The resort area is called Bahías de Huatulco and includes all nine bays. It shouldn't be confused with Santa María de Huatulco, 17 miles inland. **Santa Cruz Huatulco,** normally called just Santa Cruz, is the original coastal settlement on the bay. It has a pretty central park with a bandstand kiosk, an artisans' market by the park, a few hotels and restaurants, and a marina from where bay tours and fishing trips set sail. **Juárez** is Santa Cruz's main street, only about four blocks long in all, anchored at one end by the Hotel Castillo Huatulco and at the other by the Posada Binniguenda. Opposite the Hotel Castillo is the marina, and beyond it are restaurants housed in new colonial-style buildings facing the beach. The area's banks and a couple of convenience stores are on Juárez. It's impossible to get lost—you can see almost everything in one glance.

A mile and a half inland from Santa Cruz is **Crucecita,** a planned city that sprang up in 1985 centered on a lovely grassy plaza edged with flowering hedges. It's the residential area for the resorts, with neighborhoods of new stucco homes mixed with makeshift wooden ones and small apartment complexes. Most of the area's less expensive hotels and restaurants are here.

Until other bays are developed **Tangolunda Bay,** 3 miles east, is the focal point of development for the nine bays. Gradually, half the bays will have resorts, places where guests will arrive on a shuttle from the airport and then stay put. For now, Tangolunda has the 18-hole golf course, as well as the Club Med, Sheraton Huatulco, Royal Maeva, Holiday Inn Crowne Plaza, Casa del Mar, and Omni Zaachila hotels. Small strip centers with a few restaurants occupy each end of Tangolunda Bay. Chahue Bay, between Tangolunda and Santa Cruz, is a small bay with a marina under construction as well as houses and hotels.

GETTING AROUND   It's too far to walk between any of the three destinations of Crucecita, Santa Cruz, and Tangolunda, but there are minibus services between the towns. In Santa Cruz, catch the bus across the street from Castillo Huatulco; in Tangolunda, in front of the Holiday Inn; and in Crucecita, catercorner from the Hotel Grifer.

Fast Facts: Bahías de Huatulco

Area Code   The telephone area code is 958.

Banks   Santa Cruz has banks; there are two and both are on Juárez (Banamex and Bancomer). Their hours for changing money are generally 9am to noon weekdays.

Taxis   In Crucecita there's a taxi stand opposite the Hotel Grifer, and another on the Plaza Principal. To or from Santa Cruz, Crucecita, or Tangolunda Bay, the cost is $2.25 to $3.50, but you can often share a cab for 50¢ per person.

Telephones   The long-distance telephone office is on Calle Flamboyan near the corner of Bugambilia in Crucecita. It's open Monday through Saturday from 7:30am to 9:30pm and Sunday and holidays from 8am to 1pm.

Beaches, Water Sports & Other Things to Do
Beaches

A portion of the beach at **Santa Cruz** (away from the small boats) can be inviting as a sunning spot. Several restaurants are on the beach, and palapa umbrellas are found down to the water's edge. Jet skis can be rented for about $35 per hour. **Tangolunda Bay,** fronting the best hotels, is wide and beautiful. Theoretically all beaches in Mexico are public, however, nonguests at Tangolunda hotels may have difficulty being allowed to enter the hotel to get to the beach. At other beach locations in Mexico hotels are so busy that an outsider doesn't stand out, but that's not so at the luxury hotels in Huatulco and outsiders may be escorted back out. For about $5 one way, *pangas* from the marina in Santa Cruz will ferry you to **La Entrega Beach,** one bay over from Santa Cruz. There you'll find a row of palapa restaurants, all with beach chairs out front. Find an empty one and use that restaurant for your refreshment needs in return. A snorkel equipment-rental booth is about midway down the beach, and there's some fairly good snorkeling on the end away from where the boats arrive; be careful of wave action pushing you against the rocks.

BAY CRUISES/TOURS

Huatulco's major attraction is the coastline, that magnificent stretch of pristine bays. The only way to really grasp the beauty of the place is by taking a cruise of the bays, stopping at Chahue or Maguey Bay for a dip in the crystal-clear water and a fish lunch from one of the palapas on the beach.

The best way to arrange a bay tour is to go to the boat owners' cooperative in the red-and-yellow tin shack at the entrance to the marina. Prices are posted here, and you can buy tickets for definite times for sightseeing, snorkeling, or fishing. Prices start at $11 per person for a round-trip to La Entrega Beach and go to $17 per person, or $110 for a private all-day cruise. (La Entrega Beach, by the way, is remembered in Mexican history as the place where President Vicente Guerrero was put ashore as a prisoner after he was kidnapped in Acapulco.) Besides La Entrega Beach, there are other beaches farther away that are noted for good offshore snorkeling. These beaches, however, have no food or toilet facilities, so bring your own provisions. Boatmen at the cooperative will arrange to return to get you at an appointed time. Round-trip boat transportation to these outer beaches costs from $35–$65; a trip to see all the bays costs around $50 for about an hour without stops.

A third approach is to consult a travel agency. In Crucecita, **Sunrise Tours** (Plaza Oaxaca, Local no. 11, ☎ 958/7-0892) offers bay tours (7 bays, $20); a tour of Puerto Angel, Puerto Escondido, and associated beaches ($30); an ecotour on the Río Copalito (7 hours, $30); and an all-day tour to a coffee plantation. **Servicios Turísticos del Sur,** in both the Hotel Castillo in Santa Cruz and the Sheraton Hotel in Tangolunda (☎ 958/1-0055, ext. 784 or 788), offers similar tours.

BIRDING

Although there are no formal birding walks or tours, if birds are your interest, Huatulco will be rewarding. Before setting out, be sure to wear protective clothing (against the sun, not the birds) and sturdy shoes.

GOLF & TENNIS

The 18-hole Campo de Golf Tangolunda is adjacent to Tangolunda Bay and has tennis courts as well. The greens fee is $35 and carts cost about the same.

SHOPPING

There's a good **folk-art store** in the Sheraton Hotel, but for the most part shopping is confined to the Santa Cruz market, by the marina in Santa Cruz, and the Crucecita market, on Guamúchil half a block from the plaza in Crucecita.

ACCOMMODATIONS

Moderate and budget-priced hotels in Santa Cruz and Crucecita hotels are generally overpriced compared to similar hotels in other Mexican beach locations. The luxury beach hotels are priced at rates that are comparable to Mexico's other beach locations. Low season here is considered September, October, February, and June. During other months hoteliers may invoke high-season prices.

EXPENSIVE

✪ Zaashila

Rincón Sabroso, Bahía de Tangolunda, 70989 Hualtuco, Oax. ☎ **958/1-0460** or 800/223-5652 in the U.S. Fax 958/1-0461. 120 rms. A/C TEL TV. High season, $175 double. Low season, $100 double.

The white stucco facade of this luxurious Mediterranean-style hotel stands out from its more stately looking neighbors, and seems to fit perfectly in its beachside location. The spacious rooms are beautifully furnished with a Mediterranean flair, cool tile floors, and TV with remote control concealed in an armoire. Most have balconies and a view facing the ocean or pool.

Dining/Entertainment: The restaurant serves delicious seafood, steaks, and Oaxacan dishes. A kiosk bar/snack bar sits between it and the beach.

Services: Laundry and room service, tour desk.

Facilities: The large, free-form swimming pool on the beach extends in curves, and narrows some 50 yards.

MODERATE

Club Med

Tangolunda Bay, 70900 Santa Cruz de Huatulco, Oax. ☎ **958/1-0033** or 800/258-2633 in the U.S. Fax 958/1-0101. 500 rms. A/C. High season, $650–$670 per person per week, double occupancy (includes all meals and activities); $93 per person per night. Ask about air-inclusive packages, prices for teens, low-season discounts, and kids' free weeks.

Considering that all meals and a slew of activities are included in one price, Club Med is value-packed experience in Huatulco. It caters to all adult ages (married and single), with an atmosphere like a country club for the sports- or relaxation-minded. The setting has a spectacular view of Tangolunda Bay and lineup of hotels on the opposite side of the bay. Each room has a private patio with hammock, and all rooms have sea views. Rooms have both air-conditioning and fans, and you need both—the air-conditioning isn't very effective. Between May and early December a teen club for ages 12 to 17 offers plenty of special supervised sports and activities to keep them not only occupied but happy all day. Low-season prices make it a special bargain, though I must say that even with high-season prices you get a lot for the money.

Five restaurants feature different cuisines, with an emphasis on fresh seafood, Mexican, French, Italian, and Moroccan specialties (but not all may be open in low season). There's a nightly disco, water sports (sailing, kayaking, windsurfing, snorkeling), three swimming pools, an air-conditioned workout room with aerobics classes, three air-conditioned squash courts, a practice golf course, archery, volleyball, basketball, soccer, softball, bocce ball, billiards, Ping-Pong, a circus area with trapeze instruction, arts and crafts, and very popular activities for teens. Only excursions, deep-sea fishing, horseback riding, massage, and use of the public 18-hole golf course cost extra. The snorkeling is quite good on a coral reef on one of the club's beaches. Seven of the 12 tennis courts are lighted for night play. Unlike other Club Meds in Mexico, where you're a long distance from town, at this one you're no farther from town than the hotels across the bay; it's easy to call a taxi and go off to Crucecita on your own or to enjoy the beach and restaurants at the hotels on the bay. A taxi to town for shopping is cheaper than the hotel's boat excursion to the shopping area. However, there's so much to do here (and not so much to do in town) that most people stay within the Club Med boundaries; a stay here might mean never having to know you're in Mexico, but you'll sure enjoy the gorgeous bay and coastal setting.

Hotel Meigas Binniguenda

Blv. Santa Cruz s/n (Apdo. Postal 175), 70989 Santa Cruz de Huatulco, Oax. ☎ **958/7-0077.** Fax 958/7-0284. 76 rms. A/C TV TEL. High season, $60 single or double. Low season, $40 single or double.

This was Huatulco's first hotel, and it retains the Mexican charm and comfort that made it memorable. Rooms have Mexican tile floors, foot-loomed bedspreads, colonial-style furniture, and French doors opening onto tiny wrought-iron balconies overlooking Juárez. The TV receives Mexican channels plus HBO. There's a nice shady area around the hotel's beautiful pool in back of the lobby. The restaurant is only fair. The hotel is away from the marina at the far end of Juárez, only a few blocks from the water. They offer free transportation to a beach club at Chahue Bay.

INEXPENSIVE

Suites Begonias

Bugambilia No. 503, between Flamboyan and Chacah, Crucecita, 70989 Bahías de Huatulco, Oax. ☎ **958/7-0018.** 12 rms. FAN TV. High season, $30 single or double. Low season, $18 single or double.

The smallish suites at the Begonias are open and airy, with orange-and-black bedspreads and festive Talavera-style lamps. Two large rooms overlook Guamúchil and have table and chairs and a small balcony. It's on Bugambilia, just off the Plaza Principal.

DINING

Outside of the hotels, the best choices are in Crucecita and on the beach in Santa Cruz.

Restaurant Avalos Doña Celia

Santa Cruz Bay. ☎ **958/7-0128.** Breakfast $3–$6.75; seafood $5–$9. Daily 8:30am–10pm. SEAFOOD.

Doña Celia, an original Huatulco resident, chose to stay in business in the same area where she started her little thatch-roofed restaurant years ago. Now she's in a new building at the end of Santa Cruz's beach, serving the same good food. Among her specialties are filete empapelado, a foil-wrapped fish baked with tomato, onion, and cilantro, and filete almendrado, a fish fillet covered with a hotcake batter, beer, and almonds. The ceviche is terrific (one order is plenty for two). The Platillo a la Huatulqueño (shrimp and young octopus fried in olive oil with chile and onion and served over white rice) should satisfy any seafood lover.

♢ Restaurant Juquilita

Calle Palo Verde at Gardenia, Crucecita. No phone. Fixed price meal $2.75. Daily 6am–9pm. OAXACAN.

Don't come here if you are not hungry, or if you must have traditional eggs for breakfast. Do come here if you want something that will hold you over until late afternoon! Simmering on the stove in the back, and tended by the owner/cook (an ample and jovial motherly type from Juchitán), are chocolate, guisado (stew), black beans, chicken, and mole. Plus there are tamales and stacks of tortillas. You can tell from the clientele that they come here not because it's chic, but because of good food at the right price.

✪ Restaurante María Sabina

Flamboyan 15, Crucecita. ☎ **958/7-1039.** Main courses $2.25–$17; regional $3–$7; seafood $5–$11. Daily 1pm–midnight. SEAFOOD/OAXACAN.

This popular restaurant, which is probably the best in town, is on the far side of the Plaza Principal. The staff is super attentive and owner Jaime Negrete presides over the big open grill where the tantalizing aroma of grilled steak, ribs, chicken, and fresh fish drift throughout the cafe. Almost always full, this is where carnivores gather. The lengthy menu also features Oaxacan dishes.

BAHÍAS DE HUATULCO AFTER DARK

Bring a supply of books—Huatulco is short on entertainment. Besides the disco below, a lot of people finish off an evening at one of the eateries on Santa Cruz Bay or at **Carlos 'n' Charlie's** in Crucecita a block from the Hotel Grifer. The food is good and it's open for dinner and dancing to megaloud music nightly from 5pm to midnight.

Disco Magic Circus, Santa Cruz Bay (☎ **958/7-0017** or 958/7-0037), is across the street and a block away from the Posada Binniguenda, going toward the marina. The music is a mix of salsa and rock. Admission is $5 (free for women on Sundays and more often during low season). It's open daily from 10pm to 3am.

4

Inland to Old Mexico: Taxco & Cuernavaca

This is the land of the Aztecs and Cortés. The Taxco and Cuernavaca region, comprising parts of the states of Guerrero and Morelos, paid tribute to the Aztecs in pre-Hispanic times, and was later included in the land apportioned to Hernán Cortés after the Conquest of Mexico when he was made Marqués of the Valley of Oaxaca. His domain stretched, in sections, from Mexico City south to Oaxaca, but he spent his time primarily in this area—both near and far from Mexico City, the capital he had conquered, destroyed, and rebuilt.

Today Taxco, known for its silver shops, museums, and pictur-esque hillside colonial-era charm, is worthy of at least an overnight stay (or longer if you can spare the time). And leaving the busy vil-lage of Taxco behind for a day by retreating to Cuernava is easy to do—the drive or bus ride takes just over an hour. Visiting Cuernavaca's museums, restaurants, and surrounding villages will easily make a day's work or more, depending on your interests. And if you're staying in the leafy luxury of Las Mañanitas, you may want to stay a good long while.

1 Taxco

185 miles NE of Acapulco, 50 miles SW of Cuernavaca, 111 miles SW of Mexico City

Taxco (*tahs*-ko), famous for its silver work, sits at nearly 6,000 feet on a hill among hills, and almost everywhere you walk in the city there are fantastic views.

Taxco's renowned silver mines, first worked in the time of Cortés 4 centuries ago, were revived, for all practical purposes, by an Ameri-can, William Spratling, in the 1930s. Today its fame rests more on the over 200 silver shops, most little one-man factories, that line the cobbled streets all the way up into the hills. Whether you'll find bar-gains depends on how much you know about the quality and price of silver. But there is no doubt that nowhere else in the country will you find this quantity and variety of silver. The artistry and imagi-nation of the local silversmiths are evident in each piece.

You can get the idea of what Taxco's like by spending an after-noon, but there's much more to this picturesque town of 87,000 than just the Plaza Borda and the shops surrounding it. You'll have to stay overnight if you want more time to climb up and down its steep cobblestone streets, discovering little plazas and fine churches.

Taxco

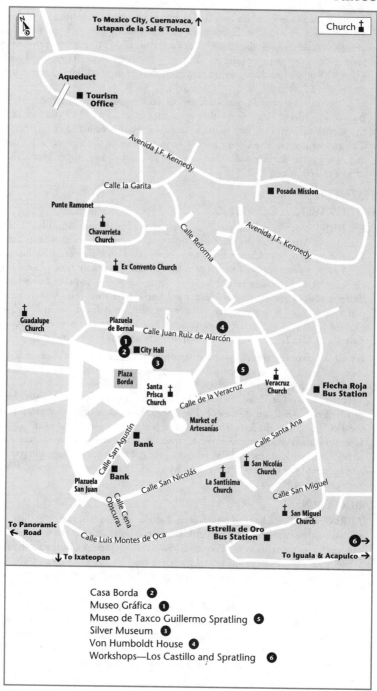

To Mexico City, Cuernavaca, Ixtapan de la Sal & Toluca ↑

Church ✝

Aqueduct

■ Tourism Office

Avenida J.F. Kennedy

Calle la Garita

■ Posada Mission

Punte Ramonet

✝ Chavarrieta Church

Calle Reforma

Avenida J.F. Kennedy

✝ Ex Convento Church

✝ Guadalupe Church

Plazuela de Bernal

Calle Juan Ruiz de Alarcón ④

① ② ■ City Hall ③

Plaza Borda

Santa Prisca Church ✝

Calle de la Veracruz

⑤

Veracruz ✝ Church

■ Flecha Roja Bus Station

Market of Artesanías

Calle Santa Ana

Calle San Agustín

Bank

San Nicolás ✝ Church

Plazuela San Juan

Bank

Calle San Nicolás

✝ La Santisima Church

Calle San Miguel

Calle Cena Obscuras

San Miguel ✝ Church

To Panoramic ← Road

Estrella de Oro Bus Station ■

⑥ →

Calle Luis Montes de Oca

↓ To Ixateopan

To Iguala & Acapulco →

Casa Borda ②
Museo Gráfica ①
Museo de Taxco Guillermo Spratling ⑤
Silver Museum ③
Von Humboldt House ④
Workshops—Los Castillo and Spratling ⑥

131

The main part of town is relatively flat. It stretches up the hillside from the highway, and although it's a steep walk, it's not a particularly long one. But you don't have to walk up and down all the hills: Vehicles make the circuit through and around the town picking up and dropping off passengers along the route. There are *burritos,* white VW minibuses that run the route from about 7am until 9pm. Taxis in town are around $1.50 to $2.

Warning: Self-appointed guides will undoubtedly approach you in the zócalo (Plaza Borda) and offer their services—they get a cut (up to 25%) of all you buy in the shops they take you to. Before hiring a **guide,** ask to see his Departamento de Turismo credentials. The Department of Tourism office on the highway at the north end of town can recommend a licensed guide for about $4 to $6 per hour walking or $14 to $20 by car.

ESSENTIALS
GETTING THERE & DEPARTING

BY BUS   Numerous bus lines run the route Zihuatanejo-Acapulco-Taxco-Cuernavaca-Mexico City, so you'll have little trouble getting a bus to or from Taxco. **From Acapulco,** both **Cuauhtémoc** and **Estrello de Oro** run several daily buses on the 4¹/₂- to 5-hour trip to Taxco. **From Mexico City,** buses to Taxco depart from the Central de Autobuses del Sur station (Metro: Tasqueña) and take 2 to 3 hours. **Estrella Blanca** and its **Líneas Unidas del Sur/Flecha Roja** lines have service to Taxco every hour or so with a variety of bus types. Your best bet is their "Plus" service for $7. These buses have air-conditioning, a TV, soft drinks, and bathrooms. **Estrella de Oro** has five (three *directo*) no-frills buses a day to Taxco for $5.50.

BY CAR   From Acapulco you have two options: Highway 95D, the new toll road through Iguala to Taxco is open. Or you can take the old two-lane road (95) that winds through villages and is slower, but it's in good condition.

From Mexico City, take Paseo de la Reforma to Chapultepec Park and merge with the Periférico, which will take you to Highway 95D on the south end of town. From the Periférico, take the Insurgentes exit and merge until you come to the sign to Cuernavaca/Tlalpan. Choose either *Cuernavaca Cuota* (toll) or *Cuernavaca Libre* (free). Continue south around Cuernavaca to the Amacuzac interchange and proceed straight ahead for Taxco. The drive from Mexico City takes about 3¹/₂ hours. Fill up with gas at Cuernavaca.

ORIENTATION

ARRIVING   Taxco has two **bus** stations. **Estrella de Oro** buses arrive at their own station on the southern edge of town. **Flecha Rojo** buses arrive at the station on the eastern edge of town on Avenida Kennedy. Both stations present a hard walk to town. If you have only a small suitcase, take a white minivan marked SANTA PRISCA or ZÓCALO from the front of either station to get to the town center. Taxis cost around 75¢ to the zócalo.

INFORMATION   The **State of Guerrero Dirección de Turismo** (☎ 762/2-6616; fax 762/2-2274) has offices at the arches on the main highway at the north end of town, useful if you're driving into town. The office is open daily from 9am to 8pm. To get there from Plaza Borda, take a combi (ZÓCALO ARCOS) and get off at the arch over the highway. As you face the arches, the tourism office is on your right.

CITY LAYOUT   The center of town is the tiny **Plaza Borda,** shaded by perfectly manicured Indian laurel trees. On one side is the imposing twin-towered, pink-stone

Santa Prisca Church, and the other sides are lined with whitewashed red-tile buildings housing the famous **silver shops** and a restaurant or two. Beside the church, deep in a crevice of the mountain, is the **city market.** Brick-paved streets fill out from here in a helter-skelter fashion up and down the hillsides. Besides the silver-filled shops, the plaza swirls with vendors of everything from hammocks to cotton candy and from bark paintings to balloons.

FAST FACTS: TAXCO

Area Code   The telephone area code is 762.

Long-Distance Phone   Farmacia Oscarin, Av. Kennedy 47 (☎ **762/2-1847**), opposite the Flecha Roja bus station, used to serve as the community long-distance telephone center. However, many small businesses now provide long-distance service, including the bus station itself. Look for the sign LARGA DISTANCIA.

Post Office   The post office moved to the outskirts of Taxco on the highway heading toward Acapulco. It's in a row of shops with a black-and-white sign reading CORREO.

Scam   Some taxi drivers at the bus station and tour guides who greet you on arrival in town receive a payoff to take you to certain hotels in Taxco. They'll even go so far as to tell you the hotel at which you have reservations is closed or in horrible disrepair in order to take you to a hotel from which they get a kickback. Proceed with your own plans and leave these guys to their dirty tricks.

Spanish/Art Classes   In 1993, the Universidad Nacional Autónoma de Mexico (UNAM) opened its doors in the buildings and grounds of the Hacienda del Chorrillo, formerly part of the Cortés land grant. Here students can study silversmithing, Spanish, drawing, composition, and history under the supervision of UNAM instructors. Classes contain between 10 and 15 students, and courses are generally for 3 months at a time. The school will provide a list of prospective town accommodations that consist primarily of hotels. As an alternative, I suggest you select an inexpensive hotel for the first several nights, then search for something more reasonable for a lengthy stay. At locations all over town are notices of furnished apartments or rooms for rent at reasonable prices. For information about the school, contact either the Dirección de Turismo (tourist office) in Taxco (see "Information," above) or write the school directly: UNAM, Hacienda del Chorrillo, 40200 Taxco, Guerrero (☎ **762/2-3690**).

EXPLORING TAXCO

Since Taxco boasts more than 200 shops selling silver, shopping for the brilliant metal is the major pastime—and the main reason most tourists come. But Taxco's cultural show is on an upward move. Besides the opulent, world-renowned **Santa Prisca y San Sebastián Church,** you have the **Spratling Archaeology Museum,** the **Silver Museum,** and the **von Humboldt House/Museo Virreynal de Taxco.** In Taxco, museums seem to have "official" hours and "real" hours, so you may find some closed when they should be open.

You also might consider taking a look at Juan O'Gorman's mosaic tile mural beside the pool at the Hotel Posada de la Misión (on the highway; go via minibus).

FESTIVALS & FAIRS

Taxco's **Silver Fair** starts the last Saturday in November and continues for one week. It includes a competition for silver sculptures from among the top silversmiths. **Holy Week** in Taxco is one of the most compelling in the country, beginning the Friday nine days before Easter with nightly processions as well as several during the day. The most riveting procession, on Thursday evening, lasts almost four hours and includes villagers from the surrounding area carrying statues of saints, followed by hooded members of a society of self-flagellating penitents chained at the ankles and carrying huge wooden crosses and bundles of penetrating thorny branches. On the Saturday morning before Easter, the Plaza Borda fills for the procession of three falls, reenacting the three times Christ stumbled and fell while carrying his cross. The **Jornadas Alarconianas,** featuring plays and literary events in honor of Juan Ruíz de Alarcón (1572–1639), a world-famous dramatist who was born in Taxco, were traditionally held in the spring, but have switched to the fall in recent years.

SIGHTS IN TOWN

Casa de la Cultura de Taxco (Casa Borda)
Plaza Borda. ☎ and fax **762/2-6617.**

Catercorner from the Santa Prisca Church and facing Plaza Borda, this was the home José de la Borda built for his son around 1759. It is now the Guerrero State Cultural Center, housing classrooms and exhibit halls where period clothing, engravings, paintings, and crafts are displayed. Traveling exhibits, such as a recent display of codices, are also on display.

Mercado Central
Plaza Borda. Daily 7am–6pm.

To the right of the Santa Prisca Church, behind and below Berta's, Taxco's central market meanders deep inside the mountain. Take the stairs off the street. Among the curio stores you'll find the food stalls and cook shops, always the best place for a cheap meal.

✪ Santa Prisca y San Sebastián Church
Plaza Borda. No phone. Free admission. Daily 8am–11pm.

This is Taxco's centerpiece parish church, around which village life takes place. Facing the pleasant Plaza Borda, it was built with funds provided by José de la Borda, a French miner who struck it rich in Taxco's silver mines. Completed in 1758 after eight years of labor, it's one of Mexico's most impressive baroque churches. Outside, the ultracarved facade is flanked by two elaborately embellished steeples and a colorful tile dome. Inside, the intricacy of the gold-leafed saints and cherubic angels is positively breathtaking. The paintings by Miguel Cabrera, one of Mexico's most famous colonial-era artists, are the pride of Taxco. A long-overdue restoration and cleaning of the interior walls has been completed, but they have become dusty again. The room behind the altar is now open and contains even more Cabrera paintings.

Guides, both boys and adults, will approach you outside the church offering to give a tour, and it's worth the small price to get a full rendition of what you're seeing. Make sure the guide speaks English well, however, and establish whether the price is per person or per tour. Give him 75¢.

✪ Silver Museum
Plaza Borda. ☎ **762/2-0558.** Admission 50¢. Daily 10am–5pm.

A recent addition is the Silver Museum, operated by a local silversmith. After entering the building next to Santa Prisca (upstairs is Sr. Costilla's restaurant), look for a sign on the left; the museum is downstairs. It's not a traditional public-sponsored museum. Nevertheless, it does a much-needed job of describing the history of silver in Mexico and Taxco, as well as displaying some historic and contemporary award-winning pieces. Time spent here seeing quality silver work will make you a more discerning shopper in Taxco's dazzling silver shops.

✪ Museo de Taxco Guillermo Spratling

Calle Veracruz. ☎ **762/2-1660.** Admission $1.50; free Sun. Tues–Sun 10am–5pm.

A plaque (in Spanish) explains that most of the collection of pre-Columbian art displayed here, as well as the funds for the museum, came from William Spratling, an American born in 1900 who studied architecture in the United States, later settled in Taxco, and organized the first workshops to turn out high-quality silver jewelry. From this first effort in 1931 the town's reputation as a center of artistic silver work grew to what it is today. In a real sense, Spratling "put Taxco on the map." He died in 1967 in a car accident. You'd expect this to be a silver museum, but it's not—for Spratling silver, go to the Spratling Ranch Workshop (see "Nearby Attractions," below). The entrance floor of this museum and the one above display a good collection of pre-Columbian statues and implements in clay, stone, and jade. The lower floor has changing exhibits.

To find the museum, turn right out of the Santa Prisca Church and right again at the corner; continue down the street, jog right, then immediately left. There it is, facing you.

✪ Von Humboldt House/Museo Virreynal de Taxco

Calle Juan Ruíz de Alarcón. ☎ **762/2-5501.** Admission $1.50. Tues–Sat 10am–5pm, Sun 9am–3pm.

Stroll along Ruíz de Alarcón (the street behind the Casa Borda) and look for the richly decorated facade of the von Humboldt House, where the renowned German scientist/explorer Baron Alexander von Humboldt (1769–1859) visited Taxco and stayed one night in 1803. The new museum houses 18th-century memorabilia pertinent to Taxco, most of which came from a secret room discovered during the recent restoration of the Santa Prisca y San Sebastián Church. It's a fascinating museum, especially if you take a guided tour; however, signs with detailed information are in both Spanish and English. The von Humboldt House has known many uses, including 40 years as a guest house run until the mid-1970s by the von Wuthenau family. To the right as you enter are two huge and very rare *tumelos* (three-tiered funerary paintings). The bottom two were painted in honor of the death of Carlos III of Spain; the top one, with a carved phoenix on top, was supposedly painted for the funeral of José de la Borda.

The three stories of the museum are divided by eras and persons famous in Taxco's history. In the *sala* (room) dedicated to José de la Borda is a copy of a painting (which hangs in the church) showing him dressed in the finery of his times, with samples of such garments in other cases. In a room of photographs are pictures of Taxco's 10 principal churches. Another room shows paintings of what workshops must have been like during the construction of Santa Prisca y San Sebastián. Another section is devoted to historical information about Don Miguel Cabrera, Mexico's foremost 18th-century artist. Fine examples of clerical garments decorated with gold and silver thread hang in glass cases. More excellently restored Cabrera paintings are hung throughout the museum; some were found in the frames you see, others were haphazardly rolled up. And, of course, a small room devoted to von Humboldt shows what this young explorer looked like and gives a short history of his sojourns through South America and Mexico.

NEARBY ATTRACTIONS

The large **Grutas de Cacahuamilpa** (Cacahuamilpa Caves) are 20 minutes north of Taxco. There are hourly guided tours daily at the caves, but these caves are much like any other you may have visited and you might not want to make the effort.

For a spectacular view of Taxco, ride the **cable cars** (*gondola*) to the Hotel Monte Taxco. Catch them across the street from the state tourism office, left of the arches, near the college campus. Take a combi marked LOS ARCOS and exit just before the arches, turn left, and follow the signs to the cable cars. Daily hours are 7am to 7pm. A round-trip ride is $3.25.

Los Castillo

5 miles south of town on the Acapulco Hwy., and in Taxco on Plaza Bernal. ☎ **762/2-1016** (workshop) or 762/2-3471 (store). Free admission. Workshop, Mon–Fri 9am–5pm; store, Mon–Fri 9am–6:30pm, Sat 9am–1pm, Sun 10am–3pm.

Don Antonio Castillo was one of hundreds of young men to whom William Spratling taught the silversmithing trade in the 1930s. He was also one of the first to branch out with his own shops and line of designs, which over the years have earned him a fine name. Besides Taxco, Castillo has shops in several Mexican cities. You can visit Don Antonio's workshop, 5 miles south of town, Monday through Friday between 9am and 5pm. Now his daughter Emilia creates her own noteworthy designs, among which are decorative pieces with silver fused onto porcelain. Emilia's work is for sale at Los Castillo, on the ground floor of the Posada de Los Castillo, just below the Plazuela Bernal. Another store, featuring the designs of Don Antonio and another daughter, Kitty, is in Mexico City's Zona Rosa, at Amberes 41.

Spratling Ranch Workshop

6 miles south of town on the Acapulco Hwy. No phone. Free admission. Mon–Sat 9am–5pm.

Spratling's hacienda-style home/workshop on the outskirts of Taxco once again hums with busy hands reproducing his unique designs. A trip here will show you what distinctive Spratling work was all about, for the designs crafted today show the same fine work—even Spratling's workshop foreman is employed again, overseeing the development of a new generation of silversmiths. Prices are high, but the designs are unusual and considered collectible. There's no store in Taxco, and unfortunately, most of the display cases hold only samples. With the exception of a few jewelry pieces, most items are available by order only. Ask about their U.S. outlets.

ACCOMMODATIONS

Compared to Cuernavaca, Taxco is a visitor's dream for an overnight-stop: charming and picturesque, with a respectable selection of well-kept and delightful hotels. However, hotel prices tend to "bulge" at holiday times (especially Easter week).

EXPENSIVE

Hacienda del Solar

Apdo. Postal 96, 40200 Taxco, Gro. ☎ and fax **762/2-0323.** 22 rms. $53–$75 double; $98 double junior suite.

Located on a beautifully landscaped hilltop with magnificent views of the surrounding valleys and the town, this hotel comprises several Mexican-style cottages. The decor is slightly different in each one, but most include bathrooms done in handmade tiles, lots of beautiful handcrafts, hand-painted folk murals, and red-tile floors. Several rooms have Gothic-vaulted tile ceilings and fine private terraces with panoramic views. Standard rooms have no terraces and only showers in the baths; deluxe rooms have sunken tubs (with showers) and terraces. Junior suites are the largest and most luxurious accommodations. The prices I quote here were given to me by the management at the hotel. The rates will be higher if you book rooms through a travel agent.

The hotel is 2½ miles south of the town center off Highway 95 to Acapulco; look for signs on the left and go straight down a narrow road until you see the hotel entrance.

Dining/Entertainment: La Ventana de Taxco restaurant overlooking the city, open for breakfast, lunch, and dinner.

Services: Laundry and room service.

Facilities: Heated swimming pool, tennis court.

INEXPENSIVE

Hotel Los Arcos

Calle Juan Ruíz de Alarcón 12, 40200 Taxco, Gro. ☎ **762/2-1836.** 21 rms. $14 single, $19 double.

Los Arcos occupies a converted 1620 monastery. The handsome inner patio is bedecked with Puebla pottery and a gaily dressed restaurant area to the left, all around a central fountain. The rooms are nicely but sparsely furnished, with natural tile floors and colonial-style furniture. You'll be immersed in colonial charm and blissful quiet. To find it from the Plaza Borda, follow the hill down (with Hotel Agua Escondida on your left) and make an immediate right at the Plazuela Bernal; the hotel is a block down on the left, opposite the Posada de los Castillo (see below).

✪ Hotel Rancho Taxco Victoria

Apdo. Postal 83, 40200 Taxco, Gro. ☎ and fax **762/2-0010.** 100 rms. $24.75 single or double standard room; $33 single or double deluxe; $41 single or double junior suite.

The Rancho Taxco Victoria clings to the hillside above town, with breathtaking views from its flower-covered verandas. It's a personal favorite partly for the views and partly because it exudes all the charm of old-fashioned Mexico. The furnishings, beautifully kept as if purchased yesterday, whisper comfortably of the hotel's heyday in the 1940s. In the guest rooms—nestled into nooks and crannies of the rambling hillside buildings—are vanities constructed of handmade tiles; local tin-craft reading lamps; old prints of Mexico and Taxco; beamed ceilings; craft work bedspreads and throw rugs; a plant or two; baths with tubs; and in many cases, small private terraces. Each standard room comes with a bedroom and in front of each is a table and chairs set out on the tiled common walkway. Each deluxe room has a bedroom and private terrace; each junior suite has a bedroom, a nicely furnished large living room, and a spacious private terrace overlooking the city. There's a lovely pool, plus an overpriced restaurant—both with a great view of Taxco. Even if you don't stay here, come for a drink in the comfortable bar/living room, then stroll on the terrace to take in the fabulous view. From Plazuela de San Juan, go up a narrow, winding cobbled street named Carlos J. Nibbi to no. 57 on the hilltop.

Hotel Santa Prisca

Plazuela de San Juan 7, 40200 Taxco, Gro. ☎ **762/2-0080** or 762/2-0980. Fax 762/2-2938. 34 rms. $22 single or double standard room; $24.75 single or double suite; $41 single or double suites nos. 25 and 26.

The Santa Prisca, one block from Plaza Borda on Plazuela de San Juan, is one of the older and nicer hotels in town. Rooms are small but comfortable, with older baths (showers only), tile floors, wood beams, and a colonial atmosphere. If your stay is long, ask for a room in the adjacent "new addition," where the rooms are sunnier, more spacious, and quieter. There is a reading area in an upstairs salon overlooking Taxco, a lush patio with fountains, and a lovely dining room done in mustard and blue.

⑤ Posada de los Castillo

Calle Juan Ruíz de Alarcón 3, 40200 Taxco Gro. ☎ **762/2-1396.** Fax 762/2-3471. 14 rms. $14 single; $18 double.

Each room in this delightful small hotel is simply but beautifully furnished with handsome carved doors and furniture; baths have either tubs or showers. Just off the lobby is a showroom of Emelia Castillo's silver and silver-porcelain pieces. (The Castillo family owns the hotel.) The manager, Don Teodoro Contreras, is a true gentleman and a fountain of information about Taxco. To get here from the Plaza Borda, go downhill a short block to the Plazuela Bernal; make an immediate right, and the hotel is a block farther on the right, opposite the Hotel Los Arcos (see above).

DINING

Taxco gets a lot of people on day-trips from the capital and Acapulco. There are not enough good restaurants to fill the demand, so prices are high for what you get.

A special note: La Taberna Restaurant, one of my favorites, was undergoing renovation, a name change (to Sotavento), and focus change (to gallery and restaurant) at press time. The menu was to be changed slightly. See if it's open when you travel; it's on the same side of the street as the post office, but just beyond it as you turn left around the bend.

VERY EXPENSIVE

Toni's

In the Hotel Monte Taxco. ☎ **762/2-1300.** Reservations recommended. Main courses $20–$35. Tues–Sat 7:30pm–1am. STEAKS/SEAFOOD.

High on a mountaintop, Toni's is an intimate and classy restaurant enclosed in a huge, cone-shaped palapa with a panoramic view of the city below. Eleven candlelit tables sparkle with crystal and crisp linen. The menu of shrimp or beef is limited, but the food is superior. Try the tender, juicy prime roast beef, which comes with Yorkshire pudding, creamed spinach, and baked potato. Lobster is sometimes available. To reach Toni's, take a combi to the convention center/tourist office, then hail a cab from there.

MODERATE

Cielito Lindo

Plaza Borda 14. ☎ **762/2-0603.** Breakfast $2.75–$6.25; main courses $4.50–$6.50. Daily 10am–11pm. MEXICAN/INTERNATIONAL.

Cielito Lindo is probably the most popular place on the plaza for lunch, perhaps more for its visibility and colorful decor than for its food—which is fine, but not great. The tables, covered in white-and-blue and laid with blue-and-white local crockery, are usually packed, and plates of food disappear as fast as the waiters can bring them. You can get anything from soup to roast chicken, enchiladas, tacos, steak, and dessert, as well as frosty margaritas.

Sr. Costilla's ("Mr. Ribs")

Plaza Borda 1. ☎ **762/2-3215.** Main courses $4.25–$11.50. Daily 1pm–midnight. INTERNATIONAL.

The offbeat decor here includes a ceiling festooned with the usual assortment of cultural flotsam and jetsam. Several tiny balconies hold a few minuscule tables that afford a view of the plaza and church (it's next to the Santa Prisca Church, above Patio de las Artesanías), and these fill up long before the large dining room does. The menu is typical Andersonese (like the other Carlos Anderson restaurants you may have encountered in your Mexican travels), with Spanglish jive and a large selection of everything from soup, steaks, sandwiches, and spareribs to desserts and coffee. Wine, beer, and drinks are served.

INEXPENSIVE

✪ Restaurante Ethel

Plazuela de San Juan 14. ☎ **762/2-0788.** Soup $1.50; main courses $3.75–$5; comida corrida $3.75. Daily 9am–10pm (comida corrida served 1–5pm). MEXICAN.

A family-run place opposite the Hotel Santa Prisca on Plazuela de San Juan, one block from Plaza Borda, Restaurante Ethel is kept clean and tidy, with white throws and colorful crumb cloths on the tables and a homey atmosphere. The hearty daily comida corrida consists of soup or pasta, meat (perhaps a small steak), dessert, and good coffee.

TAXCO AFTER DARK

Taxco's nighttime action is centered in the luxury hotels. **Paco's** is just about the most popular place overlooking the square for sipping, nibbling, people watching, and people meeting, all of which continues until midnight daily. And there's Taxco's dazzling disco, **Windows,** high up the mountain in the Hotel Monte Taxco. The whole city is on view from there, and music runs the gamut from the hit parade to hard rock. For a cover of $5 you can boogie Saturday nights from 9pm to 3am.

Completely different in tone is **Berta's,** next to Santa Prisca Church. Opened in 1930 by a lady named Berta, who made her fame on a drink of the same name (tequila, soda, lime, and honey), Berta's is traditionally the gathering place of the local gentry. Spurs and old swords decorate the walls, and a saddle is casually slung over the banister of the stairs leading to the second-floor room where tin masks leer from the walls. A Berta costs about $2; rum, the same. Open daily from 11am to around 10pm.

2 Cuernavaca

50 miles N of Taxco, 64 miles S of Mexico City

Cuernavaca, capital of the state of Morelos, has been popular as a resort since the time of Moctezuma II. Emperor Maximilian built a retreat here over a century ago. Mexicans say the town has a climate of "eternal spring," and on weekends the city is crowded with day-trippers from surrounding cities, especially the capital. On weekends the roads between Mexico City and Cuernavaca are jammed, and restaurants and hotels may be full as well. Cuernavaca has a large American colony, plus students attending the myriad language and cultural institutes that crowd the city.

Emperor Charles V gave Cuernavaca to Cortés as a fief, and the conquistador built a palace here in 1532 (now the Museo de Cuauhnahuac) and lived there on and off for half a dozen years before returning to Spain. Cortés introduced sugarcane cultivation to the area, and Caribbean slaves were brought in to work in the cane fields. His sugar hacienda at the edge of town is now the luxurious Hotel de Cortés. The economics of large sugarcane growers failed to serve the interests of the indigenous farmers and there were numerous uprisings in colonial times.

After independence, mighty landowners from Mexico City gradually dispossessed the remaining small landholders, converting them to virtual serfdom. It was this condition that led to the rise of Emiliano Zapata, the great champion of agrarian reform, who battled the forces of wealth and power, defending the small farmer with the cry of *"Tierra y Libertad!"* (Land and Liberty!) during the Mexican Revolution following 1910.

In this century, Cuernavaca has seen the influx of wealthy foreigners and of industrial capital. The giant CIVAC industrial complex on the outskirts has brought wealth to the city but also the curse of increased traffic, noise, and air pollution.

ESSENTIALS
GETTING THERE & DEPARTING

BY BUS   The **Autobuses Estrella de Oro** terminal in Cuernavaca is at Morelos Sur 900, at the corner of Tabasco, about 15 blocks south of the center of town. This is the terminal with buses to Taxco (three per day); Zihuatanejo (two per day); Acapulco, Iguala, and Chilpancingo (five per day); and Mexico City (six per day).

Numerous lines run the route Zihuatanejo-Acapulco-Taxco-Cuernavaca-Mexico City, so you'll have little trouble getting a bus to or from Cuernavaca. **Autobuses Pullman de Morelos** is the line with the most frequent departures (every 10 min.). Pullman has two stations in Cuernavaca; the downtown station is at the corner of Abasolo and Netzahualcóyotl, four blocks south of the center of town. Their other station, Casino de la Selva, is less conveniently located near the railroad station. The trip takes 1 hour.

Lineas Unidas del Sur/Flecha Roja's new terminal in Cuernavaca at Morelos 505, between Arista and Victoria, is six blocks north of the town center. Here you'll find frequent buses to Mexico City, Toluca, Chalma, Ixtapan de la Sal, Taxco, Acapulco, the Cacahuamilpa Caves, Querétaro and Nuevo Laredo.

BY CAR   Highway 95 and Toll Road 95D from Acapulco to Mexico City run right past Cuernavaca. The toll road will save you an hour but is very expensive. Acapulco's 195 miles away; Mexico City is 60 miles north.

ORIENTATION

ARRIVING   Most bus stations are within walking distance of several of my hotel recommendations.

INFORMATION   Cuernavaca's **State Tourist Office** is at Av. Morelos Sur 802, between Jalisco and Tabasco (☎ **73/14-3860** or 73/14-3920; fax 73/14-3881), half a block north of the Estrella de Oro bus station and about a 15- to 20-minute walk south of the cathedral. It's open Monday through Friday from 9am to 8pm and Saturday and Sunday from 9am to 5pm. A better bet is the City Tourism kiosk stuck in the wall of the cathedral grounds on Hidalgo close to Morelos. It's open Monday to Friday from 9am to 4pm; Saturday from 9am to 2pm.

CITY LAYOUT   In the center of the city are two contiguous plazas. The small and more formal of the two, across from the Post Office, has a Victorian gazebo (designed by Gustave Eiffel of Eiffel Tower fame) at its center. This is the **Alameda.** The larger, rectangular plaza planted with trees, shrubs, and benches is the **Plaza de Armas.** These two plazas are known collectively as the **zócalo** and are the hub for strolling vendors selling balloons, baskets, bracelets, and other crafts from surrounding villages. It's all easy-going, and one of the pleasures is grabbing a park bench or table in a nearby restaurant just to watch. On Sunday afternoons orchestras play from the gazebo. At the eastern end of the Alameda is the **Cortés Palace,** the conquistador's residence that now serves as the Museo de Cuauhnahuac.

You should be aware that this city's street-numbering systems are extremely confusing. It appears that the city fathers, during the past century or so, became dissatisfied with the street numbers every 10 or 20 years and imposed a new numbering system each time. Thus you may find an address given as "no. 5" only to find that the building itself bears the number "506," or perhaps "Antes no. 5." One grand

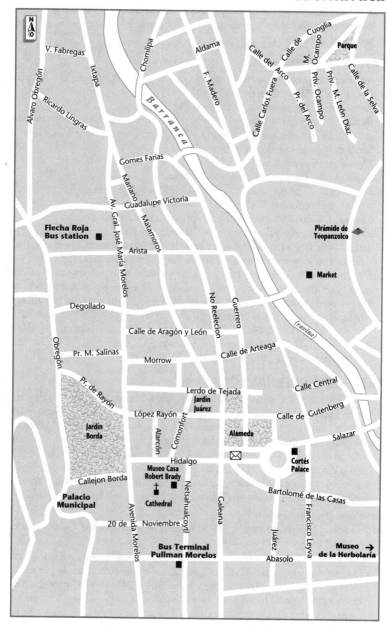

gateway I know bears no fewer than five different street numbers, ranging from 2 to 567! In my descriptions of hotels, restaurants, and sights, I'll note the nearest cross street so you can find your way to your chosen destination with a minimum of fuss.

GETTING AROUND Frequent **buses** go from downtown to all the outlying centers. Just tell a local where you want to go, and most will go out of their way to help you. **Taxis** are relatively inexpensive in Cuernavaca; $2.50 should get you from downtown to the outlying herb museum, for example. Determine the fare before taking off.

FAST FACTS: CUERNAVACA

American Express   The local representative is Viajes Marín, Edificio Las Plazas, Loc. 13 (☎ 73/14-2266; fax 73/12-9297).

Area Code   The telephone area code is 73.

Banks   Money can be changed from 9:30am to 1pm only. There are several banks in town, but the handiest to the zócalo is Bancomer at the corner of Matamoros and Lerdo de Tejada, catercorner to Jardín Juárez.

Elevation   Cuernavaca sits at 5,058 feet.

Population   Cuernavaca has 450,000 residents.

Post Office   The post office (☎ 73/12-4379) is on the Plaza de Armas, next door to the Café Los Arcos.

Spanish Lessons   As much as for its springlike weather, Cuernavaca is known for its Spanish-language schools, aimed at the foreigner. Generally the schools will help students find lodging with a family or provide a list of potential places to stay. Rather than make a long-term commitment in a family living situation, try it for a week, then decide. Below are the names and addresses of some of the schools. The whole experience—from classes to lodging—can be quite expensive, and the school may accept credit cards for the class portion. Contact the Center for Bilingual Multicultural Studies, San Jeronimo 304 (Apdo. Postal 1520), 62000 Cuernavaca, Morelos (☎ 73/17-0696); or Universal Centro de Lengua y Comunicación Social A.C. (Universal Language School), H. Preciado 332 (Apdo. Postal 1-1826), 62000 Cuernavaca, Morelos (☎ 73/18-2904 or 73/12-4902).

EXPLORING CUERNAVACA

If you plan to visit Cuernavaca on a day-trip from Mexico City, the best days to do so are Tuesday, Wednesday, or Thursday (and perhaps Friday). On weekends the roads, the city, and its hotels and restaurants are filled with people from Mexico City, and prices jump dramatically. On Monday, the Museo de Cuauhnahuac—which you definitely must see—is closed. So make it Tuesday through Friday.

You can spend one to two days sightseeing in Cuernavaca pleasantly enough. If you've come on a day-trip from Mexico City, you may not have time to make all the excursions listed below, but you'll have enough time to see the sights in town.

Catedral de la Asunción
At the corner of Hidalgo and Morelos. Free admission. Daily 8am–2pm and 4–10pm. Walk three blocks southwest of the Plaza de Armas.

As you enter the church precincts and pass down the walk, try to imagine what life in Mexico was like in the old days. Construction on the church was begun in 1533, a mere 12 years after Cortés conquered Tenochtitlán (Mexico City) from the Aztecs. The churchmen could hardly trust their safety to the tenuous allegiance of their new converts, so they built a fortress as a church. The skull-and-crossbones above the main door is not a comment on their feelings about the future, however, but a symbol for the Franciscan order, which had its monastery here in the church precincts.

Inside, the church is stark, even severe, having been refurbished in the 1960s. The most curious aspect of the interior is the mystery of the frescoes painted in Japanese style. Discovered during the refurbishing, they depict the persecution and martyrdom of St. Felipe de Jesús and his companions in Japan. No one is certain who painted them.

✪ Museo de Cuauhnahuac

In the Cortés Palace, Leyva 100. No phone. Admission $2; free Sun. Tues–Sun 10am–5pm.

The museum is housed in the Cortés Palace, the former home of the greatest of the conquistadores, Hernán Cortés. Begun by Cortés in 1530 on the site of a Tlahuica Indian ceremonial center, it was finished by the conquistador's son, Martín, and later served as the legislative headquarters for the state of Morelos. It's in the town center at the eastern end of the Jardín de los Héroes.

Once you're inside the main door, go to the right for displays of humanity's early times. The northern wing of the palace, on the ground floor, houses exhibits from the colonial era; upstairs in the northern wings are costumes, domestic furnishings, carriages, and farm implements from Mexico of the 1800s, mostly from *haciendas azucareras* (sugar plantations). There are also mementos of the great revolutionaries Francisco Madero and Emiliano Zapata.

When you get to the east portico on the upper floor, you're in for a treat. A large Diego Rivera mural commissioned by Dwight Morrow, U.S. ambassador to Mexico in the 1920s, depicts the history of Cuernavaca from the coming of the Spaniards to the rise of Zapata (1910). It's fascinating to examine this magnificent mural in all its epic detail.

Museo de la Herbolaría

Matamoros 200, Acapantzingo. ☎ **73/12-5956.** Admission $2. Daily 10am–5pm.

This museum of traditional herbal medicine, in the southern Cuernavaca suburb of Acapantzingo, has been set up in a former resort residence built by Maximilian, the Casa del Olindo, or Casa del Olvido. It was here, during his brief reign, that the Austrian-born emperor would come for trysts with La India Bonita, his Cuernavacan lover. Restored in 1960, the house and gardens now preserve the local wisdom in folk medicine. The shady gardens are lovely to wander through, and you shouldn't miss the 200 orchids growing near the rear of the property. However, the lovers' actual house, the little dark-pink building in the back, is closed. Catch combi no. 6 at the mercado on Degollado. Ask to be dropped off at Matamoros near the museum. Turn right on Matamoros and walk $1\frac{1}{2}$ blocks; the museum will be on your right.

Jardín Borda

Morelos 103, at Hidalgo. ☎ **73/14-0282** or 73/18-6372. Admission 80¢. Tues–Sun 10am–5pm.

Half a block from the cathedral is the Jardín Borda (Borda Gardens). One of the many wealthy builders to choose Cuernavaca was José de la Borda, the Taxco silver magnate, who ordered a sumptuous vacation house built here in the late 1700s. The large enclosed garden next to the house was actually a huge private park, laid out in Andalusian style with little kiosks and an artificial pond. Maximilian found it worthy of an emperor and took it over as his private preserve in the mid-1800s. After Maximilian, the Borda Gardens fell on hard times; decades of neglect followed until its recent renovation.

The paintings of the French Intervention enhance a stroll through the gardens. Here are the scenes you'll see: Emperor Maximilian and Empress Carlota arrive in Cuernavaca for the first time; then, Maximilian, while out for a ride, gets his first glimpse of La India Bonita, who was to become his lover. The next scene is of court festivities in the Borda Gardens, with courtiers taking turns rowing little boats. Finally, Maximilian's niece pleads with President Benito Juárez, after the siege of Querétaro, to spare the emperor's life. (At that time, Carlota was off in Europe, trying to round up support for her husband's cause, without result.) Juárez refused her request, and Maximilian, along with two of his generals, was executed by firing squad on the Hill of Bells in Querétaro a few days thereafter.

On your stroll through the gardens you'll see the same little artificial lake on which Austrian, French, and Mexican nobility rowed in little boats beneath the moonlight. Ducks have taken the place of dukes, however, and there are rowboats for rent. The lake is now artfully adapted as an outdoor theater, with seats for the audience on one side and the stage on the other.

The Borda Gardens have been completely restored and were reopened in October 1987 as the Jardín Borda Centro de Artes. In the gateway buildings are several galleries for changing exhibits and several large paintings showing scenes from the life of Maximilian and from the history of the Borda Gardens. There is a cafe for refreshments and light meals, and a bookstore.

Museo Casa Robert Brady

Calle Netzahualcoyotl 4. ☎ **73/18-8554.** Admission $2. Tues–Sun 10am–6pm.

This museum in a private home contains more than 1,200 works of art. Among them are pre-Hispanic and colonial pieces; oil paintings by Frida Kahlo and Rufino Tamayo; and handcrafts from America, Africa, Asia, and India. Admission includes a guide in Spanish; English and French guides are available if requested when you make your reservation.

ACCOMMODATIONS

Because so many *capitalinos* come down from Mexico City for the day or for the weekend, the hotel trade here may be heavy on weekends and holidays, light at other times. A few local hoteliers adapt their policies and prices to these shifts.

EXPENSIVE

Camino Real Sumiya

Interior Fracc. Sumiya s/n, Col. José Parres, Jiutepec, Mor. ☎ **73/20-9199** or 800/7-CAMINO in the U.S. Fax 73/20-9155. 163 rms, 6 suites. A/C MINIBAR TV TEL. $125–$135 single or double. Low-season packages and discounts available.

Sumiya's charm is its relaxing atmosphere, which is best midweek since escapees from Mexico City tend to fill it on weekends. About 7 miles south of Cuernavaca, this unusual resort, whose name means "the House on the Corner," was once the exclusive home of Woolworth heiress Barbara Hutton. Using materials and craftsmen from Japan, she constructed the $3.2 million estate in 1959 on 30 beautifully wooded acres as an exact replica of a house in Kyoto, Japan. Out of financial necessity, Hutton sold Sumiya (one of her many homes throughout the world) and its rare Asian antiques for $500,000 nearly 20 years later. The main house, a series of large interconnected rooms and decks, overlooks the grounds and contains restaurants and the lobby.

The guest rooms, which are clustered in three-storied buildings flanking manicured lawns, are plain in comparison to the striking Japanese architecture of the main house. Rooms, however, have nice Japanese accents, with austere but comfortable furnishings, scrolled wood doors, and round pulls on the armoire and closet. Three types of sliding doors in each room face the gardens; one is screened to let in Cuernavaca's cool springlike weather; another is glass; and another completely darkens the room. Each room has direct-dial long-distance phones, fax connections, three-prong electrical outlets, ceiling fans, and in-room wall safes. A kabuki-style theater on the grounds is used for special events, and beyond it lies a Japanese garden with stones placed in the same positions as the Japanese islands. Hutton's life is chronicled in *Poor Little Rich Girl*, an excellent biography by C. David Heymann (Simon & Schuster, 1984).

Cuernavaca is a $3 taxi ride away. From the freeway, take the Atlacomulco exit and follow Sumiya signs. Ask directions in Cuernavaca if you're coming from there since the route to the resort is complicated.

Dining/Entertainment: There's La Arboleda, an outdoor restaurant shaded by enormous Indian laurel trees; Sumiya, with both terrace and indoor dining; and a snack bar by the pool.

Services: Room service, business center.

Facilities: Pool, 10 tennis courts.

✪ Las Mañanitas

Ricardo Linares 107, 62000 Cuernavaca, Mor. ☎ **73/14-1466** or 73/12-4646. Fax 73/18-3672. 22 rms. TEL. $85.75 single or double; $114–$210 suite single or double. AE. Buses going north on Morelos stop within half a block of the hotel. Valet parking.

Among Cuernavaca's best-known luxury lodgings is Las Mañanitas, 5 1/2 long blocks north of the Jardín Borda. Antique headboards, gleaming polished moulding and brass accents, large baths, and superior attention to detail result in an unforgettably perfect stay. Several rooms have verdant, vine-encumbered balconies big enough for sitting and sipping while overlooking the emerald lawns where peacocks and other exotic birds strut and preen and fountains tinkle musically. Thirteen rooms have fireplaces, and the hotel also has a heated pool. After a few hours, most of the personnel address you by name.

Standard rooms are simple but charming, allowing you to splurge without paying top dollar; suites are available.

Dining/Entertainment: The restaurant, overlooking the gardens, is one of the premier dining places in the country. The restaurant serves breakfast but is open to nonguests for lunch and dinner only.

Services: Laundry and room service, concierge.

MODERATE

Hotel Hacienda de Cortés

90 Plaza Kennedy (Apdo. Postal 430), 62560 Cuernavaca, Mor. ☎ **73/15-8844** or 73/16-0867. Fax 73/15-0035. 22 suites. TEL. $39 single or double; $61 double suite; $112 imperial suite for six people. Free parking.

This hotel lies in the suburb of Atlacomulco, just off the Cuernavaca/Acapulco highway. Formerly the Hacienda de San Antonio Atlacomulco, it was used to process sugarcane during the 1600s. After several incarnations, in the 1970s it was converted into one of the country's most splendid hacienda hotels. Towering chimneys from the sugar-processing era still loom above the beautiful suites, which are all in original hacienda rooms edging the immaculate interior gardens. Each room is furnished with carefully chosen antiques, area rugs, and Mexican textiles. The vine-covered, stone-walled former grinding room is the dining room, where trios strum romantic tunes during meals. There's also outside dining. Room and laundry service are available, and there is a small secluded pool. This is a true getaway—its only drawback is its distance from town.

Hotel María Cristina

Leyva 200 (Apdo. Postal 203), 62000 Cuernavaca, Mor. ☎ **73/18-5767.** 14 rms. TV TEL. $45–$50 single or double; $50–$58 suite single or double. Free parking. Walk three long blocks to the right of the Cortés Palace or walk two blocks east (right) of Pullman Morelos bus station. It is on the southwest corner of Leyva and Abasolo.

Formerly La Posada de Xochiquetzal, the María Cristina's high walls conceal many delights: a small swimming pool, lush gardens with fountains, tasteful colonial-style furnishings, a good restaurant, patios, and large and small guest rooms. Even if you don't stay here, come for a meal.

INEXPENSIVE

⑤ Hotel Cadiz

Alvaro Obregón 329, 62000 Cuernavaca, Mor. ☎ **73/18-9204.** 17 rms. FAN. $20 single or double. Add $5 extra for TV.

Every now and then I discover a hotel with the kind of homey charm that makes me want to return. Such is the Hotel Cadiz, run by the gracious Aguilar family. You may have known it previously as the Hotel María Cristina. Each of the fresh, simple rooms is furnished uniquely, and there's a lot of old-fashioned tile and big, old (but well-kept) freestanding sinks. The grounds, set back from the street, make a pleasant respite. There is a pool and a small, inexpensive restaurant open from 9am to 4pm. From Morelos, turn left on Ricardo Linares and go past Las Mañanitas. Turn left at the first street, Obregón; the hotel is a block ahead on the right.

DINING
VERY EXPENSIVE

Casa de Campo

Abasolo 101. ☎ **73/12-4947** or 73/18-2635. Main courses $15–$25. Daily 1pm–1am. INTERNATIONAL.

The elegant Casa de Campo has become a rival of longtime favorite Las Mañanitas (see below). Like Las Mañanitas, it too comes complete with strolling peacocks and blue-and-red parrots. A converted one-story townhouse built in a U-shape around beautiful grounds, Casa de Campo spares no expense in its decor and food. Dining rooms open onto the terrace and grounds. Main courses include red snapper in creole sauce, fresh salmon, chateaubriand, and daily specials. Throughout the serving hours there's some kind of live entertainment such as a whispering violin in the garden, or soft piano music in the bar.

✪ Restaurant Las Mañanitas

Ricardo Linares 107. ☎ **73/14-1466** or 73/12-4646. Reservations recommended. Main courses $8.50–$23.50. Daily noon–5pm and 7–11pm. Buses going north on Morelos stop within half a block of the restaurant. MEXICAN/INTERNATIONAL.

Las Mañanitas sets the standard for sumptuous dining in Cuernavaca. Tables are set on a shaded terrace with a view of gardens, strolling peacocks, and softly playing violinists or a romantic trio. The decor and ambiance are lightly colonial, and the service is extremely friendly and attentive. When you arrive, you can enjoy cocktails in the cozy sala; when you're ready to dine, a waiter will present you with a large blackboard menu listing at least half a dozen daily specials. The cuisine is Mexican with an international flair, drawing on whatever fruits and vegetables are in season and offering a full selection of fresh seafood, beef, pork, veal, and fowl. Las Mañanitas is $5^{1}/_{2}$ long blocks north of the Jardín Borda.

MODERATE

Restaurant La India Bonita

Morrow 106B. ☎ **73/18-6967.** Breakfast $2–$5.25; main courses $4–$9.75. Tues–Fri 8am–10pm, Sat 9am–10pm, Sun 9am–8pm. MEXICAN.

Housed among the interior patios and portals of the restored home of former U.S. Ambassador Dwight Morrow (1920s), it is gracious, sophisticated, and definitely a Cuernavaca haven where you can enjoy the setting as well as the food. Specialties include *mole poblano* (chicken with a sauce of bitter chocolate and fiery chilies) and *filet a la parrilla* (charcoal-grilled steak). There are also several daily specials. A breakfast mainstay is the gigantic desayuno Maximiliano—a huge platter featuring enchiladas. The restaurant is two blocks north of the Jardín Juárez between Matamoros and Morelos.

✪ Restaurant Vienés

Lerdo de Tejada 4. ☎ **73/18-4044** or 73/14-3404. Breakfast $1.50–$3.25; main courses $6–$8. Daily 8am–10pm. VIENNESE.

A legacy of this city's Viennese immigrant heritage is the Restaurant Vienés, a tidy and somewhat Viennese-looking place a block from the Jardín Juárez between Lerdo de Tejada and Morrow. The menu also has Old World specialties such as grilled trout with vegetables and German potato salad; for dessert there's apfelstrudel followed by Viennese coffee. Next door, the restaurant runs a pastry/coffee shop called Los Pasteles de Vienés. Although the menu is identical, the atmosphere in the coffee shop is much more leisurely, and there the tempting pastries are on full display in glass cases.

INEXPENSIVE

La Parroquia

Guerrero 102. ☎ **73/18-5820.** Breakfast $1.75–$2.30; main courses $2.30–$4.25; comida corrida $3.25. Daily 7:30am–12am. MEXICAN/PASTRIES.

This place does great business, partly because of its great location (half a block north of the Alameda, opposite Parque Juárez), partly because of its Arab specialties, and partly because it has fairly reasonable prices for Cuernavaca. It's open to the street with a few outdoor cafe tables, perfect for watching the changing parade of street vendors and park life.

CUERNAVACA AFTER DARK

Cuernavaca has a number of cafes right off the Jardín Juárez where people gather to sip coffee or drinks till the wee hours of the morning, the best of which are Los Arcos, La Parroquia, and the Los Pasteles de Vienés (see "Dining," above). There are band concerts in the Jardín Juárez on Thursday and Sunday evenings.

  Harry's Grill, Gutenberg 5, at Salazar, just off the main square (☎ **73/12-7639**), is another addition to the Carlos Anderson chain and includes its usual good food and craziness with Mexican Revolutionary posters and jaunty waiters. Although it serves full dinners, I'd recommend you go for drinks ($1.75–$4.25). It's open daily from 1:30 to 11:30pm.

SIDE TRIPS FROM CUERNAVACA

If you have enough time, you should try to make some side trips around Cuernavaca. To the north you'll find pine trees and an alpine setting; to the east, lush hills and valleys. On the road north to Mexico City you will climb several thousand feet within half an hour into some gorgeous mountain air. If you have a car, you can go for a brisk morning hike (it's cold up there) or a lazy afternoon picnic.

TEPOZTLÁN: STREET MARKET & A MONASTERY

Less than 20 miles northeast of Cuernavaca, this Tlahuica village nearly surrounded by mountains (not to be confused with the Tepozotlán north of Mexico City) predates the Conquest. On weekends, it's a popular retreat for *capitalinos*.

  The best times to go are Saturdays and Mexican holidays when there's a sprawling outdoor **crafts market** around the central square. Tepoztlán's folk healers (*curanderos*), for which the village is well known, are often there selling medicinal herbs and other magical cures. The market is especially good during **Carnaval** (three days before Ash Wednesday), a moveable date usually in February, and around **Days of the Dead,** November 1 and 2. During Carnaval, colorfully costumed and masked dancers perform. Since outsiders flock to the town during Carnaval, plan to arrive early in the day to stake out a good observation point before things get too congested. **September 8** is the festival honoring the god of *pulque* (a fermented drink), another occasion on which there are dancers and the market is especially large.

The ruins of an **Aztec temple,** Tepozteco, honoring the god of pulque, are on a sheer rock outcropping 1,200 feet above the town. The town itself is built around a 16th-century Dominican monastery. On the street behind the monastery (actually in the back of the monastery) is the **Museo Arqueología Carlos Pellicer,** which exhibits a fine collection of pre-Hispanic artifacts. It's open Tuesday through Sunday from 9am to 5pm. Admission is $1.

There are several restaurants around the square, as well as a couple of good inns. To get here take one of the frequent buses or minivans by the Cuernavaca market. Tourists don't use these much, and other passengers generally go out of their way to be helpful and will let you know when to get off.

XOCHICALCO RUINS

About 16 miles south of Cuernavaca along Highway 95 (the "*Libre*" [no toll] road to Taxco) is the town of Alpuyeca, and 9¹/₂ miles northeast of Alpuyeca are the ruins of Xochicalco, the "House of Flowers." High on a mountaintop, Xochicalco boasts a magnificent situation and an interesting complex of buildings dating from about A.D. 600 through 900. Most interesting is the **Temple of the Feathered Serpents,** with beautiful bas-reliefs. There's also a ball court, some underground passages, and other temples. Xochicalco is of interest to archaeologists because it seems to have been the point at which the Teotihuacán, Toltec, Zapotec, and Maya cultures met and interacted. You can visit the ruins from 8am to 5pm daily. Catch a bus to the *crucero* (crossing) from the Pullman de Morelos station. Buses run frequently. From the crucero take a combi to the ruins for about $1.75. Admission is $2; additional $4.25 for use of a personal video camera.

Inland to Oaxaca City & Environs

If you want to combine some time relaxing at a low-key beach resort with an experience of the heart of Mexican culture, you could hardly make a better choice than traveling to Oaxaca State. The slightly scruffy but idyllic beach towns of Puerto Escondido and Puerto Angel and the more upscale resort at Huatulco (each covered in chapter 3) are all a short plane ride or a day-long bus ride or drive from Oaxaca City, one of Mexico's most interesting old colonial cities.

Set in a 5,070-foot-high valley amid rugged mountains, Oaxaca City has become the destination of choice for travelers seeking colonial surroundings, archaeological sites, and very creative indigenous crafts (particularly wood carvings, handwoven textiles, and pottery). It's a beautiful city, with many fine homes and shops; the purple blooms of jacaranda trees are everywhere, a contrast against the cobalt sky. The museums display gold and jade antiquities, the galleries exhibit the fine work of local artists, and the mountains and valleys of the surrounding countryside are a photographer's dream. American and European expatriates have fostered something of a bohemian subculture, and Zapotecs and Mixtecs live much as their ancestors did long ago.

Most visitors to Oaxaca (Wa-*hah*-kah) leave still unaware that the city is a booming commercial and industrial center. Prosperity has given the city a cosmopolitan touch and the outskirts of town have a definite industrial air, but Oaxaca's 800,000 residents, who call themselves Oaxaqueños (Wah-*hah*-kehn-yos), have carefully preserved the colonial beauty of the central city.

The Zapotecs came to this high valley around 800 B.C. and soon built a beautiful city and a flourishing culture at Monte Albán, 6 miles from modern-day Oaxaca city. They weren't the first people to live here: Evidence from White Cave, near Mitla, indicates the presence of primitive inhabitants in the valley as early as 10,000 B.C. Some authorities consider that Olmec influence reached the Oaxaca valley around 1200 B.C. However, it was the Zapotecs who created the city and a high-level culture, building monuments visible at the site today.

After this flowering of Zapotec culture (ca. A.D. 300–700), another tribe, the Mixtecs, built a rival center at Mitla, 36 miles away on the other side of what is today Oaxaca, and the two tribes struggled for control of the valley until they united against a powerful common enemy from the north, the Aztecs. Even together the

Oaxaca Area

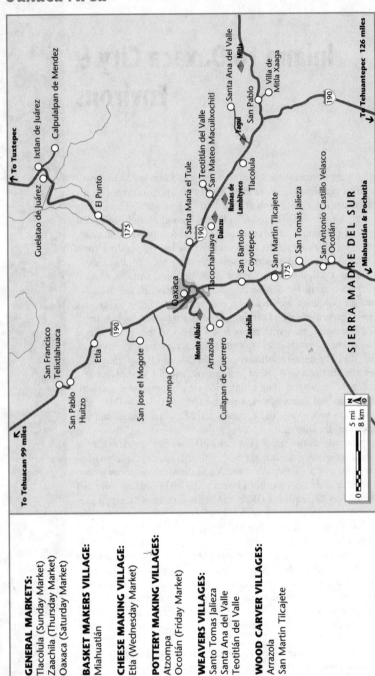

GENERAL MARKETS:
Tlacolula (Sunday Market)
Zaachila (Thursday Market)
Oaxaca (Saturday Market)

BASKET MAKERS VILLAGE:
Miahuatlán

CHEESE MAKING VILLAGE:
Etla (Wednesday Market)

POTTERY MAKING VILLAGES:
Atzompa
Ocotlán (Friday Market)

WEAVERS VILLAGES:
Santo Tomas Jalieza
Santa Ana del Valle
Teotitlán del Valle

WOOD CARVER VILLAGES:
Arrazola
San Martin Tilcajete

2-0041

two tribes were outmatched: In the late 1400s and the early 1500s Aztec influence predominated in the valley.

The local tribes didn't have to worry about the Aztecs for long, however—an even more formidable enemy appeared in 1521. After the Spanish subdued the valley, they set up a military post called Antequera here; 6 years later the town of Oaxaca was founded. Hernán Cortés was later given the title of Marqués del Valle de Oaxaca by the Hapsburg emperor Charles V, and with the title came grants of land, some of which were controlled by Cortés's descendants until the Mexican Revolution in 1910.

Two of Mexico's presidents, Porfirio Díaz and Benito Juárez, were born near Oaxaca. Nobody does much to remember Díaz these days, but monuments to Juárez are everywhere: statues, murals, streets named for him, even a Benito Juárez University. In fact, the city's official name is Oaxaca de Juárez.

A Zapotec, Juárez was born in the nearby village of Guelatao and "adopted" by a wealthy Oaxacan family who clothed, educated, and taught him Spanish in return for his services as a houseboy. He fell in love with the daughter of the household and promised he would become rich and famous and return to marry her. He managed all three, and Oaxaca adores him for it. Juárez attended law school, was the governor of the state of Oaxaca (1847–52), and later became a resistance leader and president of the republic. He is a national hero.

Oaxaca City can be so engrossing that 5 days won't be nearly enough, particularly if you go during Christmas or the Days of the Dead. Try to plan on no less than 4 days there, allowing at least 2 days for seeing the ruins, at least a day in the city itself, and a day at craft villages and markets.

1 Essentials

GETTING THERE & DEPARTING

BY PLANE   **Mexicana** (☎ **951/6-7352** or 951/6-8414; 951/1-5337 at the airport), has several daily flights to Oaxaca from Mexico City. **Aeroméxico** (☎ **951/6-1066;** 951/1-5055 at the airport) has daily flights to Mexico City. **AeroCaribe** (affiliated with Mexicana, ☎ **951/6-0229** or 951/6-0266; 951/1-5247 at the airport) flies once a day to Tuxtla Gutiérrez, Villahermosa, Mérida and Cancún. **Aviacsa** (☎ **951/3-1801**), flies once a day to Tuxtla Gutiérrez. **Aeromorelos** (☎ **951/6-0974** or 951/6-0975; 951/1-5100 and fax 951/6-1002 at the airport) flies a turboprop between Oaxaca and the Pacific coast resorts of Puerto Escondido and Bahías de Huatulco, at least once daily and more during Christmas, Easter, Days of the Dead, and the Guelaguetza. Aeromorelos flights within the state of Oaxaca can be booked in the United States through Zapotec Tours (☎ **800/444-OAXACA**). **AeroVega** (☎ **951/6-6294** or 951/6-2777), flies a 5-passenger twin-engine Aero-Commander from Puerto Escondido and Bahías de Huatulco once daily (twice if there are enough passengers). Arrangements for AeroVega are made at the Monte Albán Hotel facing the Alameda (next to the zócalo).

Inexpensive transportation from hotels in town to the airport can be arranged by **Transportes Aeropuerto Oaxaca** (☎ **951/4-4350**), located a few doors from the Hotel Monte Albán on the Alameda. They don't accept phone reservations, so drop by Monday through Saturday from 9am to 2pm or 5pm to 8pm to buy your ticket. And since the office is closed on Sunday, buy tickets on Saturday if you plan to leave on Monday. The cost is $2 from downtown hotels and around $4 from outlying hotels. The staff also charges more if you have more than two suitcases and one small carry-on.

BY BUS On long trips to and from Oaxaca, be sure to ask if your potential bus is *con escalas* (with stops), *directo* (with fewer stops), or *sin escalas* (no stops). And if you are traveling between Mexico City and Oaxaca, ask if the bus goes by way of the *autopista* (a 6-hour trip) or the federal highway (9 hours). You'll thank yourself if you've packed some water and food for longer trips (especially nonstop trips).

The first-class line **ADO** (☎ 951/5-1703 or 951/5-0903) handles most traffic north and west.

Cristóbal Colón (☎ 951/5-1214) serves the region south and east of Oaxaca—including Tuxtla Gutiérrez (five buses a day), San Cristóbal de las Casas (two overnight buses), and Huatulco, Pochutla, and Puerto Escondido on the coast (two a day, stopping at all three towns). The Cristóbal Colón bus takes 9 hours to reach Puerto Escondido because it goes by way of Huatulco; for a faster trip see below. Colón also serves the areas north and east of Oaxaca; at least 50 buses a day run to Mexico City's TAPO (East) and Central del Norte (North) stations. Another 10 go to Puebla, and 4 to Tehuacán; other destinations are Tapachula (one bus a day), Veracruz (three a day), and Villahermosa (two a day).

The deluxe **Linea UNO** (☎ 951/3-3350) has six nonstop departures daily for Mexico City using the *autopista;* the trip costs $21 one way. Also deluxe, **ADO GL** buses have five nonstop departures for Mexico City with four going to the TAPO station and one to the Norte station. A seat costs $18. The latter two feature movies, help-yourself free soft drinks, decent leg room, reclining seats, and bathroom. These are very popular so it's wise to book your seat several days in advance, especially during heavily touristed times in Oaxaca. ADO GL also has service to Puebla (three buses a day). Linea Uno buses also go to Puebla (one a day) and Veracruz (one a day).

The speediest buses to **Puerto Escondido**—which is 6 hours away over an extremely curvaceous road—leave from the terminal at Armenta y López 721 (☎ 951/4-0806) across from the Red Cross. Two lines serve the route. **Pacifico Oaxaca** buses leave daily at 8:30am and 10:30pm. One **Estrella de Valle** bus leaves at 11pm daily.

For buses to the outlying villages around Oaxaca go to the second-class bus station next to the Abastos Market. **Fletes y Pasajes,** at gate number 9, has frequent departures for Mitla and Tlacolula. **Valle de Norte** buses, at gate 29, go to Teotitlán del Valle Monday through Saturday at 11am, 12:30, 2, 3:30 and 5pm. They return at 12:30, 2, 5 and 6pm (but double-check all of these hours). To get to Teotitlán del Valle on a Sunday take a Fletes y Pasajes bus to Tlacolula, and from there (where the bus lets you off) buses leave every 20 minutes for Teotitlán del Valle. Buses for Guelatao (birthplace of Benito Juárez) leave from the second-class station several times daily. Buy your tickets a day in advance to be sure of space and a good seat. Under the breathless name of **Sociedad Cooperativo de Autotransportes Choferes del Sur** you'll find buses to Etla every 40 minutes, and to Atzompa every 30 minutes.

BY CAR The only good road connecting the coastal resorts with Oaxaca City is Highway 175, which begins at Pochutla's intersection with Highway 200, near San Angel. (Puerto Escondido is 43 miles to the west along Highway 200; Huatulco is 25 miles to the east.)

Highway 175 is paved along its entire length, and traverses expanses of banana plantations before winding up into the Sierra Madre del Sur. The drive—often affording spectacular views of misty summits—covers 149 miles and takes about 6 hours to complete.

ORIENTATION
ARRIVING BY PLANE

The airport is south of town, about a 20-minute (and $10) cab ride. **Transportes Aeropuerto Oaxaca,** Alameda de León 1A (☎ **951/4-4350**), operates an airport minibus service between the hotels in the center of town and the airport at a cost of $2 to $4 each way.

ARRIVING BY BUS

The Central Camionera first-class bus station is north of the center of town on the main highway (Calzada Niños Héroes de Chapultepec). Taxis between here and the zócalo cost about $2. If you're coming from the Pacific coast, you may arrive at the Central Camionera de Segunda Clase (second-class bus terminal) next to the Abastos Market buildings. It's 10 long blocks southwest of the zócalo. To get to the zócalo, take a taxi, or walk left out the front of the station and cross the railroad tracks. Traffic is horrendous around the station and Abastos Market.

INFORMATION

The **Municipal Tourist Office** (*Oficina de Turismo*) is at the corner of Morelos and Cinco de Mayo (☎ **951/6-4828;** fax 951/6-1550); it's open daily from 8am to 8pm. The well staffed and extremely helpful **State Tourist Office** is located across from the Alameda at Independencia 607, (corner of García Vigil; ☎ and fax **951/6-0984**). It's open daily from 9am to 3pm and 6 to 8pm.

CITY LAYOUT

Oaxaca's central historic section was laid out on a north-south and east-west grid. The cathedral faces west toward the Alameda Park, and the Palacio del Gobierno faces north overlooking the zócalo. Do not confuse the Plaza Alameda with the zócalo. Oaxaca's **Zócalo** is one of the prettiest main plazas in Mexico. The city streets change names here. North–south streets change at Independencia, while east–west streets change at Alcalá/Bustamante. Alcalá is closed to all but cross-street traffic from Avenida Independencia to Avenida Gurrión (at the Santo Domingo Church), forming a pedestrian mall. Most of the more expensive hotels, restaurants, and galleries are located north of the zócalo; the market and inexpensive hotels are south.

North, near the first-class bus station, is **Parque Paseo Juárez,** also known as El Llano. This is where families, children, teens, and lovers congregate both by day and by night: groups practicing dance steps, children learning to skate, joggers running or stretching, they are all here. Here you'll see the life of the city.

GETTING AROUND

BY BUS Buses to the outlying villages of Guelatao, Teotitlán del Valle, Tlacolula, and Mitla leave from the second-class station just north of the Abastos Market (see "Getting There & Departing," above, for details). City buses run along Juárez and Pino Suárez, Tinoco y Palacios and Porfirio Díaz, and others.

BY TAXI Colectivo taxis depart to the villages from Calle Mercadores, on the south side of the Abastos Market. You can negotiate rides to the ruins based on the number of people in your group. The average cost is around $10 per hour, which can be shared with up to five people. A regular taxi stand is along Independencia at the north side of the Alameda, while another is on Calle Murguía just south of the Hotel Camino Real. An honest, careful, and dependable English-speaking driver, **Tomás Ramírez,** can be found here, or reached at his home (☎ **951/1-5061**).

FAST FACTS: OAXACA CITY

American Express   The office, in Viajes Misca, is at Valdivieso and Hidalgo (northeast corner of the zócalo; ☎ **951/6-2700;** fax 951/6-7475). American Express office hours are Monday through Friday from 9am to 2pm and 4 to 6pm and on Saturday from 9am to 1pm. However, the travel agency is open Monday through Friday from 9am to 8pm and Saturday from 9am to 6pm. Here you will find both their travel agency and financial services office.

Area Code   The telephone area code is 951.

Bookstores   There's a good Spanish-English bookstore, Librería Universitaria, off the southeast corner of the zócalo at Guerrero 104. Most are new books, but there are a few used-book racks. Used books are even cheaper at the Biblioteca Circulante (Oaxaca Lending Library), located at Alcalá 305. For an extensive collection of books about Oaxaca, visit the Librería y Papelería Proveedora Escolar. This two-story bookstore is at Independencia 1001, at the corner of Reforma.

Consulates   Several consulates can be contacted through Grupo Consular, upstairs at Hidalgo 817 no. 4 (☎ **951/4-2744**). The U.S. Consular Agency is at Alcalá 201 (☎ and fax **951/6-4272** or 951/4-3054). Hours are Monday through Friday from 9am to 1pm.

Currency Exchange   Banks change dollars only from Monday through Friday, from 9am to 12:30pm. Look for a window saying COMPRA Y VENTA DE DIVISAS. Most banks charge a commission for cashing travelers checks, and Banpaís charges a small fee for changing dollars. There are several *casas de cambio* (money-changing storefronts) around the plaza, most of which offer a slightly lesser exchange rate than the banks. Most require a Tourist Card or passport as identification.

One such storefront is Interdisa (☎ **951/6-3399** or 951/4-3098) near the corner of Valdivieso and the zócalo, just around the corner (to the right) from the Hotel Marqués del Valle. It's open Monday through Saturday from 8am to 8pm and Sunday from 9am to 5pm.

Canadian visitors can exchange money at the above-mentioned casa de cambio and at Banamex, Bancomer, Comermex and others.

Newspapers/Magazines   The English-language newspaper *The News,* published in Mexico City, is sold at newsstands. There is a supply of English-language magazines at the Biblioteca Circulante. The monthly give-away *Oaxaca Times,* published in English, is available at the tourist offices and many hotels. Another monthly, *OAXACA,* is trilingual (English, Spanish, and French) and is widely available.

Post Office   The *correo* (main post office) is at the corner of Independencia and the Alameda Park. It is open Monday to Friday from 9am to 7pm and Saturday 9am to 1pm.

Safety   Petty crime is increasing in Oaxaca. Take normal precautions and you should have no trouble: Park your car in a lot overnight; don't leave anything in the car within view; watch your property at all times when you're waiting in the bus station; and be especially careful of very professional pickpockets in the markets and buses—they can take your wallet out of your back or front pocket, handbag, or knapsack and you won't know it until the time comes to pay for dinner. Luckily, violent crime (including mugging) is still very rare here. In most cases, the police are of little help.

Shipping   Oaxaca is a shopper's delight, and it's hard to keep from accumulating huge quantities of pottery, rugs, and other heavy goods that must be sent home. Many of the better shops can arrange shipping, but if your goods have come from the markets and villages, you'll need to ship them yourself. The first rule of shipping

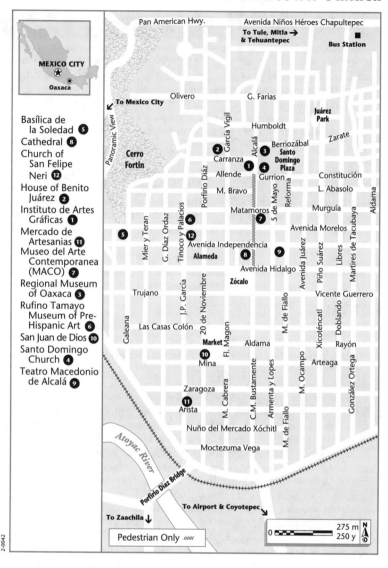

is this: You must have a receipt. That means carrying a notebook and asking merchants to write out a receipt for you when you shop. All shipped items must be stamped *"hecho en méxico"* (Made in Mexico). Mexicana airlines has a cargo office at Libres 617 (☎ 951/5-3711), open Monday through Saturday from 9am to 8pm, and it can ship your goods to any gateway cities in the United States that have U.S. customs offices. Mexicana requires eight copies of your receipts and charges a minimum of $120 for 1 to 20 kilos (2–44 lbs.) to send a package to, for example, Los Angeles. To avoid shipping, however, remember you're allowed up to two suitcases on a flight.

2 Exploring Oaxaca City

There are several very good museums, convents, and colonial buildings in Oaxaca, as well as a wonderful zócalo where the band plays every other night, and sidewalk cafes around the zócalo provide the perfect place for travelers and locals to watch the action. There are also many interesting short road trips through the surrounding countryside—to nearby ruins at Monte Albán and Mitla, or to the outlying villages for pottery, wood carving, and textiles. You'll want to visit Oaxaca's market and the various popular art shops around town; the craft work of this state is some of the finest in Mexico. Remember that most shops and museums will be closed from 2 to 4pm.

The life of the city centers around the zócalo, bordered by Avenidas Hidalgo, Trujano, Magón, and Valdivieso. Calle Magón becomes García Vigil to the north and Cabrera to the south, while Valdivieso becomes Alcalá to the north and Bustamante to the south. The white wrought-iron gazebo in the center and several fountains along the pathways make it a delightful place to walk or sit. This is the place from which to orient yourself.

To get a feel for this lovely city, I recommend walking around town to see the churches and monuments, and then (mañana) a visit to the Regional Museum and the Rufino Tamayo Museum of Pre-Hispanic Art.

FESTIVALS

Oaxaca is famous for its colorful, exuberant, and tradition-filled festivals. The most important ones are during Holy Week at Easter, the Guelaguetza in July, Días de los Muertos in November, and the Night of the Radishes and Christmas in December. Make hotel reservations at least two months in advance if you plan to visit during these times.

At festival time in Oaxaca, sidewalk stands are set up in the market areas and near the cathedral to sell buñuelos, the Mexican equivalent of a papadum (the crunchy, spiced wafers that often begin an Indian meal), only sweet. You'll be served your buñuelo in a cracked or otherwise flawed dish or bowl, and after you're finished you smash the crockery on the sidewalk for good luck. Don't be timid! After a while, you may find yourself buying more and more buñuelos—which cost about 75¢ each— just for the fun of smashing plates. Besides buñuelos, hot punch (*ponche*), loaded with fruit, and atole are served and cost about 60¢ each.

Note: If you want to come for Christmas or the Guelaguetza but rooms and transportation are booked, you may want to consider **Sanborn's Tours** for both festivals. Contact them at 2015 S. 10th St., McAllen, TX 78502 (☎ **800/395-8482**). **Remarkable Journeys,** P.O. Box 31855, Houston, TX 77231-1855 (☎ **713/721-2517** or 800/856-1993 in the U.S.; fax 713/728-8334), also arrives in time for the Night of the Radishes.

For more activities see "Oaxaca After Dark" and "Exploring the Countryside: Day-Trips from Oaxaca City" at the end of this section.

HOLY WEEK

During Holy Week (the principal activities of which begin the Thursday before Easter Sunday), figurines made of palm leaves are made and sold on the streets by village families. On Palm Sunday (the Sunday before Easter) there are colorful parades, and on the following Thursday, Oaxaca residents follow the Procession of the Seven Churches. Hundreds of the pious move from church to church, taking communion in each one to ensure a prosperous year. The next day, Good Friday, many of the barrios have "Encuentros," where groups depart separately from the church, carrying relics through the neighborhoods, then "encountering" each other back at the church. Throughout the week each church sponsors concerts, fireworks, fairs, and other entertainment.

FIESTA GUELAGUETZA

On the Mondays following the last two weekends in July, you can witness the Fiesta Guelaguetza, or Feast of Monday of the Hill. In the villages, a guelaguetza (which literally means gift) is held by a family needing to acquire the means of holding a wedding or other obligatory community celebration. Gifts are catalogued and will be repaid in kind at other guelaguetzas. In Oaxaca the custom of a guelaguetza, which includes elaborately staged regional dancing, has been a civic celebration since 1974, when the Cerro del Fortín stadium was built.

During these last two weeks in July there are fairs and exhibits, and regional dances are performed in the stadium on the Cerro del Fortín each Monday (about 10am–1pm). It's a marvelous spectacle of color, costumes, music, and dance in which the dancers toss small candies or other treats to the crowds as symbolic guelaguetzas or gifts. Some 350 different *huipils* and dresses can be seen during the performance as the villages of the seven regions of Oaxaca present their traditional dances. Admission ranges from free (in Section C) to between $50 and $75 (in Section A), and tickets must be reserved in advance through the State Tourism office (no later than May). A travel agency may be able to help you. I recommend Sections 5 and 6 in Palco A for the best seating in the Cerro del Fortín stadium. The color of your ticket matches the color of your seat. You will be sitting in strong sunlight, so wear a hat and long sleeves. At about 7:30 in the evening, following the Guelaguetza dances, a free performance of the Legend of Donaji is presented in the stadium.

On the Sunday nights before the Guelaguetza, university students present an excellent program in the Plaza de la Danza at the Soledad Church. The production is called the *Bani Stui Gulal*, and is an abbreviated history of the Oaxaca valley. The program begins at 9pm, but since the event is free and seating is limited, you should get there quite early.

DÍAS DE LOS MUERTOS

The Days of the Dead (November 1 and 2), blend Indian and Hispanic customs and trail only Easter in importance to local people. Markets brim with marigolds and offerings for altars built to honor the dead. Be sure to take one of the night cemetery tours offered around this time. An excellent one is offered out of Casa Arnel (☎ **951/5-2856,** fax 951/3-6285). They leave for Xoxo (pronounced "ho-ho") around 10pm on October 31, taking flowers and candles to be placed on tombs that have no visitors, and return about 1:30am. Cost is $15.50. They also visit other villages on the nights of November 1 and 2.

Xoxo is the most traditional on October 31, but other villages have different kinds of festivities on the next two nights, some of them quite carnival-like with masked street dancers and no cemetery vigil.

DECEMBER FESTIVALS

The December Festivals begin on the 12th, with the festival of the Virgen de Guadalupe, and continue on the 16th with a *calenda,* or procession, to many of the older churches in the barrios, all accompanied by dancing and costumes. Festivities continue on the 18th with the Fiesta de la Soledad in honor of the Virgen de la Soledad, patroness of Oaxaca state. On that night there is a cascade of fire from a "castle" erected for the occasion in Plaza de la Soledad. December 23 is the **Night**

of the Radishes, when the Oaxaqueños build fantastic sculptures out of enormous radishes (the most prized vegetable cultivated during the colonial period), as well as flowers and corn husks. Displays on three sides of the zócalo are set up from 3pm on. By 6pm, when the show officially opens, lines to see the amazing figures are four blocks long. It's well organized and overseen by a heavy police presence. On December 24, around 8:30pm, each Oaxacan church organizes a procession with music, floats, enormous papier mâché dancing figures (*caros allegoricos*), and crowds bearing candles, all of which culminate on the zócalo.

NEW YEAR'S EVE

The New Year is rung in with the Petition of the Cross, where villagers from all over come to a forlorn chapel on the hill beyond Tlacolula (about 22 miles southeast of Oaxaca, near Mitla) to light candles and express their wishes for the coming new year. Mock bargaining, with sticks and stones to represent livestock and produce, is part of the traditional way of expressing hope for the new year. Tiny symbolic farms and fields are built, proxies for dreams of real prosperity.

MUSEUMS

Institute of Graphic Arts

Alcalá 507. ☎ **951/6-6980.** Free admission (donation requested). Wed–Mon 10:30am–8pm. Closed Tues.

Also known simply as IAGO, the Institute features an outstanding national and international graphic-arts collection, which contains the works of Goya, Posada, Tamayo, Toledo, and others. Prints, drawings, and posters make up the collection and there is a fine library of over 6,000 volumes (including videos) spread over several rooms. The front gallery features traveling exhibits and there is a small bookstore. Housed in the former residence of the Toledo family, the institute is located across (catercorner to the right) from the front of the Santo Domingo Church. A small coffee and pastry shop in the back courtyard is open daily from 8am to 8pm.

Oaxaca Museum of Contemporary Art

Alcalá 202, between Matamoros and Morelos. ☎ **951/6-8499.** Free Admission (donation requested). Daily 9am–9pm.

Also known as the House of Cortés (and formerly the Museum of the City of Oaxaca), this museum is 2¹/₂ blocks north of the zócalo. It exhibits the work of contemporary artists, primarily from Oaxaca state. The museum also hosts international exhibits. If there's an opening night, join the crowd; concerts and other cultural events are also held in the main patio. A second patio has a cafe and cine club. A fine small bookstore is to your right as you enter. The beautifully restored 16th-century building housing the museum was supposedly built on the order of conqueror Hernán Cortés after receiving the title of Marqués of the Valley of Oaxaca (he died in Spain without seeing it).

Regional Museum of Oaxaca

Gurrión at Alcalá. ☎ **951/6-2991.** Admission $2; free Sun and holidays. Tues–Fri 10am–6pm. Sat, Sun and holidays 10am–5pm.

This former convent next to the Santo Domingo Church six blocks north of the zócalo has had a colorful history, including having been used as an army barracks during the War of Independence. All the rooms open onto the lovely arched interior courtyard, where the only sound is that of the fountain. There are remnants of elaborate frescoes along the walls and ceilings. The building is still magnificent, and you can feel the pervasive peacefulness of the place.

The contents of Monte Albán's Tomb 7 are probably the most popular exhibits here. Discovered in 1932, they're housed in the room immediately to the left after you enter the museum; seeing these incredible treasures first may make the rest of the rooms on the first floor more meaningful. The tomb contained the remains of 12 to 14 individuals. Some scholars believe the Zapotecs built the tomb about A.D. 500, but—though there's still debate—the tomb's contents are generally thought to be Mixtec, dating to about A.D. 1250. All agree, however, that the jewelry—made of gold (almost 8 lb.), turquoise, conch shell, amber, and obsidian—and the bowls of onyx and rock crystal are very beautiful. Some 500 pieces of jewelry and art were found, and the display is breathtaking.

A few hints on interpreting recurring visual motifs you'll see as you move through the rest of the museum (there's no guidebook to the museum, and all the plaques are in Spanish): The Zapotecs had a number system of bars and dots, similar to that of the Olmecs and the Maya, and a collection of glyphs that, perhaps, represent a calendar. Another thing to note is that most of the ceramic sculpture here has the characteristic Zapotec touches of prominent teeth, elaborate headgear (often an eagle or jaguar mask), and large earplugs. Many of the figures have mouths similar to the ones found in Olmec sculpture—it's thought that the Olmecs influenced the early development of Monte Albán.

Next stop should be the room that's straight ahead on the first floor as you enter the museum, which displays objects and artifacts that will lead you through some 8,000 years of human history in the Oaxaca valley. The next rooms are dedicated to exquisite finds from the nearby ruins of Monte Albán, the Zapotec city that flourished from 600 B.C. until beginning to decline around A.D. 800. The Mixtecs moved in and remained until the 15th century.

On the upper floor are rooms devoted to an ethnographic exhibit of regional crafts and costumes; mannequins dressed in authentic regional dress portray facets of religious, social, and cultural life. These rooms, and an exhibit devoted to the Dominican presence in Oaxaca, are not always open.

Until 1994, a portion of the convent was occupied by the military. That area has been returned to the state which has begun restoration. It will be a part of the museum.

Rufino Tamayo Museum of Pre-Hispanic Art

Av. Morelos 503. ☎ **951/6-4750.** Admission $1.50. Mon and Wed–Sat 10am–2pm and 4–7pm, Sun 10am–3pm. Closed Tues and holidays. Open all day Dec 17–30.

The artifacts displayed in this unique museum were chosen "solely for the aesthetic rank of the works, their beauty, power, and originality." The result is one of the most important collections of pre-Hispanic art in Mexico. The collection was amassed over a 20-year period by artist Rufino Tamayo, who was born in Oaxaca. The artifacts range from the preclassical period up to the Aztecs: terra-cotta figurines, scenes of daily life, lots of female fertility figures, Olmecan and Totonac sculpture from the Gulf Coast, and Zapotec long-nosed god figures. Plaques in Spanish give the period, culture, and location of each find, but you'll find yourself ignoring this information and just admiring the works and displays. Missing, however, is information on the sites where most of the figures were found, although most are noted to be from a particular area of the country. To get to the museum, walk two blocks north of the zócalo on Alcalá to Morelos, then left 2¹/₂ blocks. It's between Tinoco y Palacios and Porfirio Díaz.

CHURCHES

Basílica de la Soledad

Independencia at Galeana. No phone. Museum 25¢. Open: Museum, Mon–Sat 10am–2pm and 4–6pm, Sun 11am–2pm; Basílica, daily 7am–2pm and 4–9pm.

The Basílica, the most important religious center in Oaxaca, is seven blocks west of the zócalo. A sculpted black-stone representation of the Virgen de la Soledad, patron saint of the state, rests high on the west wall (around to the left as you face the church). A huge celebration on and around December 18th honors this patron saint, attracting penitents from all over the state. The Basílica is actually a huge complex of buildings, including a garden, convent, and museum. A small outdoor patio/theater (Plaza de la Danza), with stone and concrete step/seats, lies just in front of the church grounds; here spectators can witness the famous *Bani Stui Gulal* (see "Guelaguetza" under "Festivals," above). The original church, begun in 1582, was much damaged by the many earthquakes that occurred during the early years of the Conquest and was rebuilt between 1682 and 1690. The Basílica has four levels on the outside, each decorated with carvings of saints. The interior is an overpowering array of chandeliers, angels, gilt ceiling, paintings, and statues. A figure of La Virgen de la Soledad is above the altar in the Basílica. A copy is in the museum at the back of the church, to your right as you exit. Both statues are draped in black velvet, and the copy resides in a chapel filled with white wedding regalia made of glass, pearl, and plastic. Other items of interest include a 3-foot-square case containing innumerable miniature glass figurines (birds, angels, animals, and flowers) surrounding the Christ Child, many 18th-century *retablos* (altarpieces) expressing thanks for favors granted, and a four-panel stained-glass representation of the legend of the finding of the Virgen's carved head and hands. The garden outside the museum has a life-size metal sculpture of the legendary mule train in which the mysterious chest was found.

Cathedral of Oaxaca

Fronting the Parque Alameda. No phone. Free admission. Daily 7am–9pm.

Anchoring the east end of the Alameda is the cathedral, originally built in 1553 and reconstructed in 1773. It has an elaborate 18th-century baroque facade and a glittering interior with three naves and many side chapels. It contains a bronze sculpture above the altar, a huge pipe organ, stained-glass windows, and fine etched-glass doors.

Church of San Felipe

Tinoco y Palacios at Independencia. No phone. Free admission. Daily 8am–11pm.

This church 2¹/₂ blocks northeast of the zócalo was built in 1636 and displays all the architectural opulence of that period: The altar and nave are covered with ornately carved and gilded wood, and the walls are frescoed—ornate but not overpowering. In the west transept/chapel is a small figure of St. Martha and the dragon; the faithful have bedecked her with ribbons, praying that she assist them in vanquishing their woes (often a spouse).

San Juan de Dios

20 de Noviembre s/n, corner Aldama and Arteaga. No phone. Free admission. Daily 6am–11pm.

This is the earliest church in Oaxaca, built in 1521 or 1522 of adobe and thatch. The present structure was begun during the mid-1600s, and included a convent and hospital (where the 20 de Noviembre market is now). The exterior is nothing special but the interior has an ornate altar and paintings on the ceiling by Urbano Olivera. A glass shrine to the Virgen near the entrance and one to Christ (off to the right) are especially revered by Oaxaqueños. Because it's by the market, one block west and two blocks south of the zócalo, many of the people who visit the church are villagers who've come in to buy and sell. There's an interesting guitar mass on Sunday at 1pm.

Santo Domingo Church
Corner of Gurrión and Alcalá. No phone. Free admission. Daily 7am–2pm and 4–11pm.

There are 27 churches in Oaxaca, but you should make a special effort to see this one, next to the Regional Museum of Oaxaca, six blocks north of the zócalo. Don't judge a church by its facade. Started in the 1550s by Dominican friars and finished a century later, it contains the work of all the best artists of that period. The walls and ceiling are covered with ornate plaster statues and flowers, most of them gilded. The sun shines through the yellow stained-glass window, casting a golden glow over the whole interior. There is a large gilded rosary chapel to the right as you enter. If you are there around 11am Monday through Saturday, you are likely to hear the lovely sound of the gift shop operator singing her devotions in the Rosario chapel. It is worth timing your visit for this.

SPANISH & ART CLASSES
The **Instituto Cultural Oaxaca A.C.,** Av. Juárez 909 (Apdo. Postal 340), 68000 Oaxaca, Oax., Mexico (☎ 951/5-3404; fax 951/5-3728), offers Spanish classes for foreigners, as well as workshops with Mexican artisans such as weavers, potters, and cooks. There are also lectures emphasizing Oaxaca's history, archaeology, anthropology, and botany. Although the normal course length is 4 weeks, arrangements can be made for as short a period as a week, and the institute will arrange inexpensive housing with local families. The institute itself is housed in a lovely old hacienda next to the Pan American Highway. Even a short time at the institute will give you a better understanding of both the language and Oaxaca.

The **Instituto de Comunicación y Cultura,** Alcalá 307-12, 68000 Oaxaca, Oax. (☎ and fax **951/6-3443**), provides group or private Spanish instruction to many satisfied students. They can also arrange for a homestay with a Mexican family.

OTHER ATTRACTIONS
Teatro Macedonio de Alcalá
Independencia at Armenta y López. No phone. Open only for events.

This beautiful 1903 belle époque theater, two blocks east of the zócalo, holds 1,300 people and is still used for concerts and performances in the evening. Peek through the doors to see the marble stairway and Louis XV vestibule. A list of events is sometimes posted on the doors.

Cerro del Fortín
Díaz Ordaz at Calle Delmonte. No phone.

To take all this sightseeing in at a glance, those with cars can drive to this hill at the west of town for a panoramic view of the city, especially good just before sunset. Recognize the hill by a statue of—who else?—Benito Juárez and a stadium built to hold 15,000 spectators. The annual Fiesta Guelaguetza is held here.

You can walk to the hill as well. Head up Díaz Ordaz/Crespo and look for the Escaleras del Fortín (Stairway to the Fortress) shortly after you cross Calle Delmonte; the 180 plus steps (interrupted by risers) are a challenge, but the view is worth it.

3 Shopping in Oaxaca City

It's a toss-up as to what tourists do first in Oaxaca: see the nearby ruins, or shop. Oaxaca and the surrounding villages have some of the country's best buys in locally handcrafted pottery, wood carvings, and textiles. It's easy to buy more than you ever imagined, so come prepared with extra suitcases.

For market days in outlying villages and directions to the wood-carver and other crafts villages of importance, see "Exploring the Countryside: Day-Trips from Oaxaca City," below.

Note: Before you load down with tons of pottery, wood carvings, and weavings, keep in mind that your luggage is weighed at flight check-in. You'll be charged a fee for bags over 25 kilos (slightly over 55 lbs.). The transport bus to the airport also charges extra for passengers with overly bulky or excess baggage. See also "Shipping" under "Fast Facts" above for more information.

ARTS & CRAFTS

Several of the stores mentioned below are on the pedestrians-only Alcalá (but watch out for motorbikes), which has been closed to traffic from Independencia to Gurrión, making it a most pleasant place to browse. The Benito Juárez Market (see "City Markets," below) mainly features meat, produce, and household needs. The 20 de Noviembre Market, a block farther south, has a huge crafts section. Both markets can be accessed from either Cabrera or 20 de Noviembre streets, both of which are open to traffic.

Artesanías y Industrias Populares del Estado de Oaxaca (ARIPO)
García Vigil 809. ☎ **951/4-4030.**

The State of Oaxaca runs ARIPO, which includes a workshop and store. It is located two blocks farther up the hill beyond the Benito Juárez house. You can hear looms working in the back as you browse through the handicrafts expertly displayed in the many rooms. ARIPO has possibly the widest selection of black pottery in the city. There's also a good supply of masks, clothing, and cutlery. Open Monday through Saturday from 9am to 7pm, at the corner of Vigil and Cosijopi.

Arte y Tradición
García Vigil 406. ☎ **951/6-3552.**

Four blocks north of the zócalo and just around the corner from the FONART store, a brightly painted doorway leads one into this attractive arcade of shops with an open patio in the center. Each shop functions as a cooperative, with articles on consignment from the various villages, such as Teotitlán del Valle and Arrazola. Individuals from these villages are on hand to explain the crafts (weaving, wood carving, and the like) as practiced by their townspeople. You'll also find an excellent restaurant serving authentic Oaxacan cuisine, the Belaguetza Travel Agency, and a small bookstore. The English-speaking manager, Judith Reyes, is a real dynamo and has tremendous pride in her Mixtec heritage. The store is open daily 9am to 8pm, although the individual shop hours may vary.

FONART
M. Bravo 116. ☎ **951/6-5764.**

Oaxaca's branch of this government-supported chain is on M. Bravo at García Vigil. The name stands for *Fondo Nacional para el Fomento de las Artesanías.* Prices are fixed. Featuring a wide selection of native crafts from all over Mexico, the store is open Monday through Saturday from 9am to 2pm and 4 to 7pm. During Christmas it's open daily from 9am to 5pm.

Galería Arte de Oaxaca
Murgía 105. ☎ and fax **951/4-0910** or 951/4-1532.

Owner Nancy Mayagoitia has made this the city's best showcase for the state's leading contemporary artists. There's always something artistically exciting happening here. Open Monday through Friday from 11am to 3pm and 5 to 9pm, Saturday 11am to 3pm. You'll find it two blocks north and one block east of the zócalo.

La Mano Mágica
Alcalá 203. ☎ **951/6-4275.**

This gallery of contemporary and popular art is across from the city museum. The name means "magic hand," and it's a true celebration of Oaxacan artistic creativity. Fine exhibits of paintings by local artists occupy the front room. The back rooms are full of regional folk art by the area's best artisans, folk who carry on an inherited artistic tradition in their village homes. Pieces are personally selected by owners Mary Jane and Arnulfo Mendoza (don't miss his weavings). They can help you ship purchases anywhere in the world via DHL courier service. Located between Morelos and Matamoros opposite the Museum of Contemporary Art/MACO (House of Cortés), it's open Monday through Saturday from 10am to 1:30pm and 4 to 7:30pm.

Mercado de Artesanías
J. P. García at Zaragoza.

If the crafts section of the Benito Juárez market mentioned under "City Markets," below, leaves you wanting, this is a good place to get an overview of Oaxaca's folk arts, particularly textiles. Women and men weave rugs, belts, *huipils*, serapes, and bags on looms and display their finest work. Ask the artisans where they're from and you'll get an idea of which villages you'd like to visit. Located one block south and one block west of the 20 de Noviembre Market and four blocks south and two blocks west of the zócalo, it's open daily from 10am to 4pm.

Victor's
Porfirio Díaz 111. ☎ **951/6-1174.**

This art shop in a 17th-century monastery is managed by Sr. Ramón Fosado, who goes to the villages himself in search of the best native art. He speaks English and is very pleasant. If you're shopping for serapes and blankets, be sure to stop at Victor's to do a little research. The quality of these goods varies, but the friendly staff here is willing to tell you about the differences in materials (wool versus synthetic), dyes (natural and chemical), and designs. You should also scout around and compare the various products in the open markets. Open Monday through Saturday from 9am to 2pm and 4 to 8pm.

Yalalag de Oaxaca
Alcalá 104. ☎ **951/6-2108.**

This old mansion near the corner of Alcalá and Morelos displays a multifarious but affordable collection of art. Black pottery, Talavera ceramics, terra-cotta figurines, tin sculpture, table linens, apparel, papier-mâché sculpture, and other quality crafts from all over Mexico can be found here. Open Monday through Saturday from 9:30am to 1:30pm and 4:30 to 8pm.

CHOCOLATE & MOLE

Although Oaxaca produces some chocolate, most that is processed here comes from Tabasco and Chiapas. The state is better known for its 20 (more or less) varieties of mole (*moh*-lay), of which chocolate is often an ingredient; it comes in colors of red, yellow, black, brown, and green. Mole is used to make a sauce usually served over turkey or chicken but also as a flavoring in regional tamales. In the market area, strolling vendors sell chocolate in thick half-dollar–size cakes, usually six or eight to the package. However, you'll have more choices (and more fun deciding) if you buy it in a store specializing in chocolate. Establishments that sell fresh chocolate often also grind and mix the ingredients for mole and sell it in a paste. Mole can be found in heaps in both the Abastos and Benito Juárez markets (see "City Markets," below), at grinders on Mina, or at the Chocolate Mayordomo mentioned below. Mole keeps for a year if stored in a refrigerator.

Chocolate Mayordomo

20 de Noviembre at Mina. ☎ **951/6-1619** or 951/6-0246.

This corner store is actually a huge operation with another outlet across the street on Mina and several others throughout the city. All sell chocolate and mole and they'll mix or ground to your specifications. Here you'll find shelves of boxed chocolate either *amargo* (unsweetened) or *semidulce* (semisweet), with or without almonds and/or cinnamon, in small, hard cakes or in a soft paste. Either is used in cooking or for making hot chocolate. A half-kilo (1.1 lb) of chocolate costs around $1.50; gift boxes of plastic-wrapped fresh black or red mole are also found here for $2.50 per kilo. They make excellent gifts for friends back home. Ask General Manager Salvador Flores about chocolate—you'll learn a lot! The store is open daily from 8am to 8:30pm.

CITY MARKETS

Abastos Market

Across the railroad tracks and just south of the second-class bus station.

The Abastos Market is open daily but is most active on Saturday, when Indians from the villages come to town to sell and shop. You'll see huge mounds of dried chilies, herbs, vegetables, crafts, bread, and even burros for sale at this bustling market.

Benito Juárez Market

Bordered by Las Casas, Cabrera, Aldama, and 20 de Noviembre.

One block south of the zócalo, this covered market is big and busy every day, but especially on Saturday. The area around it is then an open street market, teeming with vendors of chilies, string, parrots, talismans, food, spices, cloth, dresses, and blankets—one of the most exciting markets in Mexico, because the people who come to sell their wares are so colorful. The bulk of the produce trade has been relocated to a new building called the Abastos Market (see above), where the local color is even more profound.

20 de Noviembre Market

Bordered by Las Casas, Cabrera, Mina, and 20 de Noviembre.

Anchored on the northwest corner by the San Juan de Dios Church and immediately south of, and truly a continuation of, the Juárez Market, this one has its own separate name. It occupies the area where once stood the convent and hospital of the San Juan de Dios Church. In addition to many food products, there are innumerable cookshops offering juices and complete meals.

4 Accommodations

Oaxaca is in the midst of a tourism boom—and a shortage of hotel rooms. You can generally arrive and find a room easily enough, but in the high tourist periods of

Easter, July, November, and December, it's best to have reservations for at least your first two nights in town.

VERY EXPENSIVE

✪ Hotel Camino Real

Cinco de Mayo no. 300, 68000 Oaxaca, Oax. ☎ **951/6-0611,** or 800/722-6466 in the U.S. Fax 951/6-0732. 91 rms. FAN TV TEL. $175 single or double standard rooms; $200 single or double superior rooms; and $245 single or double for Club rooms. Children under 12 stay free in parents' room.

Converted from the 4-centuries-old former Convent of Santa Catalina (if you listen carefully in the morning, you can hear monks chanting), this hotel is one of the most beautiful of its kind in Mexico. Through the centuries it has been used as the city municipal office, a government palace, a jail, a movie theater, and a school twice. Since becoming a hotel (as such it was first known as the Presidente), the building has been designated a "national treasure."

The hotel's two floors are decorated with frescoes and colonial relics. Mexican textiles and local pottery accent each room. Interior rooms are quieter—those with windows on the street echo with passing traffic until the wee hours. The hotel is three blocks north and one block east of the zócalo, between Murgía and Abasolo.

Dining/Entertainment: The dining room spills onto the portals in the interior courtyard and is one of the city's most pleasant places to dine. On Sundays there's a lavish brunch. The breakfast buffet changes daily but always includes Oaxacan specialties. On Friday evenings the hotel hosts a Guelaguetza—a great regional dance show and dinner buffet.

Services: Laundry and room service, travel agency.

Facilities: Swimming pool.

MODERATE

Calesa Real

García Vigil 306, 68000 Oaxaca, Oax. ☎ **951/6-5544.** Fax 951/6-7232. 77 rms. FAN TV TEL. $45 double. Free parking.

The Calesa Real, in a colonial-style building 3 1/2 blocks north of the zócalo, is popular with tour groups. One of the nicest features here is a small kidney-shaped pool in a cool courtyard. Though comfortable, furnishings in the largish rooms are nondescript, eight of the rooms on the first floor have French doors opening to the pool area; others on the second and third floors have small balconies. A second-story terrace and restaurant overlook the pool. The hotel is between Bravo and Matamoros.

Casa Colonial Bed & Breakfast

División Oriente, corner Negrete (Apdo. 640), 68000 Oaxaca, Oax. ☎ and fax **951/6-5280,** or 800/758-1697 in the U.S. Fax 951/6-7232. 15 rms. $81 double (including breakfast). Free parking.

You'll feel at home in this casa if your Spanish is limited. Owners Jane and Thornton Robison are very knowledgeable about Oaxaca and lead specialty tours to surrounding villages. Formerly a mansion, the Casa Colonial has been a private guest house for more than 20 years. Each room is individually decorated with comfortable antique furniture and private bath. There is a sala, or living room, full of books about Mexico, and the dining room has both a large family-style table and smaller individual tables. To reach the hotel from the zócalo, walk one block north on García Vigil then turn left on Independencia for six blocks. Just pass La Soledad Church, angle right for a couple of blocks; the Casa will be on your left.

⊙ Hostal de la Noria

Av. Hidalgo 918, 68000 Oaxaca, Oax. ☎ **951/4-7844,** or 800/528-1234 in the U.S. Fax 951/6-3992. 43rms. TV TEL. High season, $57 single, $66 double. Low season, $50 single, $57 double.

Behind this gracious colonial-era facade is one the city's newest hotels, complete with gracious courtyard restaurant, elegant bar and three stories (no elevator) of large rooms. Pastel-yellow walls with lavender-accent trim around the wooden doors lead to rooms overlooking either the interior courtyard or exterior streets. Rooms are large, with high ceilings, carpeting, handsome armoires for clothing, and remote control TV. Some baths have a tub/shower combination. The hotel, which is affiliated with Best Western, is two blocks east of the zócalo at the corner of Fiallo/Reforma.

Hotel Casona del Llano

Av. Juárez 701, 68000 Oaxaca, Oax. ☎ **951/4-7719** or 47703. Fax 951/6-2219. 28 rms. FAN TV TEL. $24 single; $31 double. Free parking.

In an elegant mansion with a beautiful stone veranda, this hotel definitely has curb appeal. The grand-looking but reasonably priced restaurant is on the left as you enter; there are two stories of rooms in this building as well as a new section in back that fronts a handsome inner lawn. There's no elevator. Guest quarters are tastefully decorated in pastel and earth tones, with tile floors, large windows, and rattan furniture. The Restaurant is open daily from 7am to 11pm. The hotel's across the street from El Llano, a park popular with Oaxacan families and children, but for all of the activity there, it is quiet. Located on the west side of Parque Paseo Juárez (known locally as El Llano), this hotel is a short (15-min.) walk or shorter bus ride from the zócalo. To find it from the zócalo, walk three blocks east on Hidalgo to Juárez and turn left (north) for seven blocks; it's at the corner of Humbolt.

⊙ Hotel Gala

Bustamante 103, 68000 Oaxaca, Oax. ☎ **951/41308.** Fax 951/6-3660. 36 rms. FAN TV TEL. $31 single; $36 double.

This hotel has such an impressive lobby with a sweeping staircase, and is so nicely kept, you'd expect to pay a lot more. Opened in 1992, occupying the old Hotel Ruiz, the three stories of rooms (no elevator) are carpeted and have coordinated furnishings and firm mattresses. Some rooms have windows overlooking Bustamante, and others have windows on the hall. Though some rooms have minuscule bathrooms, and in most cases there's not a lot of room for luggage, it's otherwise a very comfortable and excellently located hotel. The hotel restaurant is to the right of the front door. The Gala is half a block south of the zócalo near the corner of Bustamante and Guerrero.

Hotel Misión de Los Angeles

Porfirio Díaz 102, Col. Reforma, 68050 Oaxaca, Oax. ☎ **951/5-1500,** or 800/223-6510 in the U.S. Fax 951/5-1680. 173 rms. AC TV TEL. $45 single; $60 double.

Spread out on immaculate grounds around a large swimming pool are the several one- and two-story buildings of this resort-style hotel. The large sunny rooms, all with a patio or balcony, are nicely furnished with carpet, a game table and two chairs, and remote control television with U.S. channels. Mattresses could be better. There are two restaurants, three bars, and the disco Tequila Rock which is open Wednesday through Saturday from 9pm to 3am. The hotel is located about a half mile north of the zócalo. To find it from the Parque Juárez, walk one block north, cross the busy Calzada Ninos Heroes, and you'll see the hotel set back from the street on the right.

✪ Marqués del Valle

Portal Clavería s/n, 68000 Oaxaca, Oax. ☎ **951/6-3677** or 951/6-6294. Fax 951/6-9961. 95 rms. TV TEL. $37 single or double.

One of the most charming traditional hotels in Oaxaca, the five-story Marqués del Valle (with elevator) has large rooms built around an inner courtyard. It's across from the zócalo next to the cathedral, yet this side of the plaza isn't very noisy (except for Sunday afternoon band concerts). Rooms with French doors facing the plaza have a grand view. Be sure to try one of the coffees in the cafe under the colonnade in front of the hotel. Service is slow, but the coffee is the best in town. One tip: Walk-in customers get lower hotel rates than those who reserve ahead.

INEXPENSIVE

✪ Las Golondrinas

Tinoco y Palacios 411, 68000 Oaxaca, Oax. ☎ **951/6-8726.** Fax 951/4-2126. 24 rms. $19 single; $23 double; $27 single suite; $31 double suite.

Owned and personally managed by Guillermina and Jorge Velasco, Las Golondrinas (which means "The Swallows") has been growing more popular every year. This charming one-story hotel is situated amid rambling patios with roses, fuchsia, bougainvillea, and mature banana trees. The 24 simply furnished rooms, with windows and doors opening onto courtyards, are individually accented with Mexican crafts; all have tile floors and a small desk and chairs. The suite, with one bed, has unpainted pine furniture, a sunny shuttered window, and largish bathroom. Breakfast (nonguests welcome) is served between 8 and 10am in a small tile-covered cafe in a garden setting. Opposite the reception area is a small living room with television and guidebooks and novels to lend (not to trade). To reach the hotel, go two blocks west of the zócalo, then turn right for 4¹/₂ blocks. It's between Allende and Bravo.

Hotel Antonio's

Independencia 601, 68000 Oaxaca, Oax. ☎ **951/6-7227.** Fax 951/6-3672. 15 rms. TV. $20 single; $23 double; $26 triple.

Opened in 1991, this comfortable and conveniently located hotel was converted from an old two-story townhouse, with a lovely interior patio surrounded by an arcaded walkway. A small, colorful and cozy restaurant occupies the patio. Each room has a tile floor, colonial-style pine furniture, some with two double beds, and a small tile bath. Wall hooks solve the storage problem in rooms without closets. It's located 1¹/₂ blocks west of the cathedral, at the corner of Porfirio Díaz and Independencia.

⑤ Hotel Casa Arnel

Aldama 404, Col. Jalatlaco, 68080 Oaxaca, Oax. ☎ **951/5-2856.** Fax 951/3-6285. 30 rms (22 with bath). $5.75 single without bath, $10.75–$11.50 single with bath; $11.50 double without bath; $14.50 double with bath; apartment $150–$175 for two weeks; $300–$350 monthly. Parking $2.25 daily.

This favorite budget hotel is slightly removed from the city center but still within walking distance of most sights. The casa is a U-shaped two-story building constructed around a cool tropical garden behind the Cruz family home. Sooner or later, you'll meet a member of this large and loving family. The rooms, all with tile floors, are plain but clean and comfortable; some share a bath among four rooms. Across the street in the new wing are three additional rooms with double beds and private baths, plus four furnished apartments with fully equipped kitchens. In the apartments, stays of 15 days are allowed at half the monthly rate. Breakfast and dinner, at an extra cost (around $3), are served on the family patio. At other times the patio is a mingling place for guests, who come from all over the world.

At Christmas the family goes all out to involve guests in a traditional Mexican Christmas with posadas the 12 nights before Christmas, an elaborate room-size nativity scene, and a festive Christmas Eve dinner—all at no charge to Arnel guests. It's something special and many guests return every Christmas. The hotel also acts as a travel agent and can make tour, bus, and airline arrangements.

To get to the hotel, turn right out the front door of the first-class bus station, go two blocks, and turn right onto Aldama. The casa is seven blocks ahead on your left across from the Iglesia San Matias Jalatlaco.

Hotel Las Rosas

Trujano 112, 68000 Oaxaca, Oax. ☎ **951/4-2217.** 19 rms. $16.50 single; $20 double.

Las Rosas, formerly the Plaza Hotel, has been renovated and painted bright white. A narrow flight of stairs leads up from the street to the second-story lobby and colonial courtyard. Rooms open onto the courtyard, and some have windows; those without windows are claustrophobic. Rooms are cheerily decorated with a few regional crafts and colorful tile work. Some rooms have floor fans. There's a television in the small lobby area on the entry landing. The hotel is situated one half block west of the zócalo, between Magón and 20 de Noviembre.

Hotel Principal

Cinco de Mayo no. 208, 68000 Oaxaca, Oax. ☎ and fax **951/6-2535.** 17 rms. $18.50 single; $20 double; $24 triple.

The Principal, one block east and 2¹/₂ blocks north of the zócalo, is a longtime favorite of budget travelers, for good reason. The location, near shops, museums and restaurants, is great and rooms are clean and filled with sunlight. Six upstairs rooms have balconies. Make reservations in advance, since the hotel is often full.

Hotel Reforma

Reforma 102, 68000 Oaxaca, Oax. ☎ **951/6-0939.** 16 rms. $8.50 single; $10 double.

If you're on a tight budget, try this hotel, centrally located two blocks northeast of the plaza. Remodeled, repainted, and refurnished in 1992, the clean rooms feature brightly painted walls in pastel pink and green, tile floors, and chenille or cotton bedspreads. Some rooms are so crowded with furniture it creates a tight squeeze to the bath or requires creative luggage placement. In general, baths are small, and although the commodes are new, most don't have toilet seats; also look out for the curtainless showers, which may spray the whole bathroom. The Reforma is between Independencia and Morelos.

Hotel Santa Clara

Morelos 1004, 68000 Oaxaca, Oax. ☎ **951/6-1138.** 14 rms. $11 single; $13 double.

Opened in 1993 by the owners of the Hotel Reforma, this simple two-story hotel has a lot of charm for the few bucks you pay. Beyond the lobby is a nice paved inner courtyard with white iron tables and chairs. Rooms are in back of this, and two of them face the courtyard with big windows that let in the light. The carpeted rooms have armoires for clothing, matching furniture, and tile baths. Rooms behind the patio may be a bit dark, so check first. The hotel is near the corner of Reforma.

Hotel Virreyes

Morelos 1001, 68000 Oaxaca, Oax. ☎ **951/6-5141.** 30 rms. $8.50 single; $11 double.

The courtyard at the Virreyes is covered with painted glass that lets in such a mellow light the air seems to be colored beige. The hotel is a converted mansion that's looking a bit run down. Rooms are large, with tile floors and high ceilings, but some are very dark and have no windows. Be sure to look at your room before signing in. This is not a hotel for the light sleeper because of the street noise and the echo-chamber effect created by the enclosed courtyard. The hotel is a few steps between Juárez and Reforma.

5 Dining

Oaxaca's regional foods are among the best in Mexico. The state is known for its varieties of mole, cheese, tamales, peppers, tortillas, bread, and chocolate. *Tasajo,* a thin cut of beef, and *cecina,* a thin cut of pork, are two regional specialties. To see a magnificent array of these foods, walk through the Abastos Market on Saturday; the quantity and variety are unforgettable. When you hear women shouting *"tlayuda, tlayuda,"* take a look at the 12-inch tortillas they're selling. Oaxaca is also known for pozole Mixteco, a delightfully different version of this hearty soup that includes chicken and red mole sauce. Restaurants in the city often feature mole, tamales, and Oaxaca cheese. Fortunately, and at last, good restaurants are becoming easier to find in Oaxaca and the prices here are better than in almost any other city in Mexico.

For a snack or light breakfast, pick up your fill of pastries, cookies, sweet rolls, and breads from the large **Panificadora Bamby,** at the corner of Morelos and García Vigil, two blocks north of the zócalo. It's open daily from 7am to 9pm.

EXPENSIVE

Restaurant del Vitral
Guerrero 201. ☎ **951/6-3124.** Appetizers $2.65–$3.80; main courses $4.50–$12.50. Daily 12:30–11pm. MEXICAN/INTERNATIONAL/REGIONAL.

The building, an elegant mansion, dates from the time of Porfirio Díaz, impresses with its elegant stairway, stained- and etched-glass windows, and crystal chandeliers. White lace and pink tablecloths cover the tables, set with crystal and china. The interesting menu features cold cucumber and avocado soup; and an assortment of U.S. cuts of beef, chicken Kiev, duck with honey and cognac, brochettes, and regional specialties such as mole coloradito. The restaurant is only a block east of the zócalo, at the corner of Armenta y López.

MODERATE

La Casa de la Abuela
Av. Hidalgo 616. ☎ **951/6-3544.** Appetizers $1.50–$6.50; main courses $5–$8.25. Daily 1–11pm. MEXICAN/REGIONAL.

This upstairs restaurant overlooks both the zócalo and the Alameda. Wood-plank floors, yellow-ochre stucco walls, and dark-green cloths on chairs and tables create a rich, cozy setting in which to taste the region's foods. "Grandmother's house," as the name translates, offers *chapulines* (fried grasshoppers); huge tlayuda tortillas; empanadas with many local sauces; black bean soup; tamales; mole coloradito; *caldo de gato* (cat's stew) made with beef and pork; and much more. The entrance is a few steps west of the zócalo.

✪ Restaurant/Bar Catedral
García Vigil 105. ☎ **951/6-3285.** Breakfast $1.75–$2.75; main courses $5–$10. Daily 8am–2am. MEXICAN/REGIONAL/STEAKS.

Casually elegant, with both an open patio and interior dining, this is also a serene place to enjoy a leisurely meal. The restaurant is known for its excellent cuts of beef. Among its international selections is veal cordon bleu, and the regional choices include poblano soup, and chicken estofado which is one of the 20 moles of Oaxaca. It's 2 blocks north of the zócalo, at the corner of Morelos.

INEXPENSIVE

Cafetería Bamby

García Vigil 205. ☎ **951/6-3285.** Breakfast $1.50–$3; soups/salads $1.75–$5; main courses $3.50–$5; comida corrida $3. Daily 7am–8pm. MEXICAN.

Two and a half blocks north of the zócalo is this bright, clean, U.S.-type cafe. When you're feeling a bit homesick for home-style food, this is the place to come. Service is courteous and prompt, and the nice selection of dishes attracts both local and tourist clientele. And the bathrooms are way above average!

✪ Doña Elpidia

Miguel Cabrera 413. ☎ **951/6-4292.** Fixed-price lunch $4.15. Daily 8:30–10am, 1–5pm. REGIONAL.

This restaurant is virtually an institution in Oaxaca; Doña Elpidia, and now her son, have been catering to a refined, selective local clientele for decades. Inside the deceptively shabby-looking door is a beautiful and heavily shaded courtyard filled with birds and plants. Five tables are set out in the shaded arcade, and there are a dozen more in the indoor dining rooms. The five-course comida corrida includes a basket of bread, an appetizer, vegetable or pasta soup, a meat or enchilada course, a dessert, and Mexican coffee. There's usually a different mole daily. The place is a bit hard to find since the sign says only RESTAURANT, but it's 5½ blocks south of the zócalo, between Arista and Nuño del Mercado.

✪ Gecko Coffee Shop

Cinco de Mayo 412. ☎ **951/4-8024.** Sandwiches $1.25; desserts $1–$1.25; coffee 75¢; chocolate $1.25. Mon–Sat 7am–8pm. PASTRIES/SANDWICHES/CHOCOLATE/COFFEE.

Less than half a block south of the Santo Domingo Church is this little habit-forming gem. A variety of delicious sandwiches and pastries are served along with hot chocolate and coffee either in a small dining room or in the more ample patio. Here you have peace and quiet to sip, snack, and read or write the ever-necessary postcards. And when you finally tear yourself away, a gallery, small bookstore, and the wonderful Instituto Welte (of Oaxaca studies) are just off the patio.

⑤ Restaurant El Decano

Cinco de Mayo 210. ☎ **951/4-4153.** Appetizers $2–$5; main courses $3.25–$5.50; comida corrida $2–$2.50. Mon–Sat 9am–9pm. MEXICAN/REGIONAL.

People in the know find their way to this simple lunchroom, known primarily for its filling comida corrida. The midday repast includes a choice of two soups, then choose between entrees such as two kinds of mole, fish, stuffed squash, a small steak, or the plato Oaxaca. These are accompanied by beans, rolls, or tortillas, and followed by an ample dessert. The restaurant is 4 blocks north of the zócalo near the corner of Murgía.

⑤ Restaurant El Mesón

Av. Hidalgo 805 at Valdivieso. ☎ **951/6-2729.** Breakfast and lunch buffet $3; comida corrida $1.80; tacos $1.60–$2.80; Mexican specialties $1.35–$6. Daily 8am–1am (breakfast buffet 8am–noon; lunch buffet noon–6pm and comida corrida noon–4.30pm). MEXICAN/REGIONAL.

As you enter El Mesón you see señoritas patting out fresh tortillas, and if you sit at the counter you can watch all the kitchen preparations. The menu and prices are printed on a sheet the waitress gives you; just check off what you want and present the waitress with your selection. The food is good and reasonably priced, and it's a great place to try regional specialties. What's more, the excellent all-you-can-eat buffets include fresh fruit and at lunch fresh salads are added, plus a variety of main courses. The comida corrida is a shortened version of the lunch buffet—soup and a main course of your choice. Taco prices are per order (usually two tacos). Besides the large range of tacos, they serve some "especialidades" such as tamal Oaxaqueño, pozole, and *puntas de filete albañil* (bricklayers' beef tips). There's the regular assortment of beer and soft drinks, but this is a good place to try chocolate with water or milk (so hot and good on a chilly morning) or the equally delicious atole. The location is excellent and it's a popular meeting place for fellow travelers and locals alike.

Restaurant Las Quince Letras

Abasolo 300. ☎ 951/4-3769. Breakfast $1.75–$5.25; appetizers $1.50–$4.25; main courses $3.65–$5.25; comida corrida $3. Daily 8am–9pm. MEXICAN/REGIONAL.

Look for a bright blue entry-way with the restaurant's name painted vertically in white on it. Though it has only one small dining room, and it's a bit off the well-worn path, the restaurant has a loyal following of foreigners who know value and good taste. If you are more than a party of one, complementary *memelitas* are served while you decide what to order. This regional masa creation is similar to a sope. Here you can satisfy your longing for a fresh salad, which is huge and unadorned with dressing. The *tasajo,* prepared several ways, is cooked in a wonderful marinade. If you order the filling botana Oaxaqueña, the dozen different enticements leave barely enough room for a light dessert. To find it from the zócalo, walk north on Alcalá 4 blocks to Abasolo, then right 3 1/4 blocks. It's on the right, just past the corner of Juárez.

Restaurant T.L.C.

J. P. García at Aldama. ☎ **951/6-4331**. Breakfast $1.65–$2.50; main courses $1.35–$3.50; comida corrida $2. Mon–Sat 7am–midnight. MEXICAN.

Should you find yourself on Mina in the chocolate part of town at lunchtime, walk to the corner of J. P. García and Aldama for a treat. As a rather crowded street-corner lunchroom, it isn't particularly inviting, but the food is good. T.L.C. stands for tacos, licuados, and comida, but there's much more than that. The tostadas are a two fisted affair, the *alambre especial* features three kinds of meat and fresh vegetables, plus there are quesadillas, seafood, burgers, and tlayudas that are loaded or semiloaded. It is a block west of the markets on Aldama, and four blocks southwest of the zócalo.

6 Oaxaca City After Dark

Among the best entertainments in Oaxaca are the **band concerts** in the zócalo—and they're free, too! The state band plays on Tuesday, Thursday, and Sunday, while Monday, Wednesday, Friday, and Saturday the marimbas take over. Oaxaca has the jolliest and most active zócalo in all of Mexico, enjoyed by everyone in town, young and old, rich and poor, citizen or tourist.

A smaller version of the **Guelaguetza,** the famous regional dance of Oaxaca, is performed at the Hotel Camino Real on Friday from 7 to 10pm by a group of highly professional dancers. The cost of $28 per person includes a buffet and elaborate show. The Hotel Monte Albán presents more reasonably priced **folk dances** daily from 8:30 to 10pm for $5 for the show alone. Dinner and drinks are extra. Buy your ticket the day before; then when you enter, you'll find your name-card placed at your reserved seat.

Concerts and dance programs are offered all year long at the **Teatro Macedonio de Alcalá,** at Independencia and Armenta y López. Schedules are often posted by the front doors of the theater. The **Casa de la Cultura** (ex-convent of the Seven Princes), at the corner of Colón and G. Ortega, offers exhibits, lectures, films, and various art and music classes, as does the **Centro Cultural Ricardo Flores Magón** (Alcalá 302).

One of Oaxaca's hottest **discos** is in the **Hotel Victoria,** on the Cerro del Fortín, northwest of the center of town (☎ **951/5-2633**). It's active from 10pm until 2am on Friday and Saturday. You'll need a taxi to get there, or at least to get home. At the **Hotel Misión de los Angeles,** Calz. P. Díaz 102 (☎ **951/5-1500**), north of the Parque Juárez, the **Disco Tequila Rock** is open Wednesday through Saturday from 9pm to 3am. The **Disco Eclipse** (Calle Porfirio Díaz 219, between Matamoros and Morelos, ☎ **951/6-4236**) kicks it from Thursday through Sunday (10pm until the crowd decides to leave).

For night owls who are not up to the disco scene, there's **live music** at **El Sagrario** (Valdivieso 120, behind the cathedral; ☎ **951/4-0303**); the club provides food and beverages while (from 8pm on) you listen to salsa, guitar, and Andean panpipes. The **Terranova,** facing the zócalo at Portal Benito Juárez 116 (☎ **951/4-0533**), is a popular restaurant with live music between 8pm and 11pm. And near Santo Domingo Church is **La Candela,** Allende 211, 1¹/₂ blocks west of Santo Domingo (☎ **951/6-7933**). It's a good enough restaurant in its own right, but it's a popular nightspot with live salsa, reggae, and more, and dancing from about 9:30pm until 1:30am Tuesday through Saturday. **El Sol y La Luna,** Bravo 109 between Alcalá and Vigil, (☎ **951/4-8105**) is another good restaurant, serving crêpes, pasta, and pizza, among other things, and attracting a loyal following of diners and live-music lovers. It's open Monday through Saturday from 5pm to midnight.

7 Exploring the Countryside: Day-Trips from Oaxaca City

Monte Albán and Mitla are the two most important archaeological sites near Oaxaca, but there are several smaller ruins that are also interesting. In addition, I've mentioned a few day-trips to the more interesting villages outside Oaxaca. (For Puerto Escondido, Huatulco, and Puerto Angel, see chapter 3, "Mexico's Southern Pacific Beach Resorts.") The tourist office will give you a map showing the nearby villages where beautiful handicrafts are made. It's a fun excursion by car or bus.

MONTE ALBÁN: FABLED MOUNTAINTOP CEREMONIAL CENTER

For some 1,500 years prior to 500 B.C., the Oaxaca valleys were inhabited by more or less settled village-dwelling peoples, whose origins are mysterious. Then, between 800 and 500 B.C., a new ceramic style appeared, presumably produced by an influx of new peoples, now called Zapotec. Around 500 B.C., these peoples began to level the top of a mountain upon which to build the magnificent city we know as Monte Albán (*mon*-teh al-*ban*).

Very little of the original structures remain—they've been either obscured beneath newer structures or recycled, their stones reused. However, the Danzantes friezes (see below) are of this period.

Monte Albán was an elite center of Zapotec culture, although affected by contemporary cultures outside the valley of Mexico. You can see Olmec influence in the early sculptures; more recent masks and sculptures reflect contact with the Maya. When Monte Albán was at its zenith in A.D. 300, architectural ideas were borrowed from Teotihuacán. By around A.D. 800, the significance of Monte Albán in Zapotec cosmology began to decline. Although probably never totally abandoned, it became a mere shell of its former grandeur. Then, around the beginning of the 13th century, the remnants of this star of the valley were appropriated by the Mixtecs. The Mixtecs,

Monte Albán

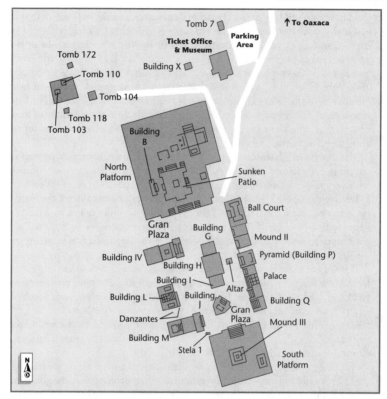

Tomb 7

↑ To Oaxaca

Parking Area

Ticket Office & Museum

Tomb 172

Building X

Tomb 110

Tomb 104

Tomb 118

Tomb 103

Building B

North Platform

Sunken Patio

Ball Court

Gran Plaza

Building G

Mound II

Building IV

Pyramid (Building P)

Building H

Palace

Building I

Altar

Building L

Building J

Gran Plaza

Building Q

Danzantes

Mound III

Building M

Stela 1

South Platform

N

who had long coexisted in the area with the Zapotecs, now imposed their own, by now more highly developed, culture. At Monte Albán, they did very little building of their own but are renowned for the treasure they left in Tomb 7.

Monte Albán covers about 15 square miles and is centered on the Great Plaza, a large grassy area that was once a mountaintop. From this plaza, aligned north-south, you can overlook the lush Oaxacan valley, a gorgeous setting for any civilization. The excavations at Monte Albán have revealed more than 170 tombs, numerous ceremonial altars, stelae, pyramids, and palaces.

Begin your tour of the ruins on the eastern side of the Great Plaza at the **I-shaped ball court.** This ball court differs slightly from Maya and Toltec ball courts in that there are no goal rings and the sides of the court are sloped. Also on the east side of the plaza are several altars and pyramids that were once covered with stucco. Note the sloping walls, wide stairs, and the ramps, which are typical of Zapotec architecture and resemble the architecture of Teotihuacán. The building is slightly out of line with the plaza (not on the north–south axis) and is thought by some to have been an observatory probably aligned with the heavenly bodies rather than with the points of the compass.

The south side of the plaza has a large platform that bore several stelae, most of which are now in the National Museum of Anthropology in Mexico City. There's a good view of the surrounding area from the top of this platform.

The west side has more ceremonial platforms and pyramids. On top of the pyramid substructure are four columns that probably held the roof of the temple at one time.

The famous **building of the Dancers (Danzantes)** is on the west side of the plaza, and is the earliest known structure at Monte Albán. This building is covered with large stone slabs carved into distorted naked figures (these are copies; the originals are protected in the site museum). There is speculation as to who carved these figures and what they represent. There is certainly a distinct resemblance to the Olmec "baby faces" seen at La Venta, in Tabasco state. The distorted bodies and pained expressions of the faces perhaps imply disease. There are clear examples of figures representing childbirth, dwarfism, and infantilism. Because of the fluidity of the figures, they became known as the Danzantes, but this is only a modern label for these ancient and mysterious carvings.

The **Northern Platform** is a maze of temples and palaces interwoven with subterranean tunnels and sanctuaries. Wander around here, for there are numerous reliefs, glyphs, paintings, and friezes along the lintels and jambs as well as the walls.

Leaving the Great Plaza, head north to the cemetery and tombs. Of the tombs so far excavated, the most famous is Tomb 7, to the east of the cemetery. Inside were found some 500 pieces of jewelry made of gold, amber, and turquoise, as well as art objects made of silver, alabaster, and bone. This amazing collection is on display at the Regional Museum of Oaxaca.

If you have a day to spend at Monte Albán, be sure to visit some of the tombs, for they contain some really magnificent glyphs, paintings, and stone carvings of gods, goddesses, birds, and serpents. Two tombs that are especially absorbing, Tombs 104 and 105, are guarded and can be entered via ladders; the guards are usually helpful about pointing out areas of special interest. Ignore the vendors hawking "original" artifacts, supposedly found at the site—if they were real, these guys would hardly need to wander around in the midday sun trying to sell them!

As you enter the site you'll see an on-site museum, a shop selling guidebooks to the ruins, a cafe, and a craft shop. I recommend you purchase one of the guidebooks. Admission to the ruins is $3.50; free on Sunday and holidays. The site is open daily from 8am to 5pm. Licensed guides charge $13.50 per person for a walking tour. Video camera permits cost $5.50.

To get to Monte Albán, take a bus from the Hotel Mesón del Angel, Mina 518, at Mier y Terán. Autobuses Turísticos makes seven runs daily, leaving at 8:30, 9:30, 10:30, and 11:30am and 12:30, 1:30, and 3:30pm. Return service leaves the ruins at 11am, noon, and 1, 2, 3, 4, and 5:30pm. The round-trip fare is $1.75. The ride takes half an hour, and your scheduled return time is 2 hours after your arrival. It's possible to take a later return for an additional $1; inform the driver of your intent (but you won't be guaranteed a seat). During high season there are usually additional buses.

THE ROAD TO MITLA: RUINS & RUG WEAVERS

East of Oaxaca, the Pan American Highway to Mitla rolls past several important archaeological sites, markets, and craft villages. En route you can visit the famous El Tule tree; the church at Tlacochahuaya; the ruins at Dainzú, Lambityeco, and Yagul; the weaver's village of Teotitlán del Valle; and the Saturday market village of Tlacolula.

Without a car, it's impossible to cover all these destinations in 1 day, and by car the route takes a very long day. On a Sunday you could combine the Tlacolula Market with all the archaeological sites, which have free admission on Sunday. Save the weaving village of Teotitlán del Valle and the church of Tlacochahuaya for another day.

Shopping at the Source: Oaxaca's Splendid Market Villages

You could spend a full week in Oaxaca just visiting the various markets held in nearby villages. Each has its specialty—cheese, produce, livestock, weaving, and pottery—and its unique character. Market days in the villages are as follows:

Wednesday	**Etla,** known for its cheese; 9¹/₂ miles north.
Thursday	**Zaachila,** ruins and agriculture; 11 miles southwest.
	Ejutla, agriculture; 40 miles south.
Friday	**Ocotlán,** pottery, textiles, and food; 18¹/₂ miles south.
Saturday	**Oaxaca,** Abastos Market.
Sunday	**Tlacolula,** agriculture and crafts (visit the chapel as well); 19¹/₂ miles southeast.

You can get to any of these craft villages by taking a bus from the second-class bus station, eight blocks west of the zócalo on Trujano. On market days these buses are crammed with passengers. If you get off a bus between destinations—say, at Dainzú on the way to Mitla or at Cuilapan on the way to Zaachila—but want to continue to the next place, return to the highway and hail a passing bus.

It's also possible to take a colectivo taxi to the villages that don't have bus service. To find a colectivo, head to the south end of the Abastos Market. On Calle Mercaderos you'll see dozens of parked maroon-and-white colectivo taxis. The town each one serves is written on the door, trunk, or windshield. There are also posted metal signs for destinations. They fill up relatively fast and are an economical way to reach the villages. Be sure to go early; by afternoon the colectivos don't fill up as fast and you'll have to wait.

Tours to all the markets as well as the craft villages and ruins can easily be arranged through **Tours Arnel,** at Hotel Casa Arnel, Aldama 404 (☎ **951/5-2856**), or **Belaguetza,** at Arte y Tradición, García Vigil 406, (☎ **951/6-3552**). There are, of course, many tour agencies in Oaxaca, but these both offer friendly, personal, English-speaking guide service at competitive prices. Three- to four-hour tours to Monte Albán or Mitla will cost about $9 per person (plus site entry). Other villages can be included at minimal cost.

Many of these historical and/or craft villages have, in the past several years, developed some truly fine small municipal museums. **San José El Mogote,** site of one of the very earliest pre-Hispanic village-dweller groups, has a display of carvings and statues found in and around the town and a display model of an old hacienda and details of its produce and social organization. **Teotitlán del Valle** is another with such a municipal museum; it features displays on the weaving process. Ask at the State Tourism Office (north side of the Alameda on Independencia) for more information on these and other museums.

The **Fletes y Pasajes** bus line (☎ **951/6-2270**) runs buses every 20 minutes from 6am to 8pm to Mitla from the second-class terminal. The terminal is eight long blocks west of the zócalo on Trujano. The trip takes an hour and 15 minutes and costs $1 each way. The driver will stop at any point along the way; let him know in advance.

SANTA MARÍA DEL TULE'S 2,000-YEAR-OLD TREE

Santa María del Tule is a small town (8 miles outside Oaxaca) that's filled with turkeys, children, and rug vendors. The town is famous for the immense **El Tule Tree,**

Shopping for Handwoven Zapotec Rugs

For centuries the Zapotecs have been among the most skilled of Mexican weavers, and now collectors worldwide are discovering their work. So it's no secret that sleuthing for the perfect rug in the weaving village of Teotitlán del Valle is a primary quest for many foreigners. The high quality rugs are reversible, and are made by families who've passed the craft on for generations.

Rug vendors and weavers with little shops begin the minute you turn left off the highway from Oaxaca to Teotitlán, and almost all of these along the stretch going into town are worth a stop. There's an artisans' rug market in town, but as you'll discover in a stroll through the dirt streets of this prosperous town, a weaver resides inside almost every house. You're welcome to knock and enter. Piles of rugs are neatly folded on tables and chairs, and they will patiently unfold them and spread them out on the floor for as long as you are willing to look.

Designs, colors, and quality vary. A few people are selling uninspired, mass produced–looking rugs made of cheap cotton or acrylic, but on the whole, craftsmanship is excellent here, with wool being the yarn of choice. The natural wool colors of white, dark brown, and black are incorporated into the rugs, and some wools are dyed using natural plants. However, most colors of blue, red, yellow, orange, and green are achieved through artificial dying.

Buying a colorfast wool rug with colorfast dyes is usually a given, but I've noticed that many shop owners will stretch the truth regarding the dyes. Perhaps because past visitors have asked for naturally dyed rugs (thinking that they're always more desirable), some store owners (not necessarily the weavers) proclaim untruthfully that the rugs are made with naturally dyed yarn. They may also proclaim that a rug with a Navajo design is instead thoroughly Zapotec. Some weavers, but more often store owners, present a bowl of dried cochineal bugs (harvesting these insects from maguey cacti is being revived in the area), as proof that the colors appearing in their rugs are natural as opposed to commercially produced. Cochineal dye was a dynamic business in pre-Hispanic times and was coveted by Europeans after the Conquest of Mexico. But the tiny insect is difficult to cultivate even now (it attracts a host of natural predators), so the dried insects are expensive to buy. Thus any rug incorporating cochineal-dyed yarn is very expensive. And in truth adeptness in using this illusive insect as a dye (or any other natural dye for that matter), is limited to only a few dye specialists in Teotitlán. Depending on the natural or manmade chemical the insect is mixed with to achieve color variation, the color can range from pale lavender to yellow and deep orange/red. Natural indigo blue, made from leaves of a plant (*indigofera anil*), is another widely touted color, but use of it too is exaggerated, even though it's grown in Oaxaca. In either case, a rug incorporating these natural dyes would lack uniformity of color, so any rug with

an *ahuehuete* tree (Moctezuma cypress) in a churchyard just off the main road. It turned 2,002 years old in 1996. The enormous ancient tree is still growing today, as is evidenced by the foliage, but pollution and a sinking groundwater level are posing a serious threat. This whole region around Santa María del Tule was once very marshy; in fact, the word *tule* means "reed." A private foundation has been established in an effort to provide protection for this survivor. Beyond El Tule is agricultural country, and at siesta time you'll see whole families resting in the shade of giant cacti.

perfectly matching blue or orange/red throughout probably isn't made with either of these natural colors. Knowledgeable collectors often prefer the irregularity of the same color in a rug which is often found when natural colors are used, however, it's also true that skilled weavers may show variations of one color in a portion of rug without using naturally died yarn; varying the same color with a different hue is an artistic weaving technique—not a ploy to fool buyers.

Traditional Zapotec rugs in pastel earth tones and with designs (usually a Greek-like fret motif) from area pyramids continue to be made; however, within the last decade a strong Navajo rug influence swept through town, radically changing local designs while deepening the colors into rich blue-greens, pale to medium yellows, strong orange-reds, handsome dark green, and dark navy to aquamarine and pale blue. These master Zapotec weavers adopted the Navajo designs readily, failing only in conquering the pleasing color combinations of the Navajos—though some weavers are excellent color designers. Purists disdain outside influence on traditional styles, but realists acknowledge the prosperity this new work brings the village. Versatile Zapotec weavers offer to weave anything to specification—show them a picture of your desired rug and the finished work demonstrates mastery of their craft. But be prepared to present rug specifications in meters, not inches or feet.

If you're a serious shopper, plan to spend the day going from house to shop to house, narrowing your choices as you go. In the warren of streets it's wise to collect names and addresses too, so you can retrace your steps if necessary. Prices start high and you're expected to bargain (that's why it can take a wearying, but very interesting, day to accomplish purchases). Cut the starting price in half and see where bargaining leads. As an example, a small bath mat–size rug costing $25 to $35 in Oaxaca, may cost $10 to $15 in Teotitlán. But there are large rugs too, some big enough to show handsomely under a dining room table or to become the centerpiece on a large wall. Price is also affected by the complication of design, and variation and number of colors. The weavers are uniformly pleasant about showing you many rugs without making you feel uncomfortable if you don't buy immediately—but don't ponder endlessly—time spent with you is time away from weaving. Besides rugs, the woven goods appear as pillow covers and are fashioned into purses with leather trim. These you'll find in shops on the main street rather than in homes.

Getting carried away while rug hunting here isn't unusual, so what a relief it is to discover that credit cards are accepted at most of the better storefront shops. But it's cash only in weaver's homes. Most people will accept dollars, but the exchange rate will be lower than you'd get at an exchange house or bank. Whatever currency you use, bring plenty—the rugs are so appealing that you'll probably buy more than you planned.

You can see the tree from outside the churchyard fence, or pay $1.50 to go inside, close to the tree.

The **Church of San Jerónimo Tlacochahuaya** is a fine example of how the Spanish borrowed from Zapotec architectural design. Inside you'll see how the church leaders artistically melded the two cultures. Note the elaborately carved altar and the crucified Christ fashioned from ground-dried corn cobs. Also, don't miss the still-functional organ (dated 1620) in the choir loft. The church is open from 10am to 2pm and 4 to 6pm. It's on the right side of the road, past El Tule Tree, and 14 miles from Oaxaca.

The Mitla bus will drop you off at the road leading into town. You can either hitch a ride with locals or walk the distance.

DAINZÚ: ZAPOTEC RUINS

Sixteen miles from Oaxaca, this site (first excavated in the 1960s) dates to sometime between 700 and 600 B.C. Increasingly sophisticated building continued until about A.D. 300. One of the major buildings was constructed against a west-facing hill; incorporated into the lower portion of this building were found some 35 carvings resembling Monte Albán's Danzantes. These carvings are now housed in a protective shed which a caretaker will unlock for interested parties. There is a partially reconstructed ball court. The site provides an outstanding view of the valley. Admission is $1.50.

Dainzú (dine-*zoo*), beautiful in the afternoon sun, lies less than a mile south of Highway 190, at the end of a mostly paved road. Look for a sign 16 miles from Oaxaca.

LAMBITYECO: ANOTHER ARCHAEOLOGICAL SITE

On the south side of Highway 190, a few miles east of the turnoff to Dainzú, is the small site of Lambityeco. Part of a much larger site containing over 200 mounds, it is thought to have been inhabited from about 600 B.C., although the fully studied part belongs to the period following the decline of Monte Albán. Of particular interest are the two beautifully executed and preserved stucco masks of the rain god Cocijo. A product of Lambityeco was salt, distilled from saline groundwaters nearby. Admission is $1.50; $5.50 for use of your video camera.

TEOTITLÁN DEL VALLE: BEAUTIFUL RUGS

This town is famous for weaving; its products can be found in the shops in Oaxaca, but if you're serious about rug shopping there's a lot of pleasure in buying them at the source and meeting the weavers in the process. Most weavers sell out of their homes and give demonstrations. The prices are considerably lower than in Oaxaca, and here you have the opportunity to visit weavers in their homes.

The church in town is well worth a visit, as is the community museum opposite the artisan's market and adjacent to the church. The museum has an interesting exhibit of natural-dye making using herbs, plants, and cochineal.

For a place to eat consider the **Restaurant Tlaminalli,** Av. Juárez 39 (☎ 951/ 4-4157), run by six lovely Zapotec sisters who serve authentic Oaxacan cuisine. Its reputation as the shrine of Oaxacan cooking brings in lots of foreigners, but my last meal there was just average. It could have been an off day. Prices on the a la carte menu seem a bit steep at $2 for soup and $5 for a smallish main course. It's on the main street as you approach the main part of town, in a red brick building on the right with black wrought-iron window covers. It's open Monday through Friday from 1 to 4pm. A bit farther on, there's another nice restaurant on the left where the main street intersects with the town center.

Direct buses make the run between Oaxaca and Teotitlán from the second-class bus station. If you're coming from or going to Mitla, you'll have to hitch or walk from the highway crossroads.

TLACOLULA: A FINE MARKET & UNIQUE CHAPEL

Located about 19 miles from Oaxaca, southeast on the road to Mitla, Tlacolula is famous for its market and **Dominican chapel,** which is considered by many to be

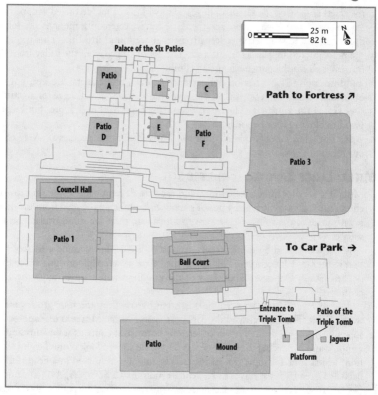

Palace of the Six Patios

Patio A

B

C

Path to Fortress ↗

Patio D

E

Patio F

Patio 3

Council Hall

Patio 1

To Car Park →

Ball Court

Entrance to Triple Tomb

Patio of the Triple Tomb

Jaguar

Patio

Mound

Platform

0 — 25 m / 82 ft

N

the most beautiful of the Dominican churches in the Americas. The wrought-iron gates, the choir loft, and the wrought-iron pulpit, considered to be unique in Mexico, are worth a look, as are the frescoes and paintings in relief. A few years ago a secret passage was found, leading to a room that contained valuable silver religious pieces. The silver was hidden during the Revolution of 1916 when there was a tide of anti-religious sentiment; the articles are now back in the church.

Sunday is market day in Tlacolula, with rows of textiles fluttering in the breeze, and aisle after aisle of pottery and baskets.

YAGUL: RUINS OF A ZAPOTEC FORTRESS

This was a fortress city on a hill overlooking the valley. It's 20 miles southeast of Oaxaca, about half a mile off the road to Mitla. There's a small sign indicating the turnoff to the left; go up the paved road to the site. The setting is absolutely gorgeous, and because the ruins are not as fully reconstructed as those at Monte Albán, you're likely to have the place to yourself. It's a good place for a picnic lunch.

The city was divided into two sections: the fortress at the top of a hill and the area of palaces lower down. The center of the palace complex is the plaza, surrounded by four temples. In the center is a ceremonial platform, under which is the Triple Tomb. The door of the tomb is a large stone slab decorated on both sides with beautiful hieroglyphs. The tomb may or may not be open for viewing.

Look for the beautifully restored ball court, typical of Zapotec ball courts (which are without goal rings). North of the plaza is the incredible palace structure built for the chiefs of the city. It's a maze of huge rooms with six patios, decorated with painted stucco and stone mosaics. Here and there you can see ceremonial mounds and tombs decorated in the same geometric patterns that are found in Mitla. This is one of the most interesting palaces in the area. The panoramic view of the valley from the fortress is worth the rather exhausting climb.

Admission is $1.25; free on Sunday and holidays. Still cameras are free, but use of a video camera will cost you $4.15. Save your receipt—it will serve for any other sites visited the same day. The site is open daily from 8am to 5:30pm, but be prepared to blow 11¢ for parking.

It's just a few miles farther southeast to Mitla. The turnoff comes at a very obvious fork in the road.

MITLA: LARGE ZAPOTEC & MIXTEC SITE

Mitla is 2³/₄ miles from the highway, and the turnoff terminates at the ruins by the church. If you've come here by bus, it's about half a mile up the road from the dusty town square to the ruins; if you want to hire a cab, there are some available in the square.

Mitla was settled by the Zapotecs around 600 B.C., but became a Mixtec bastion in the late 10th century. This city of the Mixtecs was still flourishing at the time of the Spanish Conquest, and many of the buildings were used through the 16th century.

The town of Mitla (pop. 10,000) is often bypassed by the tour groups but is worth a visit. The University of the Americas maintains the **Museum of Zapotec Art** (previously known as the Frissell collection) in town. It contains some outstanding Zapotec and Mixtec relics. Admission is $1.50. Be sure to look at the Leigh collection, which contains some real treasures. The museum is housed in a beautiful old hacienda. In a back patio is the excellent **Restaurant La Sorpresa,** Av. Juárez no. 2 (☎ **951/8-0194**); a pleasant place to relax. You can dine on the patio daily between 9am and 5pm. Breakfast costs from $3.50 and the daily lunch special costs $5.50 and includes soup, salad, a main course, and dessert. The lunch special is truly delicious and worth the bucks.

You can easily see the most important buildings in an hour. Mixtec architecture is based on a quadrangle surrounded on three or four sides by patios and chambers, usually rectangular in shape. The chambers have a low roof, which is excellent for defense but which makes the rooms dark and close. The stone buildings are inlaid with small cut stones to form geometric patterns.

There are five groups of buildings divided by the Mitla River. The most important buildings are on the east side of the ravine. The Group of the Columns consists of two quadrangles, connected at the corners with palaces. The building to the north has a long chamber with six columns and many rooms decorated with geometric designs. The most common motif is the zigzag pattern, the same one seen repeatedly on the Mitla blankets. Human or animal images are rare in Mixtec art. In fact, only one frieze has been found (in the Group of the Church, in the north patio). Here you'll see a series of figures painted with their name glyphs.

Admission to the site is $1.50; free on Sunday and holidays. Use of a video camera costs $4.25. Entrance to the museum is included in the price. It's open daily from 8am to 5pm.

Outside the ruins you'll be bombarded by vendors. The moment you step out of a car or taxi, every able-bodied woman and child for 10 miles around will come charging over with shrill cries and a basket full of bargains—heavily embroidered belts, small pieces of pottery, fake archaeological relics, cheap earrings. Offer to pay half the price the vendors ask. There's a modern handicrafts market near the ruins, but prices are lower in town.

In Mitla and on the highway going south, you'll find **mezcal outlets** (*expendios de mezcal*), which are factory outlets for little distilleries that produce the fiery cactus *aguardiente*. To be authentic, a bottle of mezcal must have a worm floating in it. The liquor is surprisingly cheap, the bottle labels are surprisingly colorful, and the taste is quite different. It is not unlike tequila—mix a shot of mezcal with a glass of grapefruit or pomegranate juice and you've got a cocktail that will make you forget the heat, even in Mitla. Watch out for the worm!

SOUTH OF MONTE ALBÁN: ARRAZOLA, CUILAPAN & ZAACHILA

ARRAZOLA: WOOD-CARVING CAPITAL

Arrazola (ar-a-*zo*-la) is in the foothills of Monte Albán, about 15 miles southwest of Oaxaca. The tiny town's most famous resident is **Manuel Jimenez,** the septuagenarian grandfather of the resurgence in wood carving as a folk art. Jimenez's polar bears, anteaters, and rabbits carved from copal wood are shown in galleries throughout the world; his home is a Mecca of sorts for folk-art collectors. Now the town is full of other carvers, all making fanciful creatures painted in bright, festive colors. Among those who should be sought out are Antonio and Ramiro Aragon; their delicate and imaginative work should rank them with Jimenez. Little boys will greet you at the outskirts of town offering to guide you to individual homes for a small tip. Following them is a good way to know the town, and after a bit you can dismiss them.

If you're driving to Arrazola, take the road out of Oaxaca City that goes to Monte Albán, then take the left fork after crossing the Atoyac River and follow the signs for Zaachila. Turn right after the town of Xoxo and you will soon be there. There are no road signs, but other travelers along the way will direct you. The bus from the second-class station in Oaxaca will let you off at the side of the road to Arrazola where it meets the highway. From there it's a pleasant 3 1/2-mile walk to the town, past a few homes, the occupants of which are wood-carvers who will invite you in for a look at their work. To return, colectivo taxis make the run to Zaachila and Oaxaca for around $2, which can be shared—it's worth it.

CUILAPAN: A DOMINICAN MONASTERY

Cuilapan (kwi-*lap*-an) is located about 10 miles southwest of Oaxaca. The Dominican friars began their second monastery here in 1550. However, parts of the convent and church were never completed due to political machinations of the late 16th century. The roof of the monastery has fallen, but the cloister and the church remain. The church is being restored and is still used today. There are three naves with lofty arches, large stone columns, and many frescoes. It is open daily from 10am to 6pm; entry is $5.50, plus $8.50 for a video camera. The monastery is visible on the right a short distance from the main road to Zaachila, and there's a sign as well. The bus from the second-class station stops within a few hundred feet of the church.

ZAACHILA: MARKET TOWN WITH MIXTEC TOMBS

Farther on from Cuilapan, 15 miles southwest of Oaxaca, Zaachila (Za-*chee*-la) has a Thursday market; baskets and pottery are sold for local household use, and the produce market is always full. Also take note of the interesting livestock section and a *mercado de madera* (wood market) just as you enter town.

Near and behind the church is the entrance to a small archaeological site containing several mounds and platforms and two quite interesting tombs. Artifacts found there now reside in the National Museum of Anthropology in Mexico City, but Tomb 1 contains carvings worth seeing.

At the time of the Spanish Conquest, Zaachila was the last surviving city of the Zapotec rulers. When Cortés marched on the city, the Zapotecs did not resist and instead formed an alliance with him, which outraged the Mixtecs, who invaded Zaachila shortly afterward. The site and the tombs are open daily from 9am to 4pm, and the entrance fee is $1.50.

To return to Oaxaca, you have a choice of walking several blocks back to the second-class bus station near the animal market or lining up with the locals for one of the colectivo taxis on the main street across from the market. I prefer the taxi.

SOUTH ALONG HIGHWAY 175
SAN BARTOLO COYOTEPEC: BLACK POTTERY

San Bartolo is the home of the black pottery you've seen in all the stores in Oaxaca. It's also one of several little villages named Coyotepec in the area. Buses frequently operate between Oaxaca and this village, 23 miles south on Highway 175. In 1953, a native woman named Doña Rosa invented the technique of smoking the pottery during firing to make it black and rubbing the fired pieces with a piece of quartz to produce a sheen. Doña Rosa died in 1979, but her son, Valente Nieto Real, carries on the tradition. It is an almost spiritual experience to watch Valente change a lump of coarse clay into a work of living art with only two crude plates used as a potter's wheel. The family's home/factory is a few blocks off the main road; you'll see the sign as you enter town. It's open daily from 9am to 5:30pm.

Black pottery is sold at many shops on the little plaza or in the artists' homes. Villagers who make pottery often place a piece of their work near their front door, by the gate, or on the street. It's their way of inviting prospective buyers to come in.

SAN MARTÍN TILCAJETE: ANOTHER WOOD-CARVING CENTER

San Martín Tilcajete is a recent addition to the tour of folk-art towns. Located about 10 miles south of San Bartolo Coyotepec, San Martín is noted, as is Arrazola, for its wood-carvers and their fantastical, brightly painted animals and dragons. The Sosa and Hernández families are especially prolific, and you can easily spend half a day wandering from house to house to see the amazing collections of hot-pink rabbits, 4-foot-long bright blue twisting snakes, and two-headed Dalmatians.

OCOTLÁN: MARKET TOWN & THE AGUILAR POTTERS

One of the best markets in the area is held on Friday in Ocotlán de Morelos, 35 miles south of Oaxaca on Highway 175. The variety of goods includes modern dishware and cutlery, hand-molded earthenware jugs, polyester dresses, finely woven cotton or wool *rebozos* (scarves), hand-dyed and tooled leather, and electronics, as well as produce. You won't find a more varied selection except in Oaxaca. On any day other than market day, you can always visit Ocotlán's most famous potters, the noted Aguilar family—Josephina, Guillermina, and Irena. On the right, just at the outskirts of Ocotlán, their row of home-workshops is distinguished by pottery pieces stuck up on the fence and the roof. Their work, often figures of daily life, is colorful, sometimes humorous, and highly prized by collectors. Visitors are welcome daily.

NORTH OF OAXACA
GUELATAO: BIRTHPLACE OF BENITO JUÁREZ

Set high in the mountains north of Oaxaca, this town has become a living monument to its favorite son, Benito Juárez. Although usually peaceful, this lovely town comes to life on Juárez's birthday (March 21). The museum, statues, and plaza all attest to the town's obvious devotion to the patriot.

To get here, a second-class bus departs from Oaxaca's first-class station six times daily. There are also several departures from the second-class station. The trip will take at least 2 hours, through gorgeous mountain scenery. Buses return to Oaxaca every 2 hours until 8pm.

Appendix

USING THE TELEPHONES

Area codes and city exchanges are being changed all over the country. If you have difficulty reaching a number, ask an operator for assistance. Mexico does not have helpful recordings to inform you of changes or new numbers.

Most **public pay phones** in the country have been converted to Ladatel phones, many of which are both coin and card operated. Instructions on the phones tell you how to use them. When your time limit for local calls is about to end (about three minutes), you'll hear three odd sounding beeps, and then you'll be cut off unless you deposit more coins. Ladatel cards come in denominations of 10, 20, and 30 New Pesos. If you're planning to make many calls, purchase the 30 New Peso card; it takes no time at all to use up a 10 peso card (about $1.65). They're sold at pharmacies, bookstores, and grocery stores near Ladatel phones. You insert the card, dial your number, and start talking, all the while watching a digital counter tick away your money.

Next is the **caseta de larga distancia** (long-distance telephone office), found all over Mexico. Most bus stations and airports now have specially staffed rooms exclusively for making long-distance calls and sending faxes. Often they are efficient and inexpensive, providing the client with a computer printout of the time and charges. In other places, often pharmacies, the clerk will place the call for you, then you step into a private booth to take the call. Whether it's a special long-distance office or a pharmacy, there's usually a service charge of around $3.50 to make the call, which you pay in addition to any call costs if you didn't call collect.

For **long-distance calls** you can access an English-speaking AT&T operator by pushing the star button twice, then 09. If that fails, try dialing 09 for an international operator. To call the United States or Canada, tell the operator that you want a collect call (*una llamada por cobrar*) or station-to-station (*teléfono a teléfono*), or person-to-person (*persona a persona*). Collect calls are the least expensive of all, but sometimes caseta offices won't make them, so you'll have to pay on the spot.

To make a long-distance call from Mexico to another country, first dial 95 for the United States and Canada, or 98 for anywhere else in the world. Then, dial the area code and the number you are calling.

To call long distance (abbreviated "lada") within Mexico, dial 91, the area code, then the number. Mexico's area codes (claves) may be one, two, or three numbers and are usually listed in the front of telephone directories. In this book the area code is listed under "Fast Facts" for each town. (Area codes, however, are changing throughout the country.)

To place a phone call to Mexico from your home country, dial the international service (011), Mexico's country code (52), then the Mexican area code (for Cancún, for example, that would be 98), then the local number. Keep in mind that calls to Mexico are quite expensive, even if dialed direct from your home phone.

Better hotels, which have more sophisticated tracking equipment, may charge for each local call made from your room. Budget or moderately priced hotels often don't charge, since they can't keep track. To avoid check-out shock, it's best to ask in advance if you'll be charged for local calls. These cost between 50¢ and $1 per call. In addition, if you make a long-distance call from your hotel room, there is usually a hefty service charge added to the cost of the call.

POSTAL GLOSSARY

Airmail   Correo Aéreo
Customs   Aduana
General Delivery   Lista de Correos
Insurance (insured mail)   Seguros
Mailbox   Buzón
Money Order   Giro Postale
Parcel   Paquete
Post Office   Oficina de Correos
Post Office Box (abbreviation)   Apdo. Postal
Postal Service   Correos
Registered Mail   Registrado
Rubber Stamp   Sello
Special Delivery, Express   Entrega Inmediata
Stamp   Estampilla or Timbre

B Basic Vocabulary

Most Mexicans are very patient with foreigners who try to speak their language; it helps a lot to know a few basic phrases.

I've included a list of certain simple phrases for expressing basic needs, followed by some common menu items.

ENGLISH-SPANISH PHRASES

English	Spanish	Pronunciation
Good Day	**Buenos días**	*bway*-nohss-*dee*-ahss
How are you?	**¿Cómo esta usted?**	*koh*-moh *ess*-tah oo-*sted*
Very well	**Muy bien**	mwee byen
Thank you	**Gracias**	*grah*-see-ahss
You're welcome	**De nada**	day *nah*-dah
Goodbye	**Adiós**	ah-dyohss

Please	**Por favor**	pohr fah-*bohr*
Yes	**Sí**	see
No	**No**	noh
Excuse me	**Perdóneme**	pehr-*doh*-ney-may
Give me	**Déme**	*day*-may
Where is . . . ?	**¿Dónde esta . . . ?**	*dohn*-day ess-tah
the station	**la estación**	la ess-tah-see-*own*
a hotel	**un hotel**	oon oh-*tel*
a gas station	**una gasolinera**	oon-nuh gah-so-lee-nay-rah
a restaurant	**un restaurante**	oon res-tow-*rahn*-tay
the toilet	**el baño**	el *bahn*-yoh
a good doctor	**un buen médico**	oon bwayn *may*-dee-co
the road to . . .	**el camino a . . .**	el cah-*mee*-noh ah
To the right	**A la derecha**	ah lah day-*ray*-chuh
To the left	**A la izquierda**	ah lah ees-ky-*ehr*-dah
Straight ahead	**Derecho**	day-*ray*-cho
I would like . . .	**Quisiera . . .**	keyh-see-*air*-ah
I want . . .	**Quiero . . .**	*kyehr*-oh
to eat	**comer**	*ko*-mayr
a room	**una habitación**	oon-nuh ha-bee tah-see-*own*
Do you have . . . ?	**¿Tiene usted . . . ?**	tyah-nay oos-*ted*
a book	**un libro**	oon *lee*-bro
a dictionary	**un diccionario**	oon deek-see-own-ar-eo
How much is it?	**¿Cuánto cuesta?**	*kwahn*-to *kwess*-tah
When?	**¿Cuando?**	*kwahn*-doh
What?	**¿Que?**	kay
There is . . . (Is there?)	**¿Hay . . .**	eye
Yesterday	**Ayer**	ah-*yer*
Today	**Hoy**	oy
Tomorrow	**Mañana**	mahn-*yawn*-ah
Good	**Bueno**	*bway*-no
Bad	**Malo**	*mah*-lo
Better (best)	**(Lo) Mejor**	(loh) meh-*hor*
More	**Más**	mahs
Less	**Menos**	may-noss
No Smoking	**Se prohibe fumar**	seh pro-*hee*-beh foo-*mahr*
Postcard	**Tarjeta postal**	tahr-*hay*-ta pohs-*tahl*
Insect repellent	**Rapellante contra insectos**	rah-pey-*yahn*-te *cohn* -trah een-sehk-tos

MORE USEFUL PHRASES

Do you speak English? **¿Habla usted inglés?**

Is there anyone here who speaks English? **¿Hay alguien aquí que hable inglés?**

I speak a little Spanish. **Hablo un poco de español.**

I don't understand Spanish very well. **No lo entiendo muy bien el español.**

The meal is good. **Me gusta la comida.**

What time is it? **¿Qué hora es?**

May I see your menu? **¿Puedo ver su menu?**

The check please. **La cuenta por favor.**

What do I owe you? **¿Cuanto lo debo?**

What did you say? **¿Mande? (colloquial expression for American "Eh?")**

I want (to see) a room . . . **Quiero (ver) un cuarto (una habitación) . . .**

    for two persons. **para dos personas.**

    with (without) bath. **con (sin) bão.**

We are staying here only . . . **Nos quedaremos aqui sola-mente . . .**

    one night. **una noche.**

    one week. **una semana.**

We are leaving tomorrow. **Partimos mañana.**

Do you accept traveler's checks? **¿Acepta usted cheques de viajero?**

Is there a laundromat near here? **¿Hay una lavandería cerca de aquí?**

Please send these clothes to the laundry. **Hágame el favor de mandar esta ropa a la lavandería.**

NUMBERS

1	**uno**	(*ooh*-noh)	17	**diecisiete**	(de-*ess*-ee-*syeh*-tay)
2	**dos**	(dohs)	18	**dieciocho**	(dee-*ess*-ee-*oh*-choh)
3	**tres**	(trayss)	19	**diecinueve**	(dee-*ess*-ee-*nway*-bay)
4	**cuatro**	(*kwah*-troh)			
5	**cinco**	(*seen*-koh)	20	**veinte**	(*bayn*-tay)
6	**seis**	(sayss)	30	**treinta**	(*trayn*-tah)
7	**siete**	(*syeh*-tay)	40	**cuarenta**	(kwah-*ren*-tah)
8	**ocho**	(*oh*-choh)	50	**cincuenta**	(seen-*kwen*-tah)
9	**nueve**	(*nway*-bay)	60	**sesenta**	(say-*sen*-tah)
10	**diez**	(dee-ess)	70	**setenta**	(say-*ten*-tah)
11	**once**	(*ohn*-say)	80	**ochenta**	(oh-*chen*-tah)
12	**doce**	(*doh*-say)	90	**noventa**	(noh-*ben*-tah)
13	**trece**	(*tray*-say)	100	**cien**	(see-en)
14	**catorce**	(kah-*tor*-say)	200	**doscientos**	(*dos*-se-en-tos)
15	**quince**	(*keen*-say)	500	**quinientos**	(*keen*-ee-ehn-tos)
16	**dieciseis**	(de-*ess*-ee-sayss)	1000	**mil**	(meal)

BUS TERMS

Bus **Autobús**

Bus or truck **Camión**

Lane **Carril**

Nonstop **Directo**

Baggage (claim area) **Equipajes**

Intercity **Foraneo**

Luggage storage area **Guarda equipaje**

Gates **Llegadas**

Originates at this station **Local**

Originates elsewhere; stops if seats available **De Paso**

First class **Primera**

Second class **Segunda**

Nonstop **Sin Escala**

Baggage claim area **Recibo de Equipajes**

Waiting room **Sala de Espera**

Toilets **Sanitarios**

Ticket window **Taquilla**

C Menu Glossary

Achiote   Small red seed of the annatto tree.

Achiote preparada   A prepared paste found in Yucatán markets made of ground achiote, wheat and corn flour, cumin, cinnamon, salt, onion, garlic, and oregano. Mixed with juice of a sour orange or vinegar and put on broiled or charcoaled fish (tikin chick) and chicken.

Agua fresca   Fruit-flavored water, usually watermelon, canteloupe, chia seed with lemon, hibiscus flour, or ground melon-seed mixture.

Antojito   A Mexican snack, usually masa-based with a variety of toppings such as sausage, cheese, beans, onions; also refers to tostadas, sopes, and garnachas.

Atole   A thick, lightly sweet, warm drink made with finely ground rice or corn and usually flavored with vanilla.

Birria   Lamb or goat meat cooked in a tomato broth, spiced with garlic, chiles, cumin, ginger, oregano, cloves, cinnamon, and thyme and garnished with onions, cilantro, and fresh lime juice to taste; a specialty of Jalisco state.

Botana   A light snack—an antojito.

Buñuelos   Round, thin, deep-fried crispy fritters dipped in sugar.

Cabrito   Grilled kid; a northern Mexican delicacy.

Carnitas   Pork that's been deep-cooked (not fried) in lard, then steamed and served with corn tortillas for tacos.

Ceviche   Fresh raw seafood marinated in fresh lime juice and garnished with chopped tomatoes, onions, chiles, and sometimes cilantro and served with crispy, fried whole corn tortillas.

Chayote   Vegetable pear or merleton, a type of spiny squash boiled and served as an accompaniment to meat dishes.

Chiles rellenos   Poblano peppers usually stuffed with cheese, rolled in a batter and baked; other stuffings include ground beef spiced with raisins.

Churro   Tube-shaped, bread-like fritter, dipped in sugar and sometimes filled with cajeta or chocolate.

Cochinita pibil   Pig wrapped in banana leaves, flavored with pibil sauce and pit-baked; common in Yucatán.

Corunda   A triangular tamal wrapped in a corn leaf, a Michoacán specialty.

Enchilada   Tortilla dipped in a sauce and usually filled with chicken or white cheese and sometimes topped with tomato sauce and sour cream (enchiladas Suizas or Swiss enchiladas), or covered in a green sauce (enchiladas verdes), or topped with onions, sour cream, and guacamole (enchiladas Potosiños).

Epazote   Leaf of the wormseed plant, used in black beans and with cheese in quesadillas.

Escabeche   A lightly pickled sauce used in Yucatecan chicken stew.

Frijoles charros   Beans flavored with beer, a northern Mexican specialty.

Frijoles refritos   Pinto beans mashed and cooked with lard.

Garnachas   A thickish small circle of fried masa with pinched sides, topped with pork or chicken, onions, and avocado or sometimes chopped potatoes, and tomatoes, typical as a botana in Veracruz and Yucatán.

Gorditas   Thickish fried-corn tortillas, slit and stuffed with choice of cheese, beans, beef, chicken, with or without lettuce, tomato, and onion garnish.

Gusanos de maguey   Maguey worms, considered a delicacy, and delicious when charbroiled to a crisp and served with corn tortillas for tacos.

Horchata   Refreshing drink made of ground rice or melon seeds, ground almonds, and lightly sweetened.

Huevos Mexicanos   Eggs with onions, hot peppers, tomatoes.

Huevos Motulenos   Eggs atop a tortilla, garnished with beans, peas, ham, sausage, and grated cheese, a Yucatecan specialty.

Huevos rancheros   Fried egg on top of a fried corn tortilla covered in a tomato sauce.

Huitlacoche   Sometimes spelled "cuitlacoche," mushroom-flavored black fungus that appears on corn in the rainy season; considered a delicacy.

Machaca   Shredded dried beef scrambled with eggs or as a salad topping; a specialty of Northern Mexico.

Manchamantel   Translated means "tablecloth stainer," a stew of chicken or pork with chiles, tomatoes, pineapple, bananas, and jícama.

Masa   Ground corn soaked in lime used as basis for tamales, corn tortillas, and soups.

Mixiote   Lamb baked in a chile sauce or chicken with carrots and potatoes both baked in parchment paper made from the maguey leaf.

Mole   Pronounced "*moh*-lay," a sauce made with 20 ingredients including chocolate, peppers, ground tortillas, sesame seeds, cinnamon, tomatoes, onion, garlic, peanuts, pumpkin seeds, cloves, and tomatillos; developed by colonial nuns in Puebla, usually served over chicken or turkey; especially served in Puebla, State of Mexico, and Oaxaca with sauces varying from red, to black and brown.

Molletes   A bolillo cut in half and topped with refried beans and cheese, then broiled; popular at breakfast.

Pan de Muerto   Sweet or plain bread made around the Days of the Dead (Nov. 1–2), in the form of mummies, dolls, or round with bone designs.

Pan dulce   Lightly sweetened bread in many configurations usually served at breakfast or bought at any bakery.

Papadzules   Tortillas are stuffed with hard-boiled eggs and seeds (cucumber or sunflower) in a tomato sauce.

Pavo relleno negro   Stuffed turkey Yucatán-style, filled with chopped pork and beef, cooked in a rich, dark sauce.

Pibil   Pit-baked pork or chicken in a sauce of tomato, onion, mild red pepper, cilantro, and vinegar.

Pipian Sauce   made with ground pumpkin seeds, nuts, and mild peppers.

Poc-chuc   Slices of pork with onion marinated in a tangy sour orange sauce and charcoal broiled; a Yucatecan specialty.

Pollo Calpulalpan   Chicken cooked in pulque, a specialty of Tlaxcala.

Pozole   A soup made with hominy and pork or chicken, in either a tomato-based broth Jalisco-style, or a white broth Nayarit-style, or green chile sauce Guerrero-style, and topped with choice of chopped white onion, lettuce or cabbage, radishes, oregano, red pepper, and cilantro.

Pulque   Drink made of fermented sap of the maguey plant; best in state of Hidalgo and around Mexico City.

Quesadilla   Flour tortillas stuffed with melted white cheese and lightly fried.

Queso relleno   "Stuffed cheese" is a mild yellow cheese stuffed with minced meat and spices, a Yucatecan specialty.

Rompope   Delicious Mexican eggnog, invented in Puebla, made with eggs, vanilla, sugar, and rum.

Salsa verde   A cooked sauce using the green tomatillo and pureed with mildly hot peppers, onions, garlic, and cilantro; on tables countrywide.

Sopa de calabaza   Soup made of chopped squash or pumpkin blossoms.

Sopa de lima   A tangy soup made with chicken broth and accented with fresh lime; popular in Yucatán.

Sopa seca   Not a soup at all, but a seasoned rice which translated means "dry soup."

Sopa Tarascan   A rib sticking pinto-bean based soup, flavored with onions, garlic, tomatoes, chiles, and chicken broth and garnished with sour cream, white cheese, avocado chunks and fried tortilla strips; a specialty of Michoacán state.

Sopa Tlalpeña   A hearty soup made with chunks of chicken, chopped carrots, zucchini, corn, onions, garlic, and cilantro.

Sopa Tlaxcalteca   A hearty tomato-based soup filled with cooked nopal cactus, cheese, cream, and avocado with crispy tortilla strips floating on top.

Sopa tortilla   A traditional chicken broth-based soup, seasoned with chiles, tomatoes, onion, and garlic, bobbing with crisp fried strips of corn tortillas.

Sope   Pronounced "*soh*-pay," a botana similar to a garnacha, except spread with refried beans and topped with crumbled cheese and onions.

Tacos al pastor   Thin slices of flavored pork roasted on a revolving cylinder dripping with onion slices and juice of fresh pineapple slices.

Tamal   Incorrectly called tamale (tamal singular, tamales plural), meat or sweet filling rolled with fresh masa, then wrapped in a corn husk or banana leaf and steamed; many varieties and sizes throughout the country.

Tepache   Drink made of fermented pineapple peelings and brown sugar.

Tikin Xic   Also seen on menus as "tikin chick," char-broiled fish brushed with achiote sauce.

Tinga   A stew made with pork tenderloin, sausage, onions, garlic, tomatoes, chiles, and potatoes; popular on menus in Puebla and Hidalgo states.

Torta   A sandwich, usually on bolillo bread, usually with sliced avocado, onions, tomatoes, with a choice of meat and often cheese.

Torta Ahogado   A specialty of Lake Chapala is made with a scooped out roll, filled with beans and beef strips and seasoned with a tomato or chile sauce.

Tostadas   Crispy fried corn tortillas topped with meat, onions, lettuce, tomatoes, cheese, avocados, and sometimes sour cream.

Venado   Venison (deer) served perhaps as pipian de venado, steamed in banana leaves and served with a sauce of ground squash seeds.

Xtabentun   (pronounced "Shtah-ben-*toon*") A Yucatán liquor made of fermented honey and flavored with anise. It comes *seco* (dry) or *crema* (sweet).

Zacahuil   Pork leg tamal, packed in thick masa, wrapped in banana leaves, and pit baked; sometimes pot-made with tomato and masa; specialty of mid-to- upper Veracruz.

Index

FROMMER'S COMPLETE TRAVEL GUIDES

(Comprehensive guides to destinations around the world, with selections in all price ranges—from deluxe to budget)

Acapulco/Ixtapa/Taxco
Alaska
Amsterdam
Arizona
Atlanta
Australia
Austria
Bahamas
Bangkok
Barcelona, Madrid & Seville
Belgium, Holland & Luxembourg
Berlin
Bermuda
Boston
Budapest & the Best of Hungary
California
Canada
Cancún, Cozumel & the Yucatán
Caribbean
Caribbean Cruises & Ports of Call
Caribbean Ports of Call
Carolinas & Georgia
Chicago
Colorado
Costa Rica
Denver, Boulder & Colorado Springs
Dublin
England
Florida
France
Germany
Greece
Hawaii
Hong Kong
Honolulu/Waikiki/Oahu
Ireland
Italy
Jamaica/Barbados
Japan
Las Vegas
London
Los Angeles
Maryland & Delaware
Maui

Mexico
Mexico City
Miami & the Keys
Montana & Wyoming
Montréal & Québec City
Munich & the Bavarian Alps
Nashville & Memphis
Nepal
New England
New Mexico
New Orleans
New York City
Northern New England
Nova Scotia, New Brunswick & Prince
 Edward Island
Paris
Philadelphia & the Amish Country
Portugal
Prague & the Best of the Czech Republic
Puerto Rico
Puerto Vallarta, Manzanillo & Guadalajara
Rome
San Antonio & Austin
San Diego
San Francisco
Santa Fe, Taos & Albuquerque
Scandinavia
Scotland
Seattle & Portland
South Pacific
Spain
Switzerland
Thailand
Tokyo
Toronto
U.S.A.
Utah
Vancouver & Victoria
Vienna
Virgin Islands
Virginia
Walt Disney World & Orlando
Washington, D.C.
Washington & Oregon

FROMMER'S FRUGAL TRAVELER'S GUIDES

(The grown-up guides to budget travel, offering dream vacations at down-to-earth prices)

Australia from $45 a Day
Berlin from $50 a Day
California from $60 a Day
Caribbean from $60 a Day
Costa Rica & Belize from $35 a Day
Eastern Europe from $30 a Day
England from $50 a Day
Europe from $50 a Day
Florida from $50 a Day
Greece from $45 a Day
Hawaii from $60 a Day

India from $40 a Day
Ireland from $45 a Day
Italy from $50 a Day
Israel from $45 a Day
London from $60 a Day
Mexico from $35 a Day
New York from $70 a Day
New Zealand from $45 a Day
Paris from $65 a Day
Washington, D.C. from $50 a Day

FROMMER'S PORTABLE GUIDES

(Pocket-size guides for travelers who want everything in a nutshell)

Charleston & Savannah
Las Vegas

New Orleans
San Francisco

FROMMER'S IRREVERENT GUIDES

(Wickedly honest guides for sophisticated travelers)

Amsterdam
Chicago
London
Manhattan

Miami
New Orleans
Paris
San Francisco

Santa Fe
U.S. Virgin Islands
Walt Disney World
Washington, D.C.

FROMMER'S AMERICA ON WHEELS

(Everything you need for a successful road trip, including full-color road maps and ratings for every hotel)

California & Nevada
Florida
Mid-Atlantic
Midwest & the Great Lakes
New England & New York

Northwest & Great Plains
South Central & Texas
Southeast
Southwest

FROMMER'S BY NIGHT GUIDES

(The series for those who know that life begins after dark)

Amsterdam
Chicago
Las Vegas
London

Los Angeles
Miami
New Orleans

New York
Paris
San Francisco